The Making of a
Stormtrooper

PETER H. MERKL

The Making of a STORMTROOPER

PRINCETON UNIVERSITY PRESS

To the Emerging Integrated Social Science History

Contents

LIST OF TABLES x

LIST OF ILLUSTRATIONS xiii

LIST OF ABBREVIATIONS xv

PREFACE xvii

ONE. Times Out of Joint 3

The Impact of the Depression 4

A Politicized Atmosphere 7

The Plight of the Young 10

Support for Weimar Democracy and Its Leaders 12

The Dragon Seed of War 15

The Fate of the Weimar Republic 18

The Final Battle of the Republic 20

TWO. The Ignorant Armies of the Night 26

The Beginnings of Paramilitary Formations 31

Communist Revolutionary Organizations 34

The *Stahlhelm*: Black-White-Red 38

A Menace to the Republic 42

Fire under the Ashes 44

The Rise of the *Reichsbanner* 49

The Red Front Fighters League (RFB) 52

The Onset of the Fighting Years 57

The KPD in the Final Phase 62

Mobilized Weimar Youth   66
The Young Plan Campaign   71
The Road to Harzburg   73
The Crisis of July 20, 1932   76
The End of the *Stahlhelm*   82
The Stormtroopers and the Other Groups   86
Converts from the Right   92
The Clash of the Private Armies   94

THREE. Chips off the Old Block   101

The *Reichswehr* and the SA   103
Three Nazi Generations   107
The Shock of the Defeat   113
Antisemitism, 1918-1919   119
Joining the Counterrevolution   121
Experiences Abroad and Overseas   128
The Occupation of the Rhineland   133
A Lower-Middle-Class Revolt?   138
Migration and Stagnation   144
Occupation and upward Mobility   148
The Social Dynamics behind the Stormtroopers   153

FOUR. The Making of Stormtroopers   160

The "Conquest of Berlin"   164
Discipline and Revolutionary Spirit   170
Stormtroopers against the Party Leadership   175
The Decapitation of the SA   181
Political Extremism and Demography   185
Unemployment and Politicization   190
A Theory of Political Deviance   194
Politicized Weimar Youth   203
SA and Hitler Youth (HJ)   210

FIVE. The Vortex of the Movement   218

Violent Youth, Violent Adults   218
Stormtrooper Antisemitism   222

The Background of Prejudice   228
Marching, Fighting, and Proselytizing   231
In the Vortex of the Movement   244
Third Reich Careers   257
The Bloodhounds of Adolf Hitler   263
The Mark of Cain   275

SIX. The Violent Face of Fascism   283

History and Political Motivation   287
Fascist Movements Compared   292
Reflections on Fascist Violence   299
Concluding Remarks   305

SELECTED BIBLIOGRAPHY   309
INDEX   325

List of Tables

II-1 Age Distribution of SPD, KPD, and NSDAP
Members 60

II-2 Reichstag Deputies 1930, by Age and Party 61

II-3 Occupations of Abel Stormtroopers, Nazi
Casualties, and the NSDAP 99

III-1 Military Elements of Pre-1933 NSDAP, SA/SS,
SA/SS Leaders Compared 109

III-2 Occupation of Abel Respondents' Fathers 150

III-3 NSDAP, KPD, and SA/SS Occupations Compared 155

III-4 Educational Levels of Abel NSDAP, SA/SS,
KPD, and KPD Leaders 156

IV-1 Reichstag Election Returns in Berlin
1924-1933 175

IV-2 German Males in the Fighting Years, by Age
and Marital Status, 1930-1933 186

IV-3 Employed and Unemployed Males by Age 188

V-1 Youthful Postures of Abel Stormtroopers and
Party Members 221

V-2 Ideological Themes of Abel SA/SS and NSDAP 222

V-3 Antisemitic Prejudice of Abel SA/SS and NSDAP 222

V-4 NSDAP Activity of Abel SA/SS and NSDAP 233

V-5 Demonstrations, Violence, and Proselytizing,
1919-1932 236

V-6 Reasons for Joining of Abel SA/SS and NSDAP 245

V-7 The Shift to Movement-Related Motives
for Joining, 1919-1933 247

V-8	Personal Introduction of Abel SA/SS and NSDAP	250
V-9	Third *Reich* Careers of Abel SA/SS and NSDAP	259
V-10	Third *Reich* Careers and Pre-1933 NSDAP Activity	277
VI-1	Starting Point, Degree of Violence, and Paramilitary Organization of European Fascist Movements	296
VI-2	Attitudes toward Nazi Movement of Abel SA/SS and NSDAP	303

List of Illustrations

1. Stormtroopers are brought in by truck for the beer-hall putsch of November 9, 1923. (Source: Deutschland Erwache)
2. The "struggle for Berlin": Dr. Goebbels speaking to the faithful. (Source: Deutschland Erwache)
3. The "struggle for Berlin": Sturmfuhrer Horst Wessel and his stormtroopers. (Source: Deutschland Erwache)
4. Adolf Hitler poses with one of the injured stormtroopers. (Source: Deutschland Erwache)
5. The SA has to change to white shirts because brown shirts are banned. 1930. (Source: Deutschland Erwache)
6. Street fight: unidentified young ruffians surround their victim on the sidewalk while passersby scatter. (Source: Zeutner, Illustrierte Geschichte des Dritten Reiches, page 27)
7. A Communist Red Front demonstration in physical confrontation with Berlin police. (Source: Bundesarchiv)
8. An election poster of Communist leader Ernst Thaelmann. (Source: Bundesarchiv)
9. Brunswick 1931: 100,000 SA men are said to be marching past Adolf Hitler. (Source: Deutschland Erwache)
10. Looking at the vast army of stormtroopers through the eyes of the leader. Dortmund 1933. (Source: Deutschland Erwache)
11. Triumphant stormtroopers march through the Brandenburg Gate. Berlin 1933. (Source: Deutschland Erwache)
12. Following the Pied Piper: Hitler Youth marching past HJ leader Baldur von Schirach. Nuremberg 1933. (Source: Deutschland Erwache)

13. SA, SS, and Stahlhelm: Stahlhelm leader Franz Seldte and Hitler. Berchtesgaden 1933. (Source: Deutschland Erwache)
14. Captain Ernst Rohm and his nemesis, Heinrich Himmler. (Source: Bundesarchiv)
15. Communists rounded up and held at bay by stormtroopers. 1933. (Source: Bundesarchiv)
16. Calling roll at concentration camp Oranienburg. 1933. (Source: Bundesarchiv)

List of Abbreviations

ADGB	General Trade Union Federation, Socialist or "Free" Trade Unions
BVP	Bavarian People's Party
DAP	German Workers Party, predecessor of NSDAP
DDP	German Democratic Party, also State Party
DHV	German Voelkisch Retail Clerks Union
DNVP	German Nationalist People's Party, Conservatives
DSP	German Social Party
DVFP	German Voelkisch Freedom Party
DVP	German People's Party
FAD	Voluntary Labor Service
Gestapo	Secret State Police
HJ	Hitler Youth
IF	Iron Front
Jungdo	Young German Order
KAPD	Communist Workers Party
KGM	Fighting Association of the *Mittelstand*
KJVD	Communist Youth League
KPD	Communist Party
Ms	Marchers
MFs	Marcher-Fighters
MFPs	Marcher-Fighter-Proselytizers
MPs	Marcher-Proselytizers
NSBO	National Socialist Factory Cell Organization
NSDAP	Nazi Party

NSDFB	National Socialist German Frontsoldiers League, formerly *Stahlhelm*
NSD St. Bd.	Nazi Student Federation
NSKK	Nazi Motor Corps
OC	Organisation Consul
PNF	Italian Fascist Party
PPF	French Popular Party (Doriot)
RFB	Red Frontfighters League, Red Front
RGO	Revolutionary Trade Union Opposition
RJ	Young Red Front
RMFB	Red Girls and Women's Federation
RNP	French National Popular Rally (Déat)
RSHA	Reich Security Main Office of SD
SA	Stormtroopers, originally *Sturmabteilung*
SA Reserve I	Formerly *Stahlhelm*
SAJ	Socialist Workers Youth
Schufo	Protective Formation, elite troops of *Reichsbanner*
SD	Security Service
SPD	Social Democratic Party
SS	Special Bodyguard of NSDAP, originally *Saalschutz*
USPD	Independent Socialist Party
VB	*Voelkisch* Observer, NSDAP newspaper

Preface

I⊤ HAS been nearly half a century since the Nazi stormtroopers marched and fought all over Germany to establish
their Third *Reich*. In spite of the huge literature on the
Nazis, surprisingly little has appeared on the active militants and the violence that contributed to Hitler's triumph,
even though he won power "legally," that is, without a
violent revolution. It is in the hope of closing this gap that
this book has been written. More specifically, I hope to shed
some light on the motivations of the average stormtrooper:
how young men came to join this organization and to develop the set of attitudes behind its militant actions. But it
is not possible to understand the motives of the stormtroopers without being aware of the other paramilitary armies of
the left and right that kept the Weimar Republic in turmoil
in its last years—the left-wing revolutionaries, the republican *Reichsbanner*, and the many militant veterans' groups
of the right, especially the *Stahlhelm*. The contrast between
the stormtroopers and these other "ignorant armies of the
night," on the other hand, illuminates the character of the
extremism of Hitler's brown shirts.

The principal resource for this inquiry into the individual
motivations of the pre-1933 stormtroopers has been the Abel
Collection of 581 autobiographical statements of early Nazis
collected by the Columbia sociologist, Theodore Abel, by
means of an essay contest. Of these 581, a total of 337 were

members of the SA (*Sturmabteilung*) or SS (*Saalschutz*) before January 1933, and it is often illuminating to contrast the stormtroopers to the mere party members. The Abel Collection, like most autobiographical sources, has certain subjective weaknesses and faults as a representative sample, which I have discussed in considerable detail in *Political Violence under the Swastika: 581 Early Nazis*.[1] At the same time, it offers us unrivaled insights into the thoughts and feelings of hundreds of thousands of Nazis whose collective actions turned out to have had a devastating impact on the twentieth century. There appears to be no better source—in fact, not even an acceptable substitute—for the material in this collection.

The present volume is not an abridgment of *Political Violence under the Swastika* but a successor, in which attention is concentrated on aspects that did not receive their due in the earlier volume. It shares with the earlier book an approach that combines quantitative social-science methods with interpretative historiography. Both books find themselves at the confluence of several trends of current historiography and social science. One is the long-standing trend to chronicle the lives of little people rather than those of great historical personalities. The new social-scientific history, in fact, tends to be a history of general conditions and not of great deeds. Many of the historians in question also use quantitative methods and sophisticated social-science models whenever their materials permit it. The individual stormtrooper, his motives, and his life may not seem to merit the attention commanded by the personality and deeds of a Hitler or a Goering. But in the mass, he becomes a major historical force and deserves to be examined with all the refinement of which the social sciences are capable.

The emphasis on using social-science methods on historical subjects, on the other hand, should not obscure the

---

[1] (Princeton: Princeton University Press, 1975), pp. 5-21. The chief flaws of the sample are: 1. the heavy bias on the hard-core Nazis who joined before September 1930; and 2. the geographic over-representation of Berlin and certain other areas.

limitations of such an approach and its heavy reliance on extant historical works. It is not possible to apply these methods successfully unless more traditional historians have first provided most of the groundwork and opened up the varied pool of sources, so their social-science-oriented successors can plumb them for motivational depths. For this reason, it is most appropriate at this point to pay tribute to the many fine historians, both German and American, whose extraordinary labors have created a situation ripe for social-science research. Their names are too numerous to list here and, in any case, they have been cited in the footnotes and bibliographic references of this book. A special debt of gratitude is owed also to the staff of the Munich *Institut fuer Zeitgeschichte*, which spared no effort in assisting my research. Last, but not least important for my efforts were reviews and correspondence relating to my earlier book on *Political Violence under the Swastika*.

The Making of a
Stormtrooper

Times Out of Joint

JULY 29, 1932, on busy *Kurfuerstendamm* in Berlin, the
weather turned hot and muggy, with a tendency toward
thundershowers. It was a Friday, payday, for many Berliners, and the bustling crowds, the strolling couples, and the
pungent summer fragrance from the hot asphalt and the
blossoms of street trees were no different from those of
other Fridays in July. And yet there was a brooding, electric
tension in the air that had nothing to do with the weather.
A time of decision had come for the Weimar Republic of
Germany, with a crucial national election only two days
away, and the people terribly divided and uncertain of what
to believe and for whom to vote.

In what, indeed, could they have placed their faith? In
the unloved republic and its liberal democratic constitution,
which thirteen years earlier had emerged from the fall of
the German empire in military defeat and revolutionary
turmoil? Should they have felt an abiding loyalty to the
leading politicians of that republic, who in their colorless
and pedestrian ways had replaced the pomp and circumstance of the empire? Or should they have placed their
faith in parliamentary democracy in the face of the threat
of dictatorship from the left and the right, while the country
was in the grip of the most devastating economic crisis in its
history? The fate of the republic, the support for its leaders

and for constitutional democracy, and the impact of the Great Depression on Weimar politics all deserve a closer look before we focus on the stormtroopers.

The Impact of the Depression

If it was payday for some people on that hot and muggy Friday, there were six hundred thousand other Berliners, and millions of Germans all over the country, who could only collect their meager unemployment dole. The Great Depression had reached its high-water mark in Germany in mid-1932. Six million people were out of work, including large numbers of skilled metal and construction workers and white-collar employees. The majority of the unemployed were young, born after the turn of the century, and there were many well-trained young people who had never landed a job or, if they had, could not hold on to it.[1] Another estimated million or two "invisible unemployed" should be added to this figure, which was substantially higher than the unemployment figures of other advanced industrial nations at the time. Shorter working hours and higher work loads for less pay were also part of the picture.[2]

Even before the crisis struck in 1929, the Weimar economy was continually wracked by economic dislocation and stagnation, which only rarely (in 1924-1925 and 1927) kept unemployment as low as five percent (generally, less than

[1] 22.8 percent of the unemployed were between 18 and 24 and, among white-collar workers, this age group amounted to 32.1 percent. See *Statistisches Jahrbuch des Deutschen Reiches, 1934*, p. 312.

[2] With 275 per 1,000 employable persons (who were one-third of the total population) unemployed at the end of 1932, Germany was ahead of the United States (207), Great Britain (186), Austria (140), Belgium (85), the Netherlands (70), and France (61). Cited in F. A. Krummacher and A. Wucher, *Die Weimarer Republik* (Munich: Desch, 1965), p. 325. As for the cutbacks in working hours and pay, trade union members in December 1931 reported 43.3 percent of their members unemployed, and another 22.9 percent on reduced hours. Civil service salaries were cut by a total of about 20 percent, and industrial salaries by about half that amount.

4

a million). During the winter months of 1929-1930 the unemployment curve dramatically began to exceed the seasonal figures of the previous year. Throughout 1930, an extra 2 million unemployed haunted Weimar politics and, following the emergency decrees of the austerity program of Chancellor Heinrich Bruening, the figure grew to 2.8 million by March 1931, and to 4.4 million in November of the same year. During the first half of 1932, finally, the curve reached its zenith of 6 million, and began to drop back to a level of 4.3 to 4.5 million during the winter before Hitler was appointed chancellor.[3]

What did all these millions of able-bodied, often well-trained, and eager German workers do when they found themselves laid off? In a country that prizes skilled work and industriousness above all, what does a person do when society suddenly has no more use for his[4] services, when he sits at home, and time hangs heavily on his hands? Siegfried Kracauer, in a newspaper report on the unemployed of 1930, paints a depressing picture of the feeling of being sidetracked from the productive activity of a lifetime, the endless queues for a few job openings, the vexing sense of waiting—waiting as a purpose in itself. Unemployment made people feel utterly helpless and dependent on a mysterious, vengeful god, or on vast, unintelligible economic processes that were grinding up their hopes and their habits of dignified living. The memory of the runaway inflation of 1923 was still very much alive in the thirties. As an individual worker or shopkeeper, a person had his or her niche of purposeful enterprise that could supply a sense of meaning and belonging. As soon as people became unemployed,

[3] These figures are calculated against the totals employed in 1929. In April 1930, 1.4 million fewer were employed than in April 1929, when 2.5 million had already been out of work. Dietmar Keese, "Die volkswirtschaftlichen Gesamtgroessen fuer das Deutsche Reich in den Jahren 1925-1936," in Werner Conze and Hans Raupach, eds., *Die Staats- und Wirtschaftskrise des Deutschen Reiches* (Stuttgart: Klett, 1967), pp. 38-39.

[4] Unemployment mostly affected males, who were often replaced by cheaper female labor.

5

they became mere particles in a vast human mass of misery, indistinguishable bodies in a waiting line.

A Berlin newspaper reported glimpses of what the unemployed there were doing in the summer months of 1932. Attendance at the popular Mueggelsee beach was up six times, and at the large Wannsee beach three times over the figures of 1924. Public libraries could barely handle the excess traffic, including thousands of customers who had never used a public library before. The public baths had the same complaint. Tent cities had grown at the edge of the city to house those unable to afford any other shelter. In the winter, there were "day rooms," "warm-up rooms," and garden cottages with inadequate heating. The Berlin city government had benches and tables set up in the city parks so people in the vast crowds could play cards while others gathered around to watch. There were always large numbers of idle men standing and loitering about in groups in public parks and squares. Women became reluctant to walk through these places for fear of being accosted or insulted. There was an air of menace about these ill-dressed and ill-kempt crowds in public places. Cigarettes took on a special meaning that no one younger than the generation of World War II would understand today. They were a ready means of making a new friend, a prize at the card game, the last thread of survival in a meaningless existence. They came in odd sizes and obscure brands, often self-rolled and of doubtful ingredients, but it was always better to have one than to be without.

The worst off among the unemployed were perhaps the listless and apathetic: lying in bed or on a sofa all day, staring at the ceiling, not wanting to get up and shave in the morning, not having the energy to go out, getting no pleasure out of the simple pastimes on the beach or in the park, and regarding everything as utterly pointless and disagreeable. The general air of run-down buildings and down-at-the heel clothing only reinforced their dispirited mood. And there was worse. Husbands and fathers sitting around at home could direct their malaise against their wives or the children. There were frequent domestic quarrels, vehement arguments with neighbors, and brawls in taverns and public places. Teenagers of working age and idle young adults became thieves, burglars, prostitutes, or pimps in order to help themselves to what society had denied them.[5] Older people became beggars or sold dry goods from door to door. Sharp deals and confidence games awaited the unwary at every turn. The demoralization of being out of work for years let out the skeletons from many a closet. Sex offenses and minor property violations multiplied, and were rarely prosecuted successfully. An army of "asocial elements" and drifters accumulated in the big city ghettos and, increasingly, in the countryside. The line between crime and misery, between viciousness and despair seemed more and more difficult to draw. Why search out and punish the small sinners, when the large-scale manipulators and crooks—real or imagined—seemed to get away with anything? The idle talk in the public squares would inevitably turn to rumors about people who allegedly profited from the widespread sufferings of others.

A Politicized Atmosphere

The brooding atmosphere of mass unemployment was eagerly exploited by the Communists (KPD) and the Nazis (NSDAP), who outdid themselves and each other in directing the latent hostility against the rich and well-educated. A pervasive hatred grew in the new proletarian masses of the unemployed against bourgeois values of achievement and culture, even against the white collars and neckties of those who still had their jobs. Although they were beginning to receive financial contributions from a few rare industrialists,[6] the Nazis were as violently opposed to German

---

[5] According to a statement of Labor Minister Syrup in January 1933, there were about 1,000,000 unemployed males and 400,000 females under the age of 25, and a critical lack of apprenticeships as well as of follow-up jobs for the young.

[6] On this highly controversial subject, see especially Henry A.

bourgeois civilization as were the Communists,[7] but they added an appeal that fell on more willing ears than at any time since the antisemitic agitation of 1919: "The Jews are our misfortune." This Nazi election slogan of the 1930 elections, blaming everything from the lost war to the Allied reparations, the Depression, and Communism on the favorite scapegoat of the Nazis, was surprisingly well attuned to the paranoid fears of secret conspiracies on the part of "international finance." One of the early Nazis in the Abel Collection,[8] a down-and-out aristocrat turned taxidriver after repeated intervals of unemployment (no. 139) put well the link between idle talk in public places and political antisemitism when he wrote,

The idle sitting-around at taxi stands, caused by the bad economic situation, led to constant political discussions among the chauffeurs [and other idlers there]. Since there was many an old soldier of like mind in the com-

Turner, Jr., "Big Business and the Rise of Hitler," in Turner, ed., *Nazism and the Third Reich* (New York: Quadrangle, 1972), pp. 91-99, where some of the popular interpretations of big-business support for Hitler are critically reviewed. As a whole, big business did not support the Nazis prior to their takeover. See also Horst Matzerath and Henry A. Turner, "Die Selbstfinanzierung der NSDAP 1930-1932," *Geschichte und Gesellschaft*, 3 (1977), 59-92, where the authors document the extraordinary degree, at least in the Rhineland, to which the Nazi party succeeded in financing itself from dues and contributions of its members during the crucial years.

[7] The Communists, curiously, were also involved in a campaign of atheism so virulent that Chancellor Bruening felt moved to decree the dissolution of all atheistic societies in May 1932. Together with the ubiquitous signs of social disintegration and the *avant-garde* art and culture of metropolitan Berlin, atheistic agitation was a major irritant to the more traditionally oriented part of the electorate, leading it to call for a strong man with a cleansing broom.

[8] The Abel Collection of autobiographical statements of pre-1933 Nazis is at the Hoover Library of War and Revolution in Stanford, California. The autobiographies bear numbers. On the representative character of this collection, see my *Political Violence under the Swastika: 581 Early Nazis* (Princeton: Princeton University Press, 1975), pp. 5-21.

Agrarian Policy Organization. These and many other Nazi interest groups were, in a sense, the first steps toward the totalitarian usurpation of all community life. This process was completed after Hitler took power, and all associations from the labor unions to sporting clubs were either undermined from within or suppressed.[10]

The NSDAP made a particular effort to attract young people, and especially unemployed youth. It had idealized the German small farmer as the archetypal German, and it paid a similar compliment to German youth. The NSDAP even called itself the "party of youth" in obvious exaggeration, and called on the Weimar gerontocracy in state and society, "Step aside, you old ones!" The NSDAP and KPD, indeed, had a substantially younger membership and leadership than the SPD, the Catholic Center party, or the old liberal People's party (DVP), the Democrats (DDP), or the Conservative party (DNVP). Most significant for us here was the successful recruitment by the NSDAP of hundreds of thousands of young stormtroopers (SA and SS) and of Hitler Youth during the Depression years.[11] Unemployed young males were put up in dormitories (*SA Heime*), where they received shelter and food in exchange for their full-time services as marchers and fighters for the brown cause. The NSDAP also maintained welfare services of sorts for its clientele, at times even asked members to look after jailed stormtroopers and their interests.

Support for Weimar Democracy and Its Leaders

Sympathetic observers outside of Germany have always wondered why there was not more loyalty to the democratic

[10] See Dietrich Orlow, *The History of the Nazi Party: 1919-1933* (Pittsburgh: University of Pittsburgh Press, 1969), pp. 164-165, 169, and 192-197.

[11] According to one source, SA membership rose from 77,000 in January 1931 to 221,000 in November 1931, and on to 445,000 in August 1932, and about 700,000 by January 1933. Andreas Werner, "SA und NSDAP, SA: 'Wehrverband,' 'Parteitruppe,' oder 'Revolutionsarmee'?" Ph.D. dissertation, Erlangen, 1964, pp. 544-552.

pany I worked for, we soon went about systematically influencing our Marxist colleagues. The conduct of the Jews in the west of Berlin and the fact that 80-90 percent of the customers were Jews was a great support for our undertaking.

This "taxicab theory of antisemitism," in which the envied, well-to-do customers are equated with the Jews, is somewhat weakened by the fact that the respondent admits to antisemitic prejudice from the days of his childhood. But his assertion that it was the economic deterioration of his circumstances that politicized his prejudiced mind is plausible. Political antisemitism in the early 1930s was bound, in any case, to lead him into the Nazi party.

Political action born from economic despair got an early start among north German farmers and small business interests. Radicalized through their plight, farmers in Schleswig-Holstein initiated tax strikes and resistance to farm foreclosures. There followed, beginning in the winter of 1928-1929, a year of bombings and confrontations with state and local officials, which soon spread to adjacent territories like Oldenburg, and even to the wine areas along the Rhine and Moselle rivers. In the end, Protestant rural areas tended to vote far more heavily for the Nazis than did urban areas. Small-businessmen such as shopkeepers, independent craftsmen, or apartment-house owners began early to defect from their traditional liberal party loyalties, as their economic position became ever more marginal, and to rally to various economically middle-class (*Mittelstand*) interest parties. The combined vote for the agrarian and middle-class parties exceeded one-tenth of the popular vote in 1928 and 1930, an element sorely missed by the moderate and republican camps. In the elections of 1932-1933, these voters all were in the fold of the NSDAP.

There was, of course, protest among the workers and unemployed, as well. Three days before the elections of July 1932, the newspapers reported "another riot of unemployed people" in Ruhla near Eisenach. There had been a major demonstration against the cutbacks in unemployment benefits; the police had intervened to stop the marchers, who then knocked down three policemen and left two others critically injured, one with eight stab wounds in his back and another with wounds in one arm and his back. In the end, the police began to shoot at the crowd, and killed an innocent passer-by. The newspapers reported this story along with the usual list of election campaign violence among Nazis, Communists, and the police. The cutbacks in the unemployment benefits had already been an issue in the bitter winter of 1928-1929, when the Unemployment Insurance Fund had to be bailed out with a loan, and again at the end of 1929, when it had a deficit of 1.5 billion marks. At this point, the trade unions resisted a cut in benefits, while the employers refused to increase their contributions, and the last parliamentary cabinet of the republic was toppled over this issue.

The Plight of the Young

Young people were particularly vulnerable to the great disillusionment of unemployment at the very outset of their career, when their outlook toward gainful employment was still being formed. The full-fledged welfare state had been completed with the Law on Employment Services and Unemployment Insurance only in 1927. After little more than two years, the impact of the Depression already forced the government to reduce the unemployment benefits, after the republican cabinet of Heinrich Mueller (SPD) fell over this issue. By 1932, unemployment payments per breadwinner had been reduced repeatedly from an average of nearly ninety marks a month to about fifty, a level of dire poverty and depressing misery that matched the overall slippage of popular income levels to about seventy-eight percent of the level of 1913. As Chancellor Bruening, whose deflationary policies and preoccupation with foreign policy issues had aggravated the unemployment problem, conceded two days before his dismissal on May 30, 1932,

Does it surprise you, ladies and gentlemen, that in the hearts and minds of the young a radicalism breaks forth which expects and instinctively hopes for improvement only through the demise and dismantling of the existing order . . . ?

When the standard of living drops to a certain low point, all inclination to listen to lectures, arguments of state, or the voice of reason will disappear with psychological necessity.[9]

Bruening had no solutions to offer for the despair of unemployment, and his successor Franz von Papen was not even sympathetic to the plight of the victims. But the extremist opposition rose to the challenge, at least at the level of propaganda. The Communists (KPD), in particular, concentrated on the employment offices, where the millions of unemployed had to appear twice a week to get a stamp for their passbooks. A Red Help organization, special unemployment committees, and the Revolutionary Trade Union Opposition (RGO) recruited large numbers of the unemployed, especially the young, and used them to distribute leaflets and to mobilize workers for strikes and against evictions from their dwellings. They also advocated such things as warm school lunches and clothing allowances in the winter. The deteriorating economic conditions made it easy for the Communists to score the Social Democrats and the Free Trade Unions (ADGB) for their support, however grudging, for the Bruening government. The Nazis eagerly learned from the KPD, and went after both the old working class and the newly proletarian middle-class and white collar unemployed. They organized their own labor organization, the National Socialist Factory Cell Organization (NSBO) and a Militant Association of Small Business (KGM), and practically took over the largest existing agricultural interest group, the *Landbund*, with their

[9] These passages are from a speech at a banquet of the foreign press to which government representatives and other prominent Germans were invited. *Frankfurter Zeitung*, May 29, 1932.

constitution of Weimar and to republican leaders among the people. It is not quite correct to assert that Germans had had no experience with democratic elections, parliaments, or the pluralism of political parties and interest groups. All of these had been present under the empire before World War I, although they had played a role subordinate to the *Kaiser*, the state monarchies, and the army. There is much evidence to suggest that prewar German society might in time have developed into a modern, progressive state in keeping with its high degree of urbanization and industrialization, if the empire had not blundered into disastrous confrontation with the West. To be sure, there were strong social tensions, especially between the rising labor movement and the established classes, and a social malaise that led the latter to yearn for an armed conflict in which Germany might win its "place in the sun." But these were not exclusive to Germany, and could probably have worked themselves out in the long run.

It is nonsense to explain Hitler's triumph by age-old German tendencies or trends in German intellectual thought. World War I was the major turning point in German political development; its consequences doomed the Weimar Republic and set the stage for the success of Adolf Hitler. The confrontation with the West and its political traditions, which in the nineteenth century had also been those of German liberalism, had a profound impact on the political attitudes of the German middle classes. The German bourgeoisie and parts of the peasantry had always combined their liberalism with a strong dose of nationalism, as is common within nations preoccupied with achieving national independence or unity in the face of dominant foreign powers. But the wave of nationalism engulfing the bourgeoisie and even the working classes in 1914 was emphatically anti-Western, and pitted, as the popular phrase went, a "people of warriors" against the "green-grocers' states" of the West. The disastrous defeat of Germany and the Allied pressure to replace the irresponsible *Kaiser* with a parliamentary regime (not to mention trying him as a war criminal) could not but pin on parliamentary democracy the image of being something alien, even though it had been prominent on the list of demands of German liberal politicians since 1915, and on the socialist agenda since 1890.

The war, of course, was also a major cause of the ensuing economic problems, including inflation, stagnation, and depression. To make matters worse, the war also initiated a gigantic swing of public opinion that took the country from a wave of pacifism and socialism in 1918 to the crest of the brown wave of *voelkisch*[12] nationalism in 1932. In 1919, shortly after the pacifistic and socialistic wave had crested, a large majority of Democrats (DDP), Centrists, and Social Democrats (SPD) proclaimed the republic and adopted the liberal democratic Weimar Constitution. Within a year, this republican majority was lost to a combination of antirepublican parties. By 1925, the famous war hero, old Field Marshal Paul von Hindenburg, was elected by a right-wing majority to the office of *Reich* president and guardian of the constitution.[13] Von Hindenburg had no particular sympathy for the republic, but served faithfully as long as there was no crisis at hand. When the Depression toppled the last parliamentary government in March 1930, and the new chancellor, Heinrich Bruening (Center), found no parliamentary majority for his cabinet or his emergency economic legislation, the octogenarian president proclaimed a state of emergency under Article 48 of the constitution, to support Bruening in lieu of a parliamentary majority. This question-

[12] This untranslatable political label denotes an integral nationalism that combined an obsession with the purity of the nation with a populistic hatred for the political, economic, and cultural establishment of Germany. See especially Martin Broszat, *National Socialism, 1918-1945* (Santa Barbara: ABC-Clio, 1966), or Fritz Stern, *The Politics of Cultural Despair* (New York: Doubleday, 1961).

[13] At the time, the republican candidate to follow the late President Friedrich Ebert (SPD) was Wilhelm Marx (Center party), who narrowly missed getting elected only because the KPD insisted on having its own candidate, Ernst Thaelmann.

able interpretation of the emergency clause formed the un-challenged constitutional basis of Bruening's and later von Papen's and von Schleicher's cabinets for nearly three years of crisis management. For the presidential campaign of 1932, moreover, the republican parties decided to cling to von Hindenburg as their candidate against the challengers: Hitler, Duesterberg (*Stahlhelm*), and Thaelmann (KPD). Hindenburg won on the second ballot, but the choice was obviously a sign of the abject weakness of the republican faith. The entire period of emergency government, more-over, was characterized by the resurgence of authoritarian political thought among the educated and in the press. There was an earnest search for authoritarian models rang-ing from a corporate state to outright dictatorship, even long before Hindenburg committed his fatal blunders of supporting von Papen and, eventually, Hitler himself for the chancellorship.

The Dragon Seed of War

The most disastrous effect of World War I, finally, consisted of the miseducation of a whole generation toward solving its problems in a military, authoritarian manner. The war generation fought in volunteer military units (Freecorps) against Polish irregulars and domestic revolutionaries in the years right after the war. In the 1930s they flocked to the Nazi party and other political right-wing organizations, bringing along a whole ideology of what it meant to be a front-line soldier fighting in the trenches. Even Bruening liked to call himself a *Frontsoldat*; President Hindenburg had been the victor of the battle of Tannenberg and, to-gether with Erich Ludendorff, a virtual military dictator of Germany during most of the war. The front-line soldier's ideology was nationalistic, undemocratic, and totally lack-ing in the kind of political insights needed in the midst of the Weimar crisis. At the same time, it fostered an assertive arrogance toward other generations, the prewar politicians, and the vast numbers who had grown up without the doubtful benefits of an education in the trenches of the Great War.

What about the republican loyalties of the postwar generation (born 1902 or later), which by 1930 amounted to one-fourth of the German adult population?[14] Were the young any more likely to support the parliamentary democracy than their elders of the war generation? Three days before the fateful *Reichstag* elections of July 31, 1932, when the NSDAP reached its highest vote in a free election (37.3 percent), an editorial in the liberal *Vossische Zeitung* pondered the ground swell of angry youth about to assert itself in the elections. The editorial writer, a pastor of the *Marienkirche* in Berlin, exhorted the republican politicians to address themselves to the political agonies of the young, however irrational they might be.

> We have always known that the imponderables of the life of the people—their sentiments, habits, hopes, or disappointments, and their prejudices—often hold more potent sway over politics than do material interests, well-founded convictions, or public necessities. A policy may be very logical and yet, psychologically, it may be a disaster.
>
> Since we have given suffrage to the young, this truth is more valid than ever. Never have generational differences been more important in German politics. . . . Our youth is anti-reason . . . , simply not interested in the philistine reasonableness of its elders . . . who in turn are too smart to make room for youth and will even close the door on its legitimate aspirations. . . .
>
> The new generation also knows nothing of liberalism and can hardly be expected to. They enjoy the most liberal of constitutions and just take its freedoms for granted. . . . What does the younger set care about democracy? They did not suffer through the winter of 1918-1919 when

[14] 23.5 percent of the eligible voters in the parliamentary elections of 1930 belonged to this group.

the [freedom] . . . of the German people hung in the balance. Now again . . . constitutional values are in danger. . . .

We old liberal democrats must take a positive approach to that which appears to trouble these new people even if they cannot always put their political problems and bellyaches very clearly.

The good pastor went on to speak about the experience of the prewar Youth Movement, which was alien to the older generation and had become so astonishingly important to all the young:

[From the tradition of the "nests" of young boys and girls, from their nature hikes and wanderings] there came the *idea of a leader* . . . and of a *Bund* of many like-minded youth groups . . . and of regional *ethnic culture* (*Volkstum*). . . . A whole new life-style thus grew from this new sense of life. . . . [Since there is no more military conscription,] *sports* and . . . a *simple and natural way of life* became important. . . . Because of the bitter experiences of unemployment of many of these youths, however, political radicalism got a hold of them by tying itself to all their favorite ideas. The idea of the leader became the promotion of the dictatorship of an unstable Austrian, the warm affection for the people became ice-cold anti-semitism, the sticking together of the youth group turned into a vicious struggle against those who dare to disagree with them . . . in short, all the unpleasantness that now separates young and old [italics in original].[15]

A wave of politicized postwar youth, in other words, had followed the hostile, authoritarian, field-grey host of World War I. Large numbers of them were among the brown stormtroopers, or had joined right-wing youth organizations of various kinds. Many preferred a Communist utopia to the republic in which they lived. Only a small number of the

[15] Dietrich Graue, "Sprecht zur Jugend," *Vossische Zeitung*, July 28, 1932, pp. 1-2. Italics in original.

postwar generation or of the war generation could be counted upon to defend their republic; very few indeed would be loyal to the republican leaders—who were, in any case, a rather colorless and uninspiring lot, and who could hardly compete with the warmed-over glories of the empire, the war heroes, or the charisma of that "unstable Austrian." Who among the young really appreciated a Friedrich Ebert, a Philipp Scheidemann, or even a Gustav Stresemann, who had guided the foreign policy of the republic with remarkable skill until his death in 1929?[16]

The Fate of the Weimar Republic

Buffeted by the stormy events, secretly still fighting the Allied powers and their treaty of Versailles, and rarely able to count on the solid support of its own citizens, the Weimar Republic stumbled along. Already in 1919, when its constitution was adopted by a vote of 262 to 75 in the National Assembly, this republic was a stepchild of public opinion. Large numbers of people on the right did not believe that the German armies had been defeated in the field of honor, but preferred to think that they had been "stabbed in the back" by red revolutionaries. The revolutionaries of the far left who preferred councils of workers and soldiers or the dictatorship of the proletariat to parliamentary democracy, felt betrayed in turn by the SPD's Ebert and Gustav Noske, who put down their uprisings against the provisional Weimar government with much bloodshed, thanks to the quickly recruited military Freecorps. About a month before the final passage of the constitution, the National Assembly had the unenviable task, under threat of Allied invasion, of ratifying the punitive Peace Treaty of Versailles, whose an-

---

[16] Ebert (SPD) was the first Weimar president and also the man who outmaneuvered the left-wing revolutionaries in the first months after the end of the war. Scheidemann (SPD) in 1918 proclaimed the republic, and Stresemann was the chancellor who reestablished the German currency after the inflation of 1923, and then, as foreign minister, guided the Weimar Republic out of its international isolation.

nexations left behind irredentist longings for the lost territories in the East, a ticking time bomb to be exploded by
the Third *Reich*. The Versailles clause attributing responsibility for the war to Germany and the Allied demands for
reparations remained thorns in the side of the republic
throughout its duration, and supplied rousing campaign issues to the antirepublican right wing.

After a momentarily successful right-wing coup d'état, the
Kapp putsch, a successful general strike to undo the putsch,
and another violently suppressed revolutionary uprising in
the Ruhr area in 1920, the national elections of that year
finally revealed the precariousness of support for the Weimar Republic. The three republican parties lost their overwhelming majority of 1919: the Social Democrats lost five
million votes, mostly to the revolutionary Independent Socialists (USPD), the liberal Democrats (DDP) lost three
million to the conservative and anti-republican People's
party (DVP), and to the German Nationalists (DNVP),
and the Center party lost about one-fourth of its strength
(two million) when its Bavarian affiliate insisted on seced-
ing as the anti-republican Bavarian People's party (BVP).
The republicans did not regain a majority of the popular
vote until the short recovery period of the Mueller cabinet
(1928-1930).

The republic staggered on from crisis to crisis, the leaders
trying to win favor with various antirepublican parties to
retain a supporting majority, while the political spectrum of
opinion drifted farther toward the right. The early confrontations with the revolutionary left soon gave way to
acute danger from the right, where various political soldiers
and Freecorps commanders began to plot against the republic and to assassinate its most prominent politicians, such as
Matthias Erzberger and Walter Rathenau. In 1923, the
French army invaded and occupied the Rhineland in order
to extract French reparations in kind rather than in the form
of the deteriorating German currency. The political and
economic shockwaves again nearly brought the republic to
its knees, as the right wing openly launched its assault on it;

the newly strengthened Communist party (KPD) attracted a substantial 12.6 percent of the vote on the far left in the May 1924 elections. If the republic survived the year 1923, it was only because of fortuitous circumstances and the bad luck of the beer-hall and paramilitary plotters on the right who somehow failed to bring off the coup de grâce.

The Final Battle of the Republic

After a short period of domestic peace and economic consolidation, 1924 to 1928, the Great Depression struck; dominant political thought turned from parliamentary democracy to images of the authoritarian state. Political opinion became increasingly polarized as the far right and far left took their struggle to the streets and meeting-halls of Germany. Now, suddenly, the Nazi party emerged from relative obscurity as one right-wing fringe group among many others, and received a stunning six-and-a-half million votes (18.3 percent) at the national elections of September 1930.[17] From that moment on, hundreds of thousands began to join the NSDAP, and its stormtroopers (SA) and Hitler Youth began to play a major role in street demonstrations, election campaigns, and meeting-hall battles all over the republic. The militant veterans' group *Stahlhelm* (steel helmet) likewise marched in the streets against the republican "system," which was the foremost target of its notorious 1928 "declaration of hatred." These two and other militant right-wing organizations, as well as Alfred Hugenberg's German Nationalists (DNVP), who had already collaborated with the Nazis in the 1929 campaign against the Young Plan of reparations, joined forces in the Harzburg Front of 1931, a preview of the coalition that brought Hitler to power in 1933. On the left, the Communist Red Frontfighters' League (RFB) fought and marched for the proletarian dictatorship and, incidentally, also against the SPD, the Versailles

[17] On a national level, Hitler became prominent only during his treason trial in connection with the beer-hall putsch, and during the combined right-wing campaign against the Young Plan of 1929.

Treaty, and the Young Plan, which, however, did not prevent it from battling the stormtroopers and the *Stahlhelm* wherever they would meet. A fourth, less militant but much larger paramilitary organization was the republican *Reichsbanner*, which was organized by the SPD and its republican friends to withstand the street pressures of the right and far left. These were the *dramatis personae* of the early thirties, from among whom we single out the stormtroopers in this book.

Germans saw this dragon seed of political battle sprout among them for years before the fateful year of 1932, when the paramilitary organizations turned first the presidential election campaign of March and early April, then the state diet elections of April, and finally the parliamentary campaign of June and July into almost daily bloody clashes, leaving many dead and wounded. Chancellor Bruening continued to ban the Nazi stormtroopers, both the SA and the bodyguard SS, as a danger to the state following the presidential campaign. But his successor, von Papen, lifted the ban on June 16. On July 20, von Papen carried out his unconstitutional coup against the republican minority government of Prussia, Germany's largest state, where the police had hitherto been able to stem the flood of right-wing political violence in the streets and meeting halls.[18] The assault on Prussia was crucial because, as in most German states, the state elections of April 24 had made the Nazis

[18] His pretext was a particularly violent clash at Altona, at which 18 persons were killed, 68 injured, and 150 arrested. The clash began when stormtroopers from Schleswig-Holstein insisted on demonstrating in the "red" districts of Altona on July 17. They drew Communist gunfire from windows and rooftops, whereupon the police, with the help of armored cars, began shooting at the snipers and at Communist barricades made of streetcars and trucks. Von Papen claimed that this episode demonstrated the inability of the Prussian government to maintain order, and made himself *Reich* commissioner for the state with full executive powers under Article 48 of the constitution. He invoked a state of emergency in Berlin and the Brandenburg area, and had the highest police officials of Berlin (who belonged to the SPD) arrested and the state ministries occupied by the army.

the largest party in the state diet, without giving it and its right-wing allies the majority needed to elect a new minister president in place of Otto Braun (SPD).[19]

Chancellor von Papen thus knocked out one of the last remaining pillars of the republic before the onrushing brown tide. The aging *Reich* president, von Hindenburg, who had hitherto refused to offer an important cabinet position to Adolf Hitler, was under intense pressure because of his apparent involvement in the East Elbian subsidy scandal. The *Reichstag* was the next target of the extremists. The liberal Prussian paper, *Vossische Zeitung*, had reported the violent excesses of left and right throughout the parliamentary election campaign with stories such as this one of July 28:

> . . . clash in the Gummersbach area between a leftist team passing out leaflets and a group of stormtroopers . . . one of the SA men stabbed to death; another seriously injured. . . .
>
> . . . near Stettin, SA raiders invaded an SPD rally and challenged the speaker to take back a remark he had made about Adolf Hitler. . . . They attacked people in the audience with chairs, injuring ten of them critically and making the meeting hall a shambles. The three gendarmes present were unable to quell the disturbance.

The *Vossische Zeitung* had every reason to view with alarm the deteriorating political life of "its" democratic republic.

In the same issue there appeared, next to an article on the high-handed coup against the Prussian government,[20]

---

[19] The 162 newly elected Nazi deputies and the 57 Communist deputies promptly started a gigantic brawl in the state diet on May 25, which ended with the Nazis victorious and singing their Horst Wessel song. Efforts by the diet's Council of Elders to punish the deputies who had started this undignified encounter were voted down by the combined majority of Nazis and Communists.

[20] As the editor saw it, the High Court's anticipated decision on the constitutionality of von Papen's coup was to be feared either way. Even if the ousted Braun government of Prussia were upheld, the *Reich* government would lose authority in the face of resurgent state

an editorial commenting on the nature of the election campaign and comparing it to previous parliamentary campaigns in Germany and elsewhere:

> There's never been such an "electoral" battle in Germany. . . . The means of the political struggle have changed ominously. After so many electoral contests [in 1932], the political slogans have lost their force. Their political messages are spent. All that remains now are their carriers, the so-called fighting organizations that are now clashing without the padding of words. Fists and brass knuckles have replaced the arguments of the debate. Terror and roving gangs characterize this electoral donnybrook. . . . There are casualties and a long list of the injured. In the midst of the capital, peaceful citizens are knocked down just because they wear a pin that aggravates the sons of Baldur [von Schirach, the Hitler Youth leader] . . . who in close league with the "Marxist subhumans" [the Nazi epithet for the Communist] have turned organized terror into the chief means of struggle in German politics—much as *Herr* von Papen would like to ignore it. If the murderous weapons of the Nazis sometimes fail to demolish their targets, this is hardly due to [his] protection but only to the hardness of many a republican head. . . . Resist dictatorship and fascism, defend the constitution and the republic!

When the ballots were counted, to the dismay of all republican forces, the NSDAP had received 13.7 million votes (37.3 percent) and the KPD 5.4 million (14.5), which gave the two extremist parties a combined majority, just as in the Prussian diet and several other state diets, to vote down any constructive actions. Two hundred thirty Nazi deputies marched in full stormtrooper uniform into the *Reichstag*.

---

particularism and left-wing radicalism. The confusion of liberals was also reflected in an article in the same issue by the famous historian Friedrich Meinecke, who fatuously praised the trade unions for their civic-mindedness (*Staatsgesinnung*) in not fighting von Papen's coup in any way other than through the courts.

Six months later, after a short interlude of declining Nazi votes[21] and a game of musical chairs played by von Schleicher and von Papen with the chancellorship, the latter persuaded President von Hindenburg to appoint Hitler chancellor, despite the many statements of Hitler and his henchmen revealing what the Nazis would do to the republic and to the rule of law once they were in power. There had been threats even before the elections of July 1932 that "heads will roll," and the first Nazi Minister President Roever of Oldenburg had said that all opponents would be "hanged." Where the Nazis first came into power, as in Oldenburg and Braunschweig,[22] they even made the stormtroopers "auxiliary policemen," who could carry out their terror with the authority of the law. After Hitler's official appointment, these "auxiliary policemen" opened the first concentration camps for their political opponents.

We can glimpse the significance of the rise of the politics of paramilitary armies by comparing the relationship between the *Reichswehr* and the stormtroopers at the beginning and at the end of this six-month period between July 1932 and January 1933. In July, *Reichswehr* Minister Kurt von Schleicher, who had just helped von Papen to become chancellor, interjected in the *Reichstag* that both the *Reichswehr* and the Prussian police would meet any strong-arm attempt by the NSDAP with armed force. Republican voices, alarmed by the concentration in Berlin of stormtrooper detachments from Pomerania and elsewhere, acclaimed von Schleicher's remark. Six months later, when

[21] In the November elections of 1932, the Nazi vote dropped to 11.7 million (33.1 percent), but the KPD vote rose by another 650,000 to 5.98 million (16.9 percent). In March 1933, however, after Hitler had been appointed chancellor and the Communists had been outlawed in connection with the *Reichstag* fire, the Nazi vote reached a total of 17.3 million (43.9 percent) after a campaign of terror and harassment of the opposition.

[22] On the rise of the Nazis in Braunschweig, see also Ernst-August Roloff, *Braunschweig und der Staat von Weimar, Politik, Wirtschaft und Gesellschaft 1918-1933* (Braunschweig: Waisenhaus Verlag, 1964), especially pp. 182-191.

Chancellor von Schleicher had failed to split the NSDAP, and proposed to hold the paramilitary armies at bay with the *Reichswehr*, a study made by his own *Reichswehr* ministry clearly showed that the *Reichswehr* would be physically unable to keep the stormtroopers and Communists under control in a state of emergency.[23] The menace of the stormtroopers had outgrown the last means to stop it.

[23] Both von Papen and von Schleicher had been flirting with the use of the *Reichswehr* to control the extremist movements. Schleicher originally commissioned the study to outmaneuver von Papen. A month later, he in turn wanted Hindenburg to authorize a state of emergency in which the support of the SPD and the trade unions would enable the *Reichswehr* to control the NSDAP and the KPD. Hindenburg refused.

The Ignorant Armies of the Night

> . . . And we are here as on a darkling plain
> Swept with confused alarms of struggle and flight
> Where ignorant armies clash by night.
>
> **From "Dover Beach" by Matthew Arnold**

No SOONER had the new Chancellor von Papen taken office and dissolved the *Reichstag*, on June 4, 1932, than he rescinded his predecessor's ban on the stormtroopers. "Shortly the streets of many cities began to echo with the shots of the warring gangs of Nazis and Communists, with the Red Fronters at first showing particular aggressiveness," according to the memoirs of the Prussian minister president, Otto Braun.[1] Attempts by the state governments to curb this explosive street warfare with state ordinances against paramilitary uniforms and demonstrations were promptly countermanded by *Reich* President von Hindenburg. There was no stopping now the daily, and even nightly clashes, brawls, assaults, and shootings among the huge private armies that had been assembled. Within a month after the ban against the SA was lifted, 99 persons were reported killed, 125 se-

[1] Otto Braun, *Von Weimar zu Hitler* (Hamburg: Reinbek, 1949), pp. 402-403. The newspaper *Münchner Neueste Nachrichten* published a daily chronicle called "Today's Clashes" filled with details from all over the country.

riously injured, and about five times that number were treated for minor injuries. Night after night, incidents occurred such as the following reported in the Berlin press on the eve of the elections:

Following an 8,000-person closed meeting of the republican Iron Front (IF) in Braunschweig, two IF men were shot down by stormtroopers in the street. The police were unable to catch the assassins.

SA troopers returning from a Hitler rally in Eberswalde attacked several passers-by wearing IF insignia, including a woman. Later they invaded the socialist *Volkshaus*, picked fights, and demolished the furniture.

In front of a KPD *Sturmlokal* (hangout), there was a shootout between Communists and Nazis. The police arrested several persons.

In Leipzig, a nocturnal clash with a KPD team putting up posters led to the fatal stabbing of a Communist locksmith, 21, by a Nazi agricultural laborer, 24, who claimed to have been acting in self-defense.

In Aachen, a Nazi poster team clashed at night with a Communist one with the result that a Nazi was fatally shot in the lungs and stomach.

A Centrist newspaper staff member in Duesseldorf was shot at by a Nazi shopkeeper, 30, who was arrested. Another Nazi was arrested for threatening passers-by with a pistol. No motive could be ascertained.

Shots were fired from a speeding truck at the home of an SPD deputy in Altona.

A local *Reichsbanner* chief was assaulted in front of the SA *Sturmlokal* in Gladbeck and had to be rescued by the police. The latter arrested his assailant, the local Nazi leader, who had a prior conviction for political offenses.

A clash occurred in Dortmund between *Reichsbanner* men and stormtroopers who pursued them on bicycles. One *Reichsbanner* man was shot to death.

27

At a rally of the *Staatspartei* (DDP) in Dessau, Nazis had occupied most of the meeting hall ahead of time so that many of the Democrats could not get in. Right after the speaker, Ernst Lemmer, began his address, the Nazi chairman of the city council gave the signal to disrupt the rally by making a deafening noise. He called on his cohorts to "throw out the speaker and the managers of the rally, the swine." The Nazis began to throw objects, hitting the speaker on the head with a beer stein, demolishing the hall, breaking up the meeting, and trying unsuccessfully to assault the speaker once more on his way out.

SA and SS stormtroopers from Frankfurt, armed with army helmets and uniforms, according to an SPD deputy in the state diet, were ready to march on the city of Darmstadt with the intention to occupy it.[2]

This was the setting just before the *Reichstag* elections, as the various private armies rested with bated breath. Since the police had forbidden demonstrations, loitering near polling stations and the like after the last big rallies, flags were the only displays on the eve of the elections. Rather than signifying joy or mourning, the flags were marks of the battling camps, which we will examine more closely in this chapter. The *Vossische Zeitung* described the scene:

> Today, one day before the probably most serious and most contested elections since 1919, red is the color of passion . . . as background for three arrows (Iron Front), the hammer and sickle, or the swastika. The old *Reich* colors black-white-red (*Stahlhelm*) have receded completely. More frequent is the black-red-gold crossed with the three arrows (*Reichsbanner*). In Wedding, at Penzlau Mountain, and in other typical workers' areas one can see whole streets in which every floor, every apartment flies

[2] From *Vossische Zeitung*, July 28, 1932, p. 7; and July 29, 1932, p. 3.

the IF flag; the KPD flag is more isolated. Even rarer, as compared to the presidential elections, are inscriptions . . . only the party numbers of the electoral lists—1, 2, and 3—but rarely words. They rely on the brief and pregnant language of symbols instead. One exception is . . . a house with a black-red-gold sign on the second floor, a banner, flanked by swastika pennants below it, reading "a defenseless people [is] a people without honor [is] a people without bread," and above it an IF flag and sign, "We demand an accounting: We want bread." How must the inhabitants of this house feel?! It seems like a simile of the whole unhappily divided German people.[3]

Election Sunday dawned clear and warm upon the battle scene in Berlin, where the police had been busy all night stopping some 250 persons who were out with paint and brushes either to deface the competitors' posters or to paint some slogans of their own on the walls. There was little violence in Berlin, although word of major clashes in the provinces came trickling in. The SA now was obviously the most dynamic of the four big private armies—the Communists/RFB, the *Reichsbanner*/Iron Front, the *Stahlhelm*, and the stormtroopers—and some of the reports sounded ominously like the Italian fascist raids of 1921/1922:

Near Stendal, stormtroopers came in trucks to raid an SPD rally, leaving 17 persons injured.

Near Frankfurt, a raid by 150 stormtroopers on a workers' colony in order to tear down an Iron Front flag left six persons injured, three of them in serious condition.

In Annweiler (Palatinate), a Nazi motor caravan was pelted with rocks by teenagers while passing through. The caravan turned around and 500 stormtroopers in-

[3] *Ibid.*, July 30, p. 2. The same issue contained further stories of violence: in Wuppertal, *Reichsbanner* and IF men guarding posters at night were assaulted by Nazis in one instance, and shot at from a car in another. Near Leipzig, at a Nazi rally, two Communist raiders fatally stabbed a stormtrooper, aged 19, and were arrested.

vaded homes along four blocks of the street, smashing all doors and windows. They inflicted numerous injuries and then fled.[4]

How was it possible for these paramilitary formations to become so prominent in Germany, where law and order had characterized public life—with rare exceptions—for half a century until 1918? Was it the attempted destruction of German militarism at the Peace Conference of 1919, or the demobilization of the huge wartime army and its limitation to 100,000 men by the treaty of Versailles that turned loose this flood of private armies? Was it the martial spirit awakened in the early years of the Great War, perhaps in its extreme embodiment, the daredevil *Sturmbataillone*, an evil ghost that would not rest?[5] The Italian equivalent, the *arditi*, also played a pivotal role in Gabrielle d'Annunzio's raid on Fiume and, later on, in the fascist movement.

To understand the rise of the Nazi stormtroopers and their role in the eventual success of Hitler, we will need to see them in the context of the major paramilitary formations of the Weimar Republic. The stormtroopers of the years 1930-1932 did not spring fully grown from Hitler's head. They had been nurtured by a full decade of paramilitary politics, and often came directly from other, similar organizations or from the rebellious ranks of organized youth. The paramilitary armies not only had a great deal in common. They fed upon each other's enmity in their development. Let us take a closer look at them as they passed through

---

[4] *Ibid.*, July 30, 1932, p. 8; and July 31, 1932, p. 3. There were, of course, also many smaller clashes resulting in deaths and injuries, including several caused by Communists and three that pitted the police against either the Communists or the stormtroopers, with considerable bloodletting on both sides. Other victims were a Center party secretary and a Conservative (DNVP) youth, both assaulted by Nazis.

[5] See the illuminating discussion and definitions of paramilitary organization by Warren E. Williams, "Paramilitarism in Interstate Relations" (Ph.D. dissertation, London, 1965), pp. 59-82, reprinted in translation in Volker R. Berghahn, ed., *Militarismus* (Cologne: Kiepenheuer & Witsch, 1975), pp. 139-151.

the crises of the Weimar Republic, until the final battles of 1932-1933, when many of them literally marched and fought all the way into the Third *Reich.*

The Beginnings of Paramilitary Formations

Short as the republican years were, there were no fewer than three distinct periods characterized by different alignments and confrontations of the four major private armies—the revolutionary left or Communists, the republican *Reichsbanner,* the nationalist *Stahlhelm,* and the Nazi stormtroopers (SA): the era of revolutionary upsurges from the left and right and their suppression (1918-1923); the years of quiet build-up of the *Reichsbanner,* the Red Front, and, last of all, the SA (1924-1929); and the period of the final showdown (1930-1933), which was dominated by the SA.

Under the democratic constitution of the Weimar Republic, the struggle for power was supposed to be carried out by the ballot alone, and not by private armies. Yet paramilitary forces came to the fore long before the early thirties—in fact, whenever the state seemed unable or reluctant to use its monopoly of force, beginning with the birth of the republic. In 1918, for example, the mighty imperial German army had a reserve of 2.7 million men ready to suppress any domestic uprisings from the left, but these reserve troops were so deeply demoralized by the wave of popular disillusionment and pacifism that they could not be counted on at the time of the armistice and at the first revolutionary stirrings. Even older garrison soldiers were swayed, and refused to fight against the domestic insurgents in Kiel, Munich, and Berlin. The impotence of the regular army was a major reason for the provisional republican government and the Army High Command to turn instead to calling for volunteer military units (Freecorps), who proved to be a mixed blessing. The Freecorps were always willing and able to fight the revolutionary left, but not exactly in defense of the new republic. They attracted many swashbuckling, imperial officers and men who perceived little dif-

31

ference between the duly elected republican government of Social Democrats, Democrats, and Catholic Central politicians and the insurgents of the far left, and who in time began to conspire against the republic.[6]

The revolutionary Spartacists, left radicals, and left Independent Socialists (USPD) later claimed to have had available a total of 120,000 militarily trained workers several weeks before the armistice of November 9, while Councils of Workers and Soldiers were undermining the old army from within. Wherever the revolutionary elements were strong, they established armed Workers' Guards (*Arbeiterwehren*) or Defense Guards (*Sicherheits-* and *Schutzwehren*) for their own Councils of Workers and Soldiers. The famed People's Marine Divisions helped themselves to substantial quantities of weapons and ammunition, including cannons, and carried the spirit of the great mutiny at Kiel to other large cities of northern and central Germany. In areas where they were particularly strong, as in Halle and Merseburg, the armed Workers' Guards of the council "kept bourgeois demonstrations and rallies under control," as we are told by recent East German sources.[7]

These first paramilitary formations of the revolutionary left turned out to be no match for the highly professional Freecorps, who defeated them in Berlin, Bremen, and Munich in 1919, and again in the great Ruhr uprising that followed the right-wing Kapp putsch of March 1920. The putsch was carried out by parts of the regular *Reichswehr* under General von Luettwitz and a Prussian senior official, Wolfgang Kapp, and collapsed when the left-wing USPD

[6] Large numbers of World War I officers (150,000) had been newly commissioned from the ranks for valor, and formed an upwardly mobile element from the prewar lower bourgeosie that after the war became prominent in the Freecorps and in patriotic and veterans' organizations. Eventually, many of these people found their way into the Nazi party.

[7] Heinz Oeckel, *Die revolutionäre Volkswehr 1918/19* (Berlin: Militaerverlag, 1968), p. 121; and also pp. 39, 47-49, 75-76, 96, and 231. In Munich, in April 1919, a red army of thirty to forty thousand had to be defeated by the Freecorps Epp.

and KPD, the republican SPD, the Democrats, and the Free Trade Unions (ADGB), in a rare show of unity, proclaimed a general strike.[8] But while the republican government returned in triumph to Berlin, the armed workers in the Ruhr, who had actually fought and defeated troops loyal to Kapp, were reluctant to accept the compromises of the republican government with the *Reichswehr*, even under the threat of further military intervention. A "red army" of eighty to a hundred thousand men had formed from local Workers' Guards in an unplanned, spontaneous manner and stood its ground for another two weeks under workers' councils.[9] Eventually, the republican government and the *Reichswehr* command ordered massed troops, including many units that had been loyal to Kapp, to march into the Ruhr and to put down what was left of the Workers' Guards. Wholesale executions and special courts finished the remainders of the Workers' Guard, as had happened in the suppression of the councils' rule in Munich a year earlier.

The parliamentary elections following the Ruhr uprising and, by implication, the earlier confrontations between the majority SPD and the left-wing USPD and other dissidents spelled disaster for the Weimar Republic. The republican SPD lost nearly half of its popular vote of 1919 to the antirepublican USPD and Communists (KPD), and this was especially true wherever there had been Freecorps expeditions against the revolutionaries. The antirepublican right-wing People's Party (DVP) and Nationalists (DNVP), with the help of the Treaty of Versailles and the government's demonstration of weakness on the occasion of the Kapp putsch, almost doubled their vote.[10] The three republican

[8] The immediate causes of the Kapp putsch were the imminent reduction of the *Reichswehr*, in accordance with the Peace Treaty of Versailles, to 100,000 men, and the decision to disband the two Freecorps, *Marinebrigaden* Ehrhardt and Loewenfeld.

[9] See Georg Eliasberg, *Der Ruhrkrieg von 1920* (Bonn: Neue Gesellschaft, 1974), pp. 103-132, and the sources cited there. The author is rather skeptical about the allegations of "red terror" under the control of these Guards. *Ibid.*, pp. 233-240.

[10] The SPD dropped from 37.9% to 21.7% while the USPD vote rose

33

parties, the SPD, the Democrats, and the Center party, thus dropped from their majority of 76.2 percent in 1919 to 43.6 percent in 1920, leaving the republican constitution without the popular majority that had created it.

Communist Revolutionary Organizations

For the development of paramilitary formations on the left, the most important effect of these early revolutionary stirrings and their suppression under orders of the republican government was the completion of the process of polarization that had begun during the war and with the extraordinary growth of the Independent Socialists (USPD) at the expense of the majority SPD.[11] The revolutionary Spartacists within the USPD from the beginning considered this party as a mere cover, and insisted on their own (Rosa Luxemburg's) idea of "spontaneous revolution," which required substantial local autonomy from any central party institutions.

In the last days of 1918 they left the USPD to establish the German Communist party (KPD), numbering a few thousand members who were deeply divided on such issues as whether to prefer Councils of Workers and Soldiers to the election of a National Constituent Assembly, on the role of political terror, and on the party's relationship to the trade unions and to the Russian Bolsheviks.[12] The slaying

---

from 7.6% to 17.9%, and the KPD, which had chosen not to compete in 1919, received 2.1%. The Center party dropped from 19.7% to 13.6%, having lost its Bavarian branch. The Democrats dropped from 18.5% to 8.3%, while the DVP rose from 4.4% to 13.9%, and the DNVP from 10.3% to 15.1%.

[11] The USPD membership soared from less than 100,000 in November 1918 to 300,000 by January 1919, and on to 750,000 by December of the same year, and nearly 900,000 a year later. Its electoral support, as we have seen, underwent similar growth between 1919 and 1920. Richard N. Hunt, *German Social Democracy 1918-1933* (New Haven: Yale University Press, 1964), pp. 198-199.

[12] See the remarks of Hermann Weber in his preface to Ossip K. Flechtheim, *Die KPD in der Weimarer Republik*, 2nd ed. (Frankfurt: EVA, 1969), pp. 26-30.

of three of its most outstanding leaders, Rosa Luxemburg, Karl Liebknecht, and Leo Joegiches, and the suppression of the Spartacist uprisings had held back the growth of the KPD during its first year. During these embattled weeks, the KPD had also organized the first political-paramilitary group, the Red Soldiers League, with the purpose of protecting revolutionary demonstrations, conducting rallies, and propagandizing the returning soldiers during the elections of Councils of Workers and Soldiers. After the collapse of the January uprising, the party had been declared illegal and, within a year, suffered the exodus of half of its membership, who formed a still more extreme but short-lived Communist Workers Party (KAPD). By the end of 1920, however, the KPD became the unwitting beneficiary of the process of polarization, as the entire left wing of the USPD went over to the KPD, suddenly making the latter a mass party of nearly four hundred thousand members.

This sudden emergence from a relatively weak fringe position explains what one historian has called "the Communist bid for power in Germany, 1921-1923,"[13] three years of futile efforts by the KPD to overthrow the Weimar Republic. For the first time the KPD seemed in a position to make good its original hope "to be the instrument of proletarian revolution in Germany." This period began with an appeal to the SPD for proletarian unity on a basis that included the establishment of "proletarian defense troops" and diplomatic relations with the Soviet Union. The SPD refused, and the republican Prussian government soon moved police and soldiers into one of the strongholds of KPD control, the Halle-Merseburg area, in order to disarm the workers. The KPD felt the time was ripe for armed resistance, and called for a general strike. There were clashes among the workers in many cities, and bombings that added to the many other troubles of the republic at that time. Some of

[13] This is the subtitle of Werner T. Angress, *Stillborn Revolution* (Princeton: Princeton University Press, 1963). See also the account in Flechtheim, *KPD*, pp. 159-190, and, on the KAPD, Olaf Ihlau, *Die roten Kämpfer* (Meisenheim: Hahn, 1969).

the wilder revolutionary elements even wanted to blow up the KPD headquarters in Halle and Breslau (Wroclaw) in order to goad the masses into action. A total of forty thousand armed workers in the Halle-Merseburg area and in Thuringia and Saxony faced seventeen thousand police and government troops. In the end, this "March action" of 1921 turned into a disaster for the KPD, which proved unable to mobilize the hoped-for millions of non-Communist workers.

Following this debacle, the KPD for a while made common cause with the SPD, the USPD, and the trade unions. This popular front at times even implied the defense of the republic by the KPD against the threat from the radical right, which in 1921 and 1922 assassinated the finance minister, Matthias Erzberger, and the foreign minister, Walther Rathenau. The KPD, which at its beginnings had spurned the trade unions altogether, had by 1922 gained a strong foothold in the Free Trade Unions (ADGB), and was quite successful whenever it chose to mobilize workers for massive street demonstrations and other forms of direct action. In 1922, also, a guard service was created to protect Communist rallies and functionaries.

The crisis year of 1923, with the French invasion of the Rhineland and the financial collapse of the German economy, once more spurred the KPD to revolutionary enthusiasm. Early in the year, the KPD began to raise a paramilitary army of Proletarian Hundreds under the leadership of cadres composed of active KPD members and the guard service (*Ordnerdienst*). In Central Germany, even the SPD agreed to cooperate in forming Proletarian Hundreds. Several hundred thousand men were estimated to be ready for the next wave of revolution, until the Prussian government outlawed the Proletarian Hundreds on May 12.[14] The party, moreover, reinterpreted its mission as a national liberation struggle against French imperialism—arm in arm with the French Communists against the bourgeoisie—culminating in the "Schlageter policy" of fighting shoulder to shoulder

[14] See Kurt G. P. Schuster, *Der Rote Frontkämpferbund 1924-1929* (Duesseldorf: Droste, 1975), and the sources used there.

with the radical right against the French occupation.[15] During the few weeks of the Schlageter policy, the Communist newspaper *Rote Fahne* and other KPD publications actually carried articles by right-wing politicians and writers such as the author of the book *The Third Reich*, Moeller van den Bruck. Meanwhile, a prominent Communist leader, Ruth Fischer, attacked the Jews in her diatribes against capitalism. But the party also organized a big wave of strikes leading up to the Berlin general strike of August 1923, all in protest against runaway inflation and other economic aspects of the crisis. The momentum of the KPD campaign against the bourgeois coalition government of Chancellor Cuno finally succeeded in toppling the government, but only to find itself blocked when the SPD entered a grand coalition under Chancellor Stresemann.

Nevertheless, the KPD was still on the rise in membership, voters, and trade union support. Most important, the party was deeply involved in clandestine military preparations for a "German October revolution." The Executive Committee of the Communist International had decided that the time had come to overthrow what it took to be the German equivalent of the Russian rivals to the Bolsheviks back in 1917. With appropriate instructions and assistance from Moscow, the KPD built up a secret military organization (*M-Apparat*), collected arms, and planned to mobilize a red army from the Proletarian Hundreds under the leadership of a Russian-German Revolutionary Committee (*Revko*). An army of fifty to sixty thousand was to intercept the assault of *Reichswehr* units and right-wing paramilitary organizations in Central Germany from the south, while the revolutionary workers would take over in the Ruhr area and in Berlin. A general strike was indeed proclaimed on September 27 in the Ruhr. At the same time, the KPD introduced three ministers into the left-wing SPD state govern-

---

[15] The "Schlageter policy" was so named after the executed Free-corps officer Albert Leo Schlageter, who to all nationalistic elements had become a martyr of national indignation and of the clandestine struggle against the French.

ment of Saxony, with the intention of acquiring access to weapons and control of police forces. Another three entered the Thuringian state government. The Proletarian Hundreds were to be armed, and further guard units were to be established to prepare and protect a general strike throughout Germany. But Stresemann was watchful, and with one stroke undercut the plotting of both the radical left and radical right by declaring a state of emergency, and giving the army under General von Seeckt complete control—which, for example, took away the power of the Saxonian cabinet over the state police. The regional *Reichswehr* commander was instructed to demand that the Proletarian Hundreds be disarmed and, when the Saxonian government refused, the *Reichswehr* marched into the state and deposed the coalition government. The revolt had collapsed again before it had really started. Only in Hamburg, where Ernst Thaelmann insisted on going through with the plans for an armed uprising, were there open hostilities between a handful of insurgents and the police. The final result of the whole undertaking was that the KPD was once more outlawed for a considerable period, and that its internal politics fell completely under the sway of the Stalinist left.

The Stahlhelm: Black-White-Red

The chief antagonists of the revolutionary left had been not only the republican governments and, at their behest, the Freecorps and the *Reichswehr* troops. Local defense leagues and vigilante organizations also fought the "reds." From the Freecorps, the *Reichswehr*, and the *Einwohnerwehr*, personal ties and shared convictions led to the formation of the numerous nationalistic and veterans' organizations that characterized the early years of the republic.[16] The same Central German area of Halle-Merseburg and Magdeburg in which the left was so strong and active from

[16] This was true especially after *Einwohnerwehr* and Freecorps were dissolved. See also James H. Diehl, *Paramilitary Politics in Weimar Germany* (Bloomington: University of Indiana Press, 1977).

the outset also spawned the militant *Stahlhelm* veterans. There were larger veterans associations, such as the *Kyff-haeuser* League of Veterans, and more war-like shock troops, such as the Freecorps, other irregular units (*Zeit-freiwillige*), and the *Einwohnerwehren*, who were the actual combat troops against the revolutionary left in the early days. And there were political adventurers like the Captains Ehrhardt or Rossbach with their Freecorps, who far more directly went after the high stakes of nationalistic politics. But among the multitude of traditional right-wing and veterans' organizations of the Weimar republic, the *Stahlhelm* stands out as the purest embodiment of the glories of the imperial army and of the militaristic spirit of the war effort.

The spirit of the *Stahlhelm* was captured best by an early pamphlet of the organization appealing to the legendary frontsoldier:

Comrade:

Do you remember how we stuck it out together under the heaviest enemy fire, shoulder to shoulder, keeping our German faith in true comradeship? Is this comradeship to end the same minute we take off the field-grey coat? Shouldn't we continue this proven battle-hardened comradeship, which is part of the best that we brought home from this long war?

Do you recall, while we were defending Germany's borders out there at the risk of our lives, how many of those who stayed home took away our jobs and our income; how war-and-revolution racketeers filled their pockets; and how incompetent and dishonest elements pushed themselves into the leading positions? Don't you want to help us to see to it now that the front soldiers receive the economic and political positions they deserve after their titanic struggle against a world of enemies?

Are you aware that criminal and alien elements want to arouse the lowest instincts of the people and plunge Germany into a civil war? Won't you help us maintain law and order so that we can all go peacefully about the work

39

our country needs so badly to hold off a total breakdown and to give a hand to the fatherland?

Join our ranks as a comrade![17]

The Stahlhelm, League of the Frontsoldiers

The monarchistic, antirepublican tenor of the *Stahlhelm* was not present from the beginning, although there was a strong antirevolutionary note, with the usual solicitude for the well-being and the interests of the veterans.[18] Beginning with the imposition of the Treaty of Versailles in early summer of 1919, however, an ultranationalistic realignment took place in most veterans' organizations and Freecorps, which combined bitterness about the harsh terms of the treaty with hatred toward the republican parties that had signed it. In particular, the limitation of the *Reichswehr* to one hundred thousand men, and, perhaps, four thousand officers spelled the end of the hopes of hundreds of thousands of professional military men for the continuation of their careers. This affected particularly the large number of young officers who had been promoted from the ranks during the war and were far too young to be pensioned off. Large numbers of officers and subofficer grades ended up among the four hundred thousand Freecorps fighters, where they often made up whole units. Cadets and academic youth in the Freecorps and other units had also been hoping for military or at least civil service careers.[19] It took little insight for all these men to see that they would be out in the street as soon as the Freecorps had done their job of suppressing insurrection and protecting the eastern borders.

[17] Quoted in Hans Henning Freiherr Grote, ed., *Deutschlands Erwachen* (Essen: Nationale Vertriebsstelle Ruhrland, 1933), p. 293.

[18] The Magdeburg *Stahlhelm* even volunteered to supply trained men for the police functions of the local Council of Workers and Soldiers. Volker Berghahn, *Der Stahlhelm, Bund der Frontsoldaten* (Duesseldorf: Droste, 1966), pp. 13-17.

[19] Guenter Paulus, in "Die soziale Struktur der Freikorps in der ersten Monaten nach der Novemberrevolution," *Zeitschrift für Geschichtswissenschaft*, 3 (1955), 685-704, also mentions unemployed young workers and retail clerks among the typical Freecorps recruits.

Meanwhile, the republican government understandably preferred to accept only reliable elements into the new mini-
Reichswehr, and the question of which veterans' organizations were acceptable sources of recruits was politically
very explosive. Thus radical factions of discontented veterans grew in the early *Stahlhelm*, as in many another veterans' group, and set the organization on a militantly antirepublican course.

The two most important *Stahlhelm* leaders, Franz Seldte
and Theodor Duesterberg, to some extent characterize the
trends in the *Stahlhelm*. Seldte, a Magdeburg manufacturer,
had been a bourgeois reserve officer before the war, and
became a decorated invalid as a result of it. He was close to
the National Liberals before 1918 and to the People's party
(DVP) after it. His *Stahlhelm* career represents both a moderate, bourgeois strain and the perversion of bourgeois values in the empire and, eventually, in the hands of Hitler.
Duesterberg, by way of contrast, was a product of the
Potsdam cadet corps and an eminently successful staff officer before and during the war. He joined the conservative
DNVP in Halle, and soon thereafter the *Stahlhelm* there,
which had been shaped by the prolonged and intense fighting against the revolutionary left. Duesterberg represented
the imperial officer in all his military glory, with an uncom-
promising *voelkisch* extremism and a total lack of understanding for the great changes that had overcome German
society in 1918. But he also possessed a sense of integrity
that a mere Hitler could not shake. Together, the two *Stahlhelm* leaders represented the dominant features of respectable prewar German society that had been hardened by the
war and set to an unrelenting vendetta against the Weimar
republic.

As the organization grew across the country and new
locals were initiated under the imperial black-white-and-
red war flag, it soon became clear that the *Stahlhelm* was to
be counted among the increasing number of right-wing foes
of the republic. It had not taken sides in the Kapp putsch,
but many members had participated in the subsequent

Ruhr battles. The *Stahlhelm* was prominent in the 1920 attempts to unite all the conservative veterans' organizations, and profited notably from the suppression of *Orgesch*[20] and of local vigilante groups (*Einwohnerwehr*), many of whose members ended up joining the *Stahlhelm*. The heterogeneous impulses and origins of many of the new recruits made for considerable confusion, and for complex interrelationships with other groups. But all the members yearned for military ostentation and, under the general ban on maneuvers and drills, found street demonstrations and even street fighting very attractive. In addition, large numbers of juveniles and nonveterans, even women, wanted to join this organization, originally devoted only to World War I veterans. Eventually, a youth organization, the Scharnhorst League (and, to a lesser degree, another group, the *Wehrwolf*) accommodated the young until the establishment of *Jungstahlhelm*, which grew to a prodigious one hundred thousand members by 1930. The women were accommodated in the *Koenigin-Luise-Bund* and other groups, since it would have gone against the grain of the all-male youth and veterans' culture of the Weimar republic to mix the sexes.

A Menace to the Republic

By the time of the assassination of Walther Rathenau, in 1922, the *Stahlhelm* was already caught up in the retaliatory actions of the republican government. Friedrich Otto Hoersing, the Social Democratic *Oberpraesident* of the province of Saxony, outlawed the *Stahlhelm* there, and Minister of the Interior Carl Severing extended the action to the whole state of Prussia, despite the *Stahlhelm*'s protestations of innocence. Back in circulation early in 1923, it was augmented by many converts from other outlawed organizations, and was once more in the throes of radical factionalism that

[20] The Organisation Escherich (Orgesch) was a major national congeries of veterans and right-wing associations that had grown up in Bavaria.

42

gainsaid the leadership's assurances of loyalty to the republic. Toward the government, the *Stahlhelm* solemnly declared that it rejected putsch plans of any sort, had no arms or armed units, and maintained no links to other putschist groups or parties, such as the German *Voelkisch* Freedom party (DVFP).[21] The actual position of the *Stahlhelm* with regard to the republic was somewhere between the cautious course of Seldte, who received moral support from Stresemann's DVP, and Duesterberg's campaign to "fight for the equal rights of nationalist and *voelkisch* circles to the streets which are presently dominated ruthlessly by the Reds."[22] Many *Stahlhelm* members also became involved in active resistance and sabotage teams fighting against the French occupation of the Ruhr area, in contrast to the passive resistance of the government.

When the right-wing agitation and conspiracies of that turbulent year of 1923 finally came to a head in October, the *Stahlhelm* sent a telegram to Chancellor Stresemann, calling on him to establish a national dictatorship, and offering its unqualified support. But Stresemann shied away from the suggested dissolution of the *Reichstag*, the overthrow of Social Democratic rule in Prussia, and an extreme German nationalist course against the republic. Von Seeckt was at first reported to be more receptive to these plans because they had broad backing from nationalists in north and south,[23] but he backed off when there was an isolated military putsch attempt by a Major Ernst Buchrucker and his Black *Reichswehr*. Some *Stahlhelm* men were involved in this venture. Many local units of the organization, including that of Halle (Duesterberg), were seething with an activist

21 See Berghahn, *Stahlhelm*, pp. 35-39. *Stahlhelm* leader Seldte's declarations of republican loyalty formed a stark contrast to the sentiment of some of the groups in the organization, especially in Halle, where Duesterberg had become *Gaufuehrer*.

22 Quoted in Berghahn, *Stahlhelm*, pp. 38-39.

23 Later dictatorial proposals of a close collaborator of Seldte's contained elaborate details about specific measures and policies. See *Der Stahlhelm* (periodical), January 15, 1924, p. 4, and Berghahn, *Stahlhelm*, p. 51.

fervor that Seldte could hardly contain. The collapse of Hitler's beer-hall putsch, however, also doomed Duesterberg's and the Munich *Stahlhelm's* plans for seizing the initiative.[24] Hitler, too, had miscalculated badly when he thought he could force his erstwhile nationalist and *Reichswehr* allies to fall in line behind him in a Mussolini-style "March on Berlin." Instead of the conspirators, General von Seeckt became the military dictator, with the support of President Ebert. This ended all further plotting. The *Stahlhelm* narrowly escaped being outlawed again, and had to settle down to the quiet years of the republic.

Fire under the Ashes

Thus ended the era of Communist and fascist putsches. The beleaguered republic recovered economically and politically for what appeared at the time to be a long period of consolidation, after which it was expected that it would no longer exhibit the state of weakness and confusion that had tempted the would-be Lenins and Mussolinis of Germany. Yet it was precisely in these early middle years of the republic that the radical right, the radical left, and the republicans began to gird themselves in a systematic fashion for the final struggle.

For the *Stahlhelm*, the era was characterized by relative quiescence, although it was involved, along with other right-wing organizations, in the plans for a secret eastern army that was to augment the *Reichswehr* in case of a conflict with Poland.[25] At the same time, this façade of legality could not hide the increasingly political and ideological enmity of the *Stahlhelm* toward the new republican *Reichsbanner*, the Catholic Center party, and the alleged Jewish domination of German business and culture. *Voelkisch* ideology and, in northern Germany, old Prussian prejudices

[24] See esp. Harold J. Gordon, *Hitler and the Beer Hall Putsch* (Princeton: Princeton University Press, 1972), pp. 250-253.

[25] See Thilo Vogelsang, *Reichswehr, Staat und NSDAP* (Stuttgart: DVA, 1962), pp. 46, 53.

44

accounted for many of these sentiments; the anti-Catholic coloration of these groups was, in contrast, quite counter-productive in the Catholic parts of Germany. Antisemitism had come to the fore only in 1922, when *voelkisch* elements in Halle began to question Jewish membership in *Stahl-helm*. It led to the adoption of an exclusionary clause in 1924, and to antisemitic agitation and boycott activities in some localities, notably in Berlin, where the former *Stahl-helm* leader Count Helldorf had joined the Nazi storm-troopers.[26] Meanwhile, the *Stahlhelm* was preoccupied with the Dawes Plan of Reparations (1924), which to the right wing was merely the Versailles *Diktat* on the installment plan. Opposing the Dawes Plan and the Treaty of Locarno also implied hatred for Stresemann and his DVP, which had adopted a more moderate, republican course. In spite of the sworn aversion of the *Stahlhelm* to political parties, more-over, the organization found itself willy-nilly drawn into electoral politics in the quiet years between 1924 and 1928. The center of decision making had moved back to the par-ties and representative institutions. The presidential nomi-nation of old soldier von Hindenburg was by no means de-cided by the *Stahlhelm* or any other veterans' organization, however much their members revered him. The *Stahlhelm* could only jump on a bandwagon not of its construction.[27]

The *Stahlhelm* had benefited from a great influx of new members in 1924, which brought the total membership to about 260,000. But instead of producing greater activism, this surge led to an extended phase of disorganization and laxity in many locals, where beer busts and card-playing evenings outweighed the more political occasions. Flag consecrations and the massive annual Frontsoldiers' Days

[26] See Berghahn, *Stahlhelm*, pp. 64-67. On the other hand, the heavy-handed attempts to form partisan coalitions in 1926 ended in humiliating retreats. *Ibid.*, pp. 86-87.

[27] The *Stahlhelm* and kindred groups were reluctant to choose the popular field marshal for fear of helping thereby to consolidate the legitimacy of the republic. Duesterberg's *voelkisch* activism, in any case, went far beyond the Prussian conservatism of von Hindenburg.

45

degenerated into patriotic posturing, strutting in uniform, and swashbuckling gestures. The odd combination of the experience of the trenches and of the defeat of 1918 with bourgeois nationalism seemed a poor recipe for the pursuit of political power. To be sure, there were many new intellectual interpretations of the frontsoldiers' mission, especially along "national-revolutionary" or "conservative-revolutionary," even "national bolshevik" lines,[28] but there were hardly any ideas capable of immediate political realization. There was, however, no mistaking the hostility of *Stahlhelm* members to any kind of parliamentary democracy, and their inclination toward authoritarian government along corporative, fascist lines, and toward some sort of ethnocentric imperialism. The exaggerated leadership cult, which seized the Communists and the Social Democratic *Reichsbanner* only in about 1929-1930, raised its swollen head in the *Stahlhelm* as early as 1925, when the traditional *Vorsitzender* (chairman) became a *Fuehrer*. While the strong emotions and the political naiveté of the "frontsoldier generation" were unlikely to produce anything very profound or lasting, there was a general turning against the Wilhelminian past, often expressed with the abrasive bitterness of a growing generation gap. The young veterans, and even more the nonveterans of the *Jungstahlhelm*, began to look at their elders and superior officers with scorn.

The transition to the final assault on the republic was marked by a solemn resolution in October 1926 of the Executive Board of the *Stahlhelm* to "get into the system" (*Hinein in den Staat*), which was at first widely interpreted to mean that the organization was following the example of the DVP, which had moved from monarchistic opposition

[28] See, for example, Klemens von Klemperer, *Germany's New Conservatism* (Princeton: Princeton University Press, 1957), or Armin Mohler, *Die konservative Revolution in Deutschland, 1918-1932* (Stuttgart: EVA, 1950). The finer distinctions between varieties of this genre bore little relevance to particular sets of institutions or policies other than that some were still monarchistic, while others spoke of charismatic popular leaders and a Third *Reich*.

to a responsible role in the government. It soon became clear, however, that the true intention was to penetrate and take over "the system" from within. At the following Front-soldiers' Day in Berlin, in May 1927, when no fewer than 132,000 *Stahlhelmers* tried to impress the capital with their presence, this intention became plain.[29] Navy Captain Ehr-hardt's *Bund Wiking* was partly brought into the *Stahlhelm*, and a student (*Langemarck*) and a workers' group, *Stahl-helm Selbsthilfe* (Self-Help), were founded. The latter was a propaganda organization and aimed at the long-standing goal of "conquering the German working classes," or at least alienating them from the SPD and KPD.

The *Stahlhelm* also urged the right-wing parties to put up *Stahlhelmers* as candidates in the impending state and fed-eral elections, with respectable results: fifty-one of the sev-enty-three DNVP candidates elected to the *Reichstag* in 1928 were *Stahlhelm* members, and so were nine of forty-five DVP deputies and five others. In the Prussian *Landtag*, fifty-five deputies of the DNVP, nine of the DVP and two others were *Stahlhelmers*. However, these impressive num-bers hardly implied that the *Stahlhelm* could rely on more than a few of these deputies to do its bidding. The national election had been a humiliating defeat for the right wing. The *Stahlhelm* therefore chose to hold another monster rally of 138,000 in Hamburg, and other massive rallies through-out Germany, at which the frontsoldiers expressed their hatred for the "system" and vowed to fight it.[30] This "decla-ration of hatred" constituted a kind of declaration of war upon the republic, which was widely noted and commented

[29] The state and municipal authorities were so apprehensive about this seeming attempt at "occupying" the capital, that they seriously considered suppressing the rally. See the pictorial material on this and the Frontsoldiers Days in Franz Seldte, ed., *Der Stahlhelm*, 2nd ed. (Berlin: Stahlhelmverlag, 1933), p. 194, and pp. 167, 185-203.

[30] Berghahn, *Stahlhelm*, pp. 111-112. Stresemann interpreted the evolution of the organization in 1928 as "the foundation of a fascist party," and induced all DVP deputies to resign from the *Stahlhelm*. *Ibid.*, pp. 115-121. The rank and file of the DVP did not share his view.

upon. The organization also toyed with the idea of a constitutional referendum to abolish parliamentary government in favor of a stronger president.

In the same year, the organization also conducted a drive for funds and demands of amnesty for the imprisoned *Feme* murderers, right-wing assassins of the years 1922 and 1923. It was symptomatic of the condition of the respectable bourgeoisie that conservatives and liberals of all sorts should applaud this action. On a more symbolic level, the *Stahlhelm* took the occasion of the seventieth birthday of the deposed *Kaiser* to reiterate its loyalty and reaffirm the continued validity of the *Stahlhelm* soldiers' oaths on His Imperial Majesty, an action that placed republican civil servants among the *Stahlhelmers* in a most ambiguous position—not to mention President Hindenburg, an honorary member and patron of the *Stahlhelm*.[31]

It may seem difficult to imagine a group that would make the *Stahlhelm* seem innocuous by comparison. Yet this was emphatically true of the *voelkisch* groups, including the Nazis, who seemed to be able to top every position of the *Stahlhelm*. They regrouped their forces in 1925 under the leadership of Hitler, this time without reliance on the help of army units or other paramilitary organizations. They began with a small but well-organized and nation-wide party organization, and took care that the stormtroopers would be thoroughly under the control of the party. From their 1923 debacle and from the Kapp putsch they had learned that they could not win by illegal force, but would have to attempt to gain power by legal means. At the same time, the disillusionment of the defeat tended to wash most of the lukewarm, opportunistic elements out of the Nazi movement, leaving only the diehards who did not mind belonging to what most people considered a tiny lunatic

---

[31] The *Stahlhelm* maintained close relations with von Hindenburg, and, on the occasion of his eightieth birthday, helped to present the old *Junker* with an East Prussian estate, Neudeck, which had been bought with funds raised by several right-wing groups including the *Stahlhelm*.

fringe. Many rough and ready former Freecorps fighters and violent elements from other movements of the radical right found their way to the swastika in those days.

The Rise of the Reichsbanner

In the same "quiet period," the republican parties established a paramilitary organization, the *Reichsbanner Schwarz-Rot-Gold*. The founder was the same Social Democratic *Oberpraesident* Hoersing, who had controlled the police troops in the Halle-Merseburg area during the "March action" of 1921, and had outlawed the *Stahlhelm* there in 1922. The *Reichsbanner* was established in February 1924 for "the defense against possible attacks by political enemies on the constitution or republic."[32] It was the largest paramilitary army of its time, with between 1.5 and 3.5 million members, but it was dependent on the procurement of arms, which the *Reichsbanner* hoped to obtain from the republican government in Prussia or the *Reich* government. Its members, leadership, and financial support came mainly from the SPD and the Free Trade Unions, and only to a small extent from the Democrats and the Center party.

The reference to the black-red-gold flag of the 1848 revolution and the Weimar Republic was deliberate, and *Reichsbanner* lore also attempted to co-opt some of the heroes of the nationalist wars of liberation against Napoleon in the hope of building up a symbolic genealogy for a national-republican guard. There was a great deal of receptiveness for paramilitary organization among the highly organized Social Democratic associations and trade unions, whose mass membership had been as much involved in the war as were the militarists of the right. The Workers Sports Associations alone numbered half a million able-bodied young people, and the youth organization of the *Reichsbanner*, the *Jungbanner*, eventually enrolled half a million eighteen- to

[32] See Friedrich Otto Hoersing, "Das Reichsbanner Schwarz-Rot-Gold" in Bernard Harms, ed., *Volk und Reich der Deutschen*, 2 vols. (Berlin: Hobbing, 1929), II, 182.

twenty-five-year olds, not to mention another 220,000 younger people and 150,000 Red Falcons under fourteen. The partisan Socialist Workers Youth (SAJ) had 56,000 members in 1933.

There was, however, a general reluctance among the republican leadership to build up paramilitary formations. There had been earlier attempts to organize republican soldiers or guard associations back in 1919, but they tended to be in an uncertain position between the much stronger insurgents of the left and the Freecorps. Back in 1919, also, the SPD newspaper *Vorwaerts* had in vain urged loyal workers to join the vigilante *Einwohnerwehr* and protective associations, and not to leave them to the right-wing elements. The large number of veterans who enrolled in the *Reichsbanner*, in any event, shows clearly that the whole war generation and the entire legacy of the war were not all on the side of the nationalistic opposition to the republic. The *Reichsbanner's* mere existence, but also its huge rallies and demonstrations throughout the country seemed for a while to build up a breakwater against the storms of both radical extremes, who often combined forces in attacking the republic. On the other hand, this republican guard was not entirely welcome in many quarters of the SPD, especially among the pacifistic left, where it was seen as the worst kind of compromise with the militarism and nationalism of the day. The dominant forces in the heterogenous *Reichsbanner* were, indeed, not given to socialist orthodoxy, and frequently found common ground or at least mutual respect with militant right-wing organizations such as the *Stahlhelm* veterans or the *Jungdeutscher Orden* (*Jungdo*).

The *Reichsbanner* was also viewed with misgivings by such SPD dignitaries as the Prussian minister of the interior, Carl Severing, who frowned on its violence, and was reluctant to encourage a republican paramilitary formation for fear of having to concede equal rights to the antirepublican forces. Only the impact of the right and left-wing assaults of 1923, notably Hitler's beer-hall putsch, persuaded the Prussian minister to consider, still grudgingly, that the republic might be in need of paramilitary help. The minor participation of the other republican parties, the Center and Democratic parties, in this "suprapartisan veterans association" for the defense of the republic clinched the argument in favor of the *Reichsbanner*. For a while, the youth organizations of the parties involved also discussed merging, which would have assured the republican guard of broader support, but nothing came of it.[33]

No sooner had the *Reichsbanner* risen in all its might than the acute antirepublican threat died down. The quiet years of the republic gave less justification to militant republican rallies and demonstrations. Still, there were occasions such as the Day of the Hundred Thousand in Magdeburg in 1925, the celebration of the foundation of the organization, the annual Constitution Day parades (which competed with the pseudo-patriotic German Days of the right), the torchlight parades on the occasion of the transfer of President Ebert's body from Berlin to Heidelberg, and especially the eighty-year commemoration of the 1848 National Constituent Assembly in Frankfurt in 1928, when the *Reichsbanner* claimed to have marched 150,000 uniformed members past St. Paul's church, the site of the historic gathering. The *Reichsbanner* deserves credit for having brought the flag and spirit of the republic close to many small towns and villages that had never been exposed to it before. The organization also stood its ground in the presidential election campaign of 1925, when it could campaign for a common republican candidate, Wilhelm Marx (Center).[34]

Despite its huge size and massive public displays, the *Reichsbanner* languished in spirit and membership in those quiet years. A grave internal crisis involving rash promises

[33] See Karl Rohe, *Das Reichsbanner Schwarz-Rot-Gold* (Duesseldorf: Droste, 1966), pp. 40-43, 47-52. An important aspect of this suprapartisan, republican character was also that it replaced de facto the hopes for a left-wing popular front of the SPD, the ADGB, and the KPD.

[34] Rohe, *Reichsbanner*, pp. 78-80. There were also isolated instances where local *Reichsbanner* units campaigned for SPD candidates in other elections.

of *Reichsbanner* support for the Austrian Republican *Schutzbund* in 1927 and 1929 demonstrated both its "greater German" character and the tenuous consensus it commanded. The socialist left, and especially the Socialist Workers Youth (SAJ), which lost many members to the simple-minded militaristic appeal of the *Reichsbanner* youth (*Jungbanner*), disavowed its anti-Communism and its stress on national solidarity above the class struggle. Its bourgeois allies in the Center and Democratic parties began to feel uneasy in an organization composed almost exclusively of SPD supporters, even though the *Reichsbanner* was careful never to engage in religious or ideological debates or in disputes with the clergy. A subtle undertow of political and class polarization aggravated the latent cleavages in the whole war generation, and its militaristic camaraderie in the final years.[35] Eventually, the *Reichsbanner* turned into the Iron Front, and awaited the fatal assault upon the republic.

The Red Front Fighters League (RFB)

The most virulent private armies of the earlier period, those of the revolutionary left, adopted a much less flamboyant posture in the middle years, without forgoing its paramilitary organization. The outlawing of the KPD in 1923-1924 had also involved disarming and dissolving the Proletarian Hundreds, militant guard troops open to the entire left but under Communist control. With their potential red army gone, the Communists needed a new and more centralized paramilitary organization that could protect their rallies and speakers, demonstrate in the streets, engage in canvassing and propaganda during elections, and, most of all, stand its ground against the paramilitary shocktroops of the right. This organization was the Red Front (Fighters League), and its youth group, Young Red Front, which were both

[35] The *Reichsbanner* had characteristically adopted the veteran-style address "Kamerad," rather than the traditional socialist "Genosse," which the Nazis developed into the populistic "Volksgenosse."

open to non-Communists. The Red Front (RFB) was nominally autonomous but closely linked to the KPD. Founded in Halle late in 1924 and taken over by Thaelmann in 1925, the Red Front soon grew to a hefty 150,000 members, only to decline again after 1927. In the 1930s, the RFB was the principal antagonist of the Nazi stormtroopers in the streets of Berlin, Hamburg, Saxony, and the Ruhr, seasoned in countless physical clashes and electoral campaigns against the growing brown menace. But it also clashed often with the police, the *Reichsbanner*, and with the paramilitary organizations of the nationalistic right, such as *Stahlhelm* and other militant veterans groups. In fact, there was a pattern of combined attacks by Nazis and the RFB on the *Reichsbanner* in many places.

When the ban on the KPD was allowed to lapse in mid-1924, the Proletarian Hundreds continued to be outlawed. But some of their remains in the Halle area took on the name Red Front Fighters League. And it was there, on May 11, that a pitched battle occurred between massive forces of KPD demonstrators and the police, resulting in eight dead, sixteen seriously injured, and hundreds arrested. The occasion had been a "German Day," a massive patriotic rally of *Stahlhelm, Wehrwolf,* and other right-wing groups in Halle, which had been authorized in spite of the ban on open-air demonstrations occasioned by the labor unrest of the preceding months. The KPD had promptly called for an antifascist "Workers Day," and brought in thousands of counterdemonstrators to match the large forces of the right. Despite the ensuing bloodbath at the hands of the police, the party ended the day by calling on the workers to seek more confrontations with "the fascists" at several impending German Days in other towns.

The RFB took on its characteristic style as a partisan army of agitators and propagandists in the presidential campaign of 1925, in which Thaelmann was a candidate. Its political purpose was still veiled under the military organization and rituals and the militaristic rhetoric of the *Rote Fahne*, which called Thaelmann "the iron, red fist which will shatter the enemies of the working class," and called the RFB "disciplined columns," "marching in measured rhythm, with flags and standards . . . fighters without arms," and "soldiers of the revolution."[36] Its statute expressly rejected "illegal armament," and gave as its main goal "the cultivation of class consciousness and of the memories of the war for the purpose of defense against nationalist, military propaganda for further imperialistic wars."[37] Like other veterans' organizations, the RFB also promised to look out for the interests of veterans, especially those of the disabled and of the dead soldiers' families, and to maintain friendly contacts with proletarian veterans' groups abroad. In fact, the RFB's chief contacts abroad were symbolic exchanges of messages and delegates with the Soviet army. The RFB engaged in major demonstrations, but rarely in the kinds of military drill and field maneuvers that would have given the authorities a good excuse to suppress it under the provisions of the Peace Treaty and the Law for the Protection of the Republic. (There were, indeed, almost continuous attempts by right-wing forces to get the RFB outlawed. They were motivated in part by general right-wing fears and by the desire to justify paramilitary buildup on the right. They were also motivated by the wish to deflect the Allies' insistence on suppressing *Stahlhelm* and similar right-wing paramilitary groups to the RFB.) RFB members were also supposed to carry their propaganda and recruitment drive into workers' sports organizations and trade unions, and, most of all, into the mighty *Reichsbanner*, which was viewed as the most obvious target of the KPD policy of "socialist unity from below," that is, without the consent of the SPD, *Reichsbanner*, or trade union leaders.

Ernst Thaelmann emphasized from the beginning the long-range revolutionary character of the RFB as an instrument of the class struggle, as distinct from putschist expectations of it as an immediate military tool. This left the

[36] *Rote Fahne*, no. 71, March 28, 1925.

[37] See Schuster, *Der Rote Frontkämpferbund*, p. 261, and pp. 66-67.

organization free to pursue its assignments of agitation and propaganda without raising immediate fears of attempted coups, as in the earlier years of the KPD. In 1927, for example, the RFB columns of men in green Russian shirts, jackboots, army belts, and caps with the red star dominated the patriotic *Stahlhelm* rally in Berlin with their raised fists, as they had haunted other right-wing German Days before.[38] Their demonstrations and massive flag displays became a routine sight in many big cities, as did the violent clashes that were frequently the result. Typical examples of RFB rallies were its huge *Reich* meetings every Pentecost in Berlin, when some 20,000 to 40,000 uniformed RFB members would parade with 140 marching bands and 780 flags before vast crowds. At the third such rally in 1927, crowds estimated between 60,000 and 250,000 saw 40,000 members (24,000 in uniform) carrying 1500 flags. Tens of thousands had come on special trains and on trucks from all over the country.[39] It is difficult to say how much of the spectacular increase of the KPD in "red Berlin," from 19.6 percent of the popular vote in 1924 to 37.1 percent in November 1932, can be attributed to these grandiose displays.[40] It is enough to point to the Nazi "conquest of Berlin" by means of monster rallies, which netted only 24.6 percent of the popular vote in July of 1932.

Women were also in the RFB at first, but in later years they formed their own Red Women and Girls League (RMFB), wearing red scarves in rallies and demonstrations, and directing the League's energy to women's issues, includ-

[38] See Hannes Heer, *Thaelmann* (Hamburg: Rowohlt, 1975), pp. 96-98, where as many as 70 to 80 percent of RFB members are said not to have been in the KPD in 1927. See also Karl Dietrich Bracher, *Die Auflösung der Weimarer Republik*, 4th ed. (Villingen: Ring, 1964), pp. 145-146.

[39] Schuster, *Der Rote Frontkämpferbund*, pp. 80-81.

[40] Berlin was the only electoral district in which the KPD vote ever exceeded 30 percent. Districts with more than 20 percent in the thirties were Merseburg (27.1 percent in 1932), Duesseldorf-East (28.3 percent), Potsdam, Westphalia-South, Duesseldorf-West, Leipzig, Chemnitz, and Hamburg.

55

ing the legalization of abortion. Both RFB and RMFB were expected to help recruit and indoctrinate future KPD members.

More significant in quantity and participation in street violence was the Young Red Front (RJ), the youth organization of the RFB for the sixteen to twenty-year-olds. As the KPD had its dedicated Communist Youth (KJVD) of about forty thousand souls (1932), and even a children's group (Young Spartacus) of twenty-five thousand (1930), the RJ had twenty-five thousand young men below voting age, who were among the most active elements of the entire movement. Their independent temper expressed itself in friction with the adult RFB and with their "teachers" in the RJ, in the wearing of Russian army coats and yellow bandoleers instead of the RFB uniform, in cover names (pretending the organization was illegal), and in aggressive violence toward the police and other paramilitary organizations. The RJ uniforms, drums, and fifes were so appealing, in fact, that whole locals of the KJVD changed over to the RJ, and the KJVD leadership had to work to keep others from imitating the marching bands and uniforms of RJ. The Young Red Front also developed well-conceived programs for training its youth leaders and indoctrinating its members. Apart from the usual Communist and RFB issues, there were strong overtones of the old prewar Youth Movement in the RJ statute: sports, hiking, and discussions were to make amends for the social and cultural ravages of the war and postwar periods. And each RJ member was exhorted to fight pornography, the cinema, nicotine, and alcohol because of their pernicious influence on body and soul of young workers.

The propensity of the RJ for violence was well put by RJ leader Werner Jurr, who wrote in 1928, "RJ groups regularly patrol the streets every night. Woe to the member of a fascist organization who dares show his face. Tearing off his insignia and a good licking take only moments."[41] Physical

[41] Quoted by Schuster, *Der Rote Frontkämpferbund*, p. 128, see also p. 132.

56

combat with "bourgeois" groups, even with the *Reichsbanner*, and frequently with the police were an indispensable part of RJ life. The police soon learned to schedule rival Communist and right-wing parades many blocks apart, since both parties tended to insist on demonstrating the same day. The police also tried to keep the Communist demonstrations away from the well-known stormtrooper *Sturmlokale* (hangouts), and the Nazi demonstrations out of Communist neighborhoods as far as possible. But somehow the militants of both colors always found each other before or after the event, if not during it. From the Communist point of view, of course, the police of Prussia were the "social fascist police" of the SPD government.

The Onset of the Fighting Years

The wave of strikes of 1928 had involved a good deal of political disturbance between *Reichsbanner* and RFB in Berlin, so that the Social Democratic city government passed an ordinance prohibiting all political demonstrations. This ordinance was still in force on May 1, 1929, the traditional day for socialist labor demonstrations, when the KPD chose to ignore it. The Social Democratic chief of police ordered the Communist demonstrators dispersed by force, whereupon barricades were erected in "red" Wedding and Neukoelln, and pitched battles continued for days, leaving 25 dead, 160 injured, and 1,200 arrested. Forty-eight policemen also suffered injuries. For the first time since 1923, the KPD again began to speak of "a revolutionary situation" and an "armed uprising," although its burning hatred against the "social fascists" of the SPD was hardly new. The Social Democratic minister of the interior, in any case, outlawed the RFB, and his action was promptly followed by the other German state governments.[42]

[42] See Hermann Weber, *Die Wandlung des deutschen Kommunismus*, 2 vols. (Frankfurt: EVA, 1969), I, 223-224, and Siegfried Bahne, "Die Kommunistische Partei Deutschlands," in Erich Matthias and Rudolf Morsey, eds., *Das Ende der Parteien, 1933* (Duesseldorf:

Although it had been outlawed, the RFB obviously did not disappear. It underwent a drastic reorganization along military lines. It had been meant "for veterans and people trained in the use of arms who believe in the class struggle" from the beginning. Now it formed storm battalions of 350 to 400 men, not unlike the stormtroopers, and three such battalions were to form a regiment. There were also special technical troops, and there were probably very intimate connections to the military apparatus (*AM-Apparat*, formerly *M-Apparat*) under the Comintern. The illegal RFB men continued to fight their antagonists in the streets of the Weimar Republic, and especially in Berlin, Hamburg, the Ruhr, and Central Germany. RFB membership had declined drastically as a result of the prohibition, but the extraordinary influx of the unemployed and the very high turnover in KPD and RFB makes it probable that it completely recovered in the worst crisis years of 1931-1932. Still, the RFB and the *AM-Apparat* were hardly ever a match for the Nazi onslaught and its conservative helpmates.

The militant stance of the Red Fronters was a symbol of proletarian revolutionary consciousness and as much a foil for proletarian belligerency as for bourgeois fears.[43] RFB members were made to recite the following oath to their flag:

> We class-conscious proletarians take this oath: To use every effort fighting to free all workers from capitalist exploitation, repression, and persecution. With iron discipline and obedience we shall follow all orders and instructions required by the struggle for the interests of the proletariat.
> May the deepest contempt of the working classes and harshest judgment of revolutionary justice hit anyone who

---

Droste, 1960), pp. 667-668. The Prussian government had been preparing this step for nearly a year.

[43] See also H. Duenow, *Der Rote Frontkaempferbund* (East Berlin: MNV, 1958), and Ernst Posse, *Die politischen Kampfbuende Deutschlands*, 2nd ed. (Berlin: Junker & Duennhaupt, 1931), pp. 68-70.

is unfaithful to the Red Flag or who betrays the interests of the proletariat. On, you front fighters, out with your chest. We are swearing on red, victorious or dead. Dedicated to the great class struggle, we are the red pioneers of a new age. Victory or death, a solemn oath. We live or die for you, you red flag of the dictatorship of the proletariat.

The romantic and melodramatic overtones of this oath were not all that different from those of right-wing youth. Such militant sentiments were probably also shared by many Communists who were not actually in the RFB. After the RFB was outlawed, moreover, such sentiments may well have served to rally many a desperate soul among the mass of the unemployed to the Communist banner, and to ease the further conversion of some to the stormtroopers.

As we draw nearer the final battle of the republic, we should note the parlous state of the KPD in the final years of the republic, the "fighting years" of the stormtroopers and of the NSDAP. Ever since the early years, when the KPD and USPD often seemed to be the true heirs of the prewar SPD, the Communist party had undergone drastic change. In 1923, the KPD came close to rivaling the SPD in many areas, even though the SPD had inherited the rest of the USPD a year earlier. With four thousand ADGB functionaries and Communist majorities in 60 union locals, the KPD could boast a strong toehold in the Free Trade Unions. It also had majorities in 80 German communes and pluralities in another 170, which gave it a total of six thousand elected communal officials such as mayors and councilmen. It was particularly strong in certain industries with a tradition of labor militancy, such as mining, metals, railroads, navigation, construction, printing, textiles, chemicals, and in agriculture and forestry. Apart from its revolutionary activism, it differed from the SPD mostly in being substantially younger and, perhaps, in being less rooted in the more traditional unions and in industries organized early in German industrial history. Since the SPD had come to power in the

59

early years of the republic, moreover, it had been able to occupy many important local bureaucratic and union positions, to the exclusion of the Communists.[44]

In their vital statistics, insofar as they are known, the two arch rivals for socialist working-class support were not very different, except with regard to age. The SPD had a major problem of attracting the younger generation, which instead flocked to the KPD, or even to the still younger Nazis (Table II-1). The generational division was particularly

TABLE II-1 Age Distribution of SPD, KPD, and NSDAP Members (percent)

	SPD 1926	SPD 1930	KPD 1927	NSDAP 1933
Under 25	7.7	7.8	12.3 ⎫	
25-30	9.6	10.3	19.5 ⎭	42.7
30-40	25.3	26.5	32.7	27.2
40-50	30.4	27.3	21.9	17.2
50-60	20.2	19.6 ⎫		⎧ 9.3
Over 60	6.8	8.5 ⎭	13.6	⎩ 3.6
Totals	100.0	100.0	100.0	100.0

NOTE: The information on Table II-1 comes from Hunt, *German Social Democracy*, pp. 106-107, and Wienand Kaasch, "Die soziale Struktur der KPD," *Kommunistische Internationale*, 19 (1928), 1066. Hunt quotes the Socialist youth leader Erich Ollenhauer to the effect that, due to the larger base of the SPD, these figures still mean that in 1931 there were 80,000 SPD members under twenty-five and a total of 320,000 under thirty-five, more than the entire KPD membership. The NSDAP figures are from NSDAP, *Parteistatistik*, 2 vols. (Reichsorganisationsleiter, 1935), I, 155-162, which also shows its youthful character to be particularly pronounced in northern Germany, where most of the confrontations in the early thirties occurred.

pronounced among the party and union leaders at all levels; the old SPD stalwarts simply refused to give younger talents a chance. But this was true also of all the other parties, with

[44] See also Richard A. Comfort, *Revolutionary Hamburg, Labor Politics in the Early Weimar Republic* (Stanford: Stanford University Press, 1966), chapter 7, and especially Flechtheim, *KPD*, pp. 311-322.

the result that, for example, in 1930 the *Reichstag* deputies under forty years of age were almost all KPD or NSDAP members. All deputies were distributed as in Table II-2. It is difficult to imagine a more striking manifestation of the generation gap.

TABLE II-2   Reichstag Deputies 1930,
by Age and Party (percent)

	NSDAP	KPD	SPD	Center (BVP)	DDP	DVP	DNVP	Others
Under 40	68.6	71.4	14.0	11.5	26.7	6.7	7.3	8.6
40-50	20.0	26.0	34.3	28.7	13.3	30.0	24.4	37.1
Over 50	11.4	2.6	51.7	59.8	60.0	63.3	68.3	54.3
Totals	100.0	100.0	100.0	100.0	100.0	100.0	100.0	100.0

SOURCE: Computed from the figures supplied by Sigmund Neumann, *Die Parteien der Weimarer Republik* (Stuttgart: Kohlhammer, 1965; the original appeared in 1932), p. 133. The DDP included a few relatively young *Jungdo* members.

As for occupational composition, the SPD had changed considerably between the prewar era and 1930 in the share of petty bourgeois and especially white-collar employees. From a share of 93.2 percent blue-collar workers in 1905-1906, the party had dropped to 76.9 percent workers in 1930, while its petty bourgeois component had grown from 6.4 to 21.2 percent; intellectuals and civil servants had also entered and helped to make it "respectable." Many of these recent petty bourgeois additions were actually former workers who had become local government cooperative or union officials. The KPD was somewhat more proletarian in the early Weimar years, but not by much. There was always a disproportionate share of skilled and semi-skilled workers in both parties, belying the charge that the SPD represented the "labor aristocracy" and the KPD mostly unskilled labor. More important still, the KPD was not really the party of factory workers from the biggest enterprises in Weimar Germany. It tended to recruit members from small and medium firms and, moreover, suffered a rapid decline in the percentage of factory workers in its ranks after 1928. From a share of 63 percent in 1928, the factory workers in the KPD dropped to 52 percent in 1929, 32 percent in 1930, 20-22 percent in 1931, and 11 percent in 1932, largely because of the rising number of unemployed among the KPD. This was the "class character" of the most violent antagonists of the SA.

The KPD in the Final Phase

The Depression had a much greater impact on mobilization of the extreme left than on the recruitment of Nazis. The KPD had always had high percentages of unemployed workers among its members. The onset of the Great Depression in 1930 and 1931 evidently increased this share to around four-fifths of the entire membership.[45] The party had indeed become a party of the unemployed, of the lowest victims of the capitalistic business cycle. Combined with an annual turnover rate ranging between one-third and one hundred percent this meant that the party was built on sand. Even in the Communist stronghold of Halle-Merseburg, in 1927, before the turnover accelerated, almost forty percent of the membership had been in the party less than three years. According to Hermann Weber, as many as a million people may have joined and then left the party during the republic. In the last three years, on the other hand, membership once more rose from about 100,000 in 1929 to 200,000 in 1931, and 290,000 at the time of the *Reichstag* elections in 1932. By the end of 1932, the membership may have been as high as 360,000.

If the membership was largely new and unpredictable, the party cadres were not much more stable. They were again and again subjected to purges and expulsions at the

[45] See Kaasch, "Die soziale Struktur," pp. 1052-1056, and the comments of Weber, *Die Wandlung*, I, 243 and 282. The unemployed in Berlin-Brandenburg were already 25 percent in 1924 and 15 percent in 1925, when the Middle Rhine area had a rate of 50 percent. The KPD was in this period notably unsuccessful in carrying through its plans to penetrate large enterprises with KPD cells, in part for the same reason.

caprice of factional struggles in the party and in the Comintern, where Stalin was involved in outmaneuvering and excommunicating his rivals. At typical delegate conferences in 1932, for example, in Berlin two-fifths of the delegates were new KPD members, and all but one-fourth had been members for less than three years.[46] Under these circumstances, the only beneficiary was the Comintern-approved national leadership, which no longer had to fear disagreement from the ranks or the cadres. To make matters ludicrous, the KPD had decided to build up party leader Thaelmann from a pedestrian mediocrity into a charismatic folk hero to rival the charismatic appeal of Adolf Hitler. Some of the regional leaders were similarly dubbed *"Fuehrer* of the Ruhr Proletariat," and the like.

This, then, was the force that believed it could conquer the republic and, *en passant*, stem the Nazi tide. With inept leadership, inexperienced cadres, poor coordination, and masses of followers of uncertain indoctrination, what gave the KPD hope against the brown phalanx? There was, first, the rising electoral curve, which favored the party almost regardless of its obvious failures and mistakes. With the benefit of new masses of unemployed created by the depression, the national vote for the KPD climbed from 3.2 million (10.6 percent) in 1928 to 4.6 million (13.1 percent) in 1930, and to 6 million (16.9 percent) in November 1932. To be sure, the NSDAP had gotten more than twice that number in the July elections, but between July and November it lost 2 million of its nearly 14 million voters again, and the KPD leaders honestly thought they could see a silver lining. Their old archival, the SPD, had all along lost votes in almost the exact proportion as the KPD gained them and, by the November elections of 1932, the KPD Central Committee predicted that the latest Social Democratic losses spelled "the historic decline of the SPD" and, by implication, a free trajectory toward the Communist utopia. Two months later,

[46] Weber, *Die Wandlung*, ɪ, 244, 286-289, also recounts the 1930 purge of the staff of the *Bezirksleitung* of Berlin-Brandenburg, which only one fourth of the functionaries survived.

the last Communist attempt to call for a general strike collapsed as Hitler became chancellor. Communist demonstrations were outlawed. And despite some efforts at military organization and rumors of another imminent uprising, the illegal RFB was clearly not up to offering armed resistance.[47]

To be sure, the KPD also had a broad base in some other mass organizations, especially the Revolutionary Trade Union Opposition (RGO), the party's last foray into Weimar trade union politics.[48] Before 1925, too, the KPD had had its own unions, but their decline from 250,000 members in 1922 to 60,000 in 1925 induced the party to lead them back into the giant (6 million) ADGB. With the determined anti-SPD course of 1929, however, the RGO began to run its own candidates for the Works Councils against those of the ADGB. The RGO proved moderately successful, amassing a membership of 312,000 by April of 1932, but it also suffered from a high turnover. The hopes for "organizing the unorganized," especially by means of the local unemployment commissions of RGO and KPD among the unemployed, and for penetrating German industry with factory cells were never realized to any appreciable extent. In November 1932, finally, there occurred the disgraceful Berlin transport workers strike, when the RGO struck for five days shoulder to shoulder with the Nazi labor organization, NSBO, against the ADGB and the SPD city government.[49]

There is no more telling way to chronicle the futility of the Communist struggle against the fascist menace than to juxtapose KPD policy toward the rival SPD with KPD statements regarding fascism. The Communist hatred for the SPD was understandable under the circumstances, and the

[47] Bahne, "Die Kommunistische Partei," pp. 681-690.

[48] There was also the International Red Help for the support of persecuted Communists; International Workers Help for helping and propagandizing workers, especially strikers; and several cultural associations.

[49] Thaelmann called this strike "the strongest, most positive, revolutionary achievement to date of the RGO and KPD," Bahne, "Die Kommunistische Partei," pp. 679-681.

epithet of "social fascists" can be traced back to earlier days, when the Freecorps were known as the "Noske dogs" in reference to SPD Defense Minister Gustav Noske, who had first unleashed them against the revolutionary left. From 1929 on, however, the KPD campaign of hatred for the "social fascists" and their "Hoersing bandits" (*Reichsbanner*) was highlighted by the steady advance of the real fascists, whom the KPD was apparently unable to recognize as a menace until it was too late. The year of 1929, in any case, was a turning point because of the onset of the Great Depression and the impressive showing of the united right-wing forces in the initiative against the Young Plan of reparations. The KPD fulminated against the "fascism" of the grand coalition cabinet, including the SPD, and its policies of reconciliation with the West under the Locarno Treaty and the Young Plan. The KPD may have perceived an anti-Soviet bias in these policies, but had clearly placed itself on the side of the real fascists and their anti-Young Plan campaign. The 1930 KPD Program for the National and Social Liberation of the German People confirmed this impression.

At the time of the first Nazi landslide, in the elections of 1930, the KPD grandly announced that it alone had been victorious because its vote had surpassed that of the SPD in several districts.[50] The first emergency cabinet of Chancellor Bruening, which was tolerated by the SPD, was called "a fascist dictatorship" in the KPD press. In 1931, the KPD even joined a campaign of the antirepublican right to overthrow the SPD government of Prussia, which had refused to lift the ban against the RFB in Prussia. The coming to power of Chancellor von Papen was billed as the arrival of fascist dictatorship, while the SPD continued to be called the "moderate wing of fascism." Yet when von Papen carried out his coup against the Prussian government, the KPD

[50] In Berlin, Merseburg, Cologne, and Duesseldorf the KPD had a higher vote than the SPD. See esp. Flechtheim, *KPD*, pp. 255-264. Weber also stresses the unceasing appeals to the SPD rank and file to make common cause with the KPD against the SPD leadership. Weber, *Die Wandlung*, I, 241-242.

all of a sudden called for a general strike and expected the SPD and the ADGB to join it.[51] The Communists paid dearly for their errors of judgment once the Nazis came to power—with more than a little help from them.

Mobilized Weimar Youth

This story would not be complete without a brief mention of the highly mobilized Weimar youth, which had no parallels outside of Germany. Not only the vast paramilitary armies before and next to the SA, but also the seemingly unlimited reservoir of spontaneously organized, younger males contributed in the end to the mushroom growth of the stormtroopers. Let us briefly survey the youth groups that were to be sources of SA recruits. More than four-fifths of the stormtroopers of the Abel Collection were in a youth group before they were twenty-six years old.[52]

German organized youth culture sprang into existence with unbelievable rapidity in the two decades before 1914. From its modest beginnings with the bourgeois *Wandervogel* (1901), the autonomous groups of the Youth Movement were estimated to number about sixty thousand by 1914, and the total of religious, sports, trades, patriotic, and political youth groups may have amounted to two million on the eve of the war.[53]

[51] Flechtheim, *KPD*, pp. 265-272, 277-278. In February 1932, Thaelmann had still called the SPD a "twin of the NSDAP." Weber, *Die Wandlung*, I, 242. Before the Prussian *Landtag* elections of May 1932, the KPD called the SPD "the most active factor of the fascistization of Germany." Bahne, "Die Kommunistische Partei," p. 669.

[52] The ages of youth group members ranged from the beginning teens to twenty-five and, among particular individuals and youth leaders, far beyond. For the large political organizations, the age range assigned the "party youth" varied widely, and frequently overlapped with the typical stormtrooper age of eighteen to thirty years. For the Abel study, we simply called all voluntary memberships in social groups (other than the military and trade unions) youth group memberships if the respondent was twenty-five or younger at the time.

[53] See Walter Z. Laqueur, *Young Germany*, (New York: Basic Books, 1962), p. 15 who cites H. Siemering, *Die deutschen Jugend-*

The war proved a shattering and politicizing experience for this generation, which began to flock to various postwar political groups from the extreme left[54] to the *voelkisch-nationalistic* right.[55] Many held back from partisan politics altogether, but did not hesitate to join protective associations and Freecorps. Organized Catholic youth, which was loyal to the republic, numbered nearly half a million, and Protestant youth, which was lukewarm or even hostile to the republic, three-quarters of a million.[56] The total member-

pflegeverbaende (Berlin: 1918). There is a rich literature on this subject as documented selectively in the German edition of Laqueur's book and the book by Willibald Karl, *Jugend, Gesellschaft und Politik im Zeitraum des I. Weltkrieges* (Munich: Stadtarchiv, 1973). See especially the encyclopedic three-volume *Dokumentation der Jugendbewegung*, of which the third volume, *Die Deutsche Jugendbewegung 1920 bis 1933: Die buendische Zeit*, edited by Werner Kindt (Duesseldorf: Diederichs, 1974), deals with the Weimar Republic.

[54] Kindt, *Die Deutsche Jugendbewegung*, pp. 1010-1049. The SAJ had 56,000 members in 1933, the Communist Youth (KJVD), founded 1919, 40,000 in 1932, the *Jungspartakus* (for children) 25,000 in 1930, and the *Rote Jungfront*, the youth group of the Red Frontfighters League outlawed in 1929, 25,000 in 1930. The Socialists also had the *Jungbanner*, the youth group of the republican *Reichsbanner*, with 220,000 members under 18 and 495,000 between 18 and 25 in 1930, as well as the Red Falcons, with a membership of 150,000, mostly 10 to 14-year olds.

[55] The right-wing youth numbered about 250,000 in 1930, of which the largest components were *Jungstahlhelm*, with 100,000, and *Kyffhaeuserjugend*, with 65,000, both youth associations of prominent veterans' leagues. The *Bismarckjugend* (DNVP) had 40,000, and the *Hindenburgjugend* (DVP) 12,000 members. See the notes and sources in Peter D. Stachura, *Nazi Youth in the Weimar Republic* (Santa Barbara: ABC-Clio Press, 1975), pp. 114-115.

[56] The Catholic Young Men's Association had 342,000 members in 1918, and 387,000 by 1930. Many young Catholics were enrolled simultaneously in Catholic sports, farm, scouting (*St. Georg's Pfadfinder*) and some youth movementlike hiking groups. If we include the Catholic workers' youth organizations (*Werkjugend* and Kolping associations), about 1.5 million boys and girls belonged to Catholic youth groups. See Lawrence D. Walker, *Hitler Youth and Catholic Youth, 1933-1936* (Washington, D.C.: Catholic University of America Press, 1970), pp. 25-28. On Protestant groups, see Kindt, *Die*

ship of all organized youth groups in 1927 was close to five million, most of whom were at least touched by the alternative life-style of the Youth Movement that implied a rejection of bourgeois values and institutions, and a rather ambiguous relationship to the politics of the republic.

A typical example of the political attitudes within the Youth Movement was the attitude of the Young German Order (*Jungdo*). *Jungdo* constituted something of a crossroads of the conservative-nationalist and liberal-democratic strains among bourgeois youth. Formally founded in 1920, it tied together the enthusiastic volunteers of 1914, the product of the prewar Youth Movement, with the politicized, confused postwar generation. Its founder and leader, Artur Mahraun (1890-1950), grew up in the prewar Youth Movement, and deeply absorbed its love of nature and appreciation of German ethnic and cultural history. As a young Prussian lieutenant, he lived the new ethos of the *Bund*, of replacing authoritarian command with a consensual type of authority based on the creation of a sense of community and on the leader's personal concern for the educational development of his charges. Under his leadership, the group went through a metamorphosis from a "Bolshevik-fighting" Freecorps hostile to all partisan politics to a merger with the republican Democratic party (DDP) in the 1930 elections. This reluctant foray into partisan electoral politics turned into a disaster, both because of lack of success in the 1930 elections and because of the mutual recriminations between the seasoned Democratic politicians and the *Jungdo* leaders attempting to present a new political life-style.

The Order called its subgroups by the curious labels of brotherhoods and sisterhoods, and the leaders were grand

---

Deutsche Jugendbewegung, pp. 517-769, and Stachura, *Nazi Youth*, pp. 105-108, 115, n. 59 and p. 116, n. 64. By the end of 1929, Protestant youth included some 700,000 members in its various associations, of which the largest were the Evangelical Young Men's Associations and the Evangelical-Lutheran Young Women's Associations in Prussia. The Bible Circles, which were pro-Nazi, only numbered about 20,000.

masters, headed by the *Hochmeister*, Mahraun. It adopted a flag featuring a black cross with flared arms like a crusader's cross on a white octagon, and its frequent rallies were dominated by countless such placards and by flags carried by men in grey windbreaks, and wearing military caps and belts. Young Brotherhoods added the sixteen to twenty-year-olds to the frontsoldiers and, in many places, there was a Young Troop of twelve to sixteen-year-olds.[57] Christianity and *voelkisch* beliefs were important to *Jungdo* members, and there was some early antisemitism. Yet in its later clashes with the "demagogic antisemitism" of the Nazis, the Order emphatically squashed the crypto-Nazi tendencies in its midst.[58] In mid-1921, *Jungdo* membership was already estimated at seventy thousand, and by 1922 it boasted rallies of ten thousand with ten marching bands and seventy-five flag teams. At the same time, the Youth Movement style in organization and activities clearly prevailed over the typical veterans' activities of military drills and wartime commemorations and reminiscences.[59] Later rallies, such as the one in Leipzig in 1925, brought together thirty-five thousand brothers and sisters, although the Order had begun its long decline in membership from an estimated five hundred thousand in 1922-1923 to less than fifty thousand in 1930. During the electoral venture of 1930, there was once more a shortlived upturn.[60] In the final years, *Jungdo* occupied

[57] See Klaus Hornung, *Der Jungdeutsche Orden* (Duesseldorf, Droste: 1958), pp. 11-18.

[58] Alexander Kessler, *Der Jungdeutsche Orden in den Jahren der Entscheidung 1928-1930* (Munich: Lohmueller, 1975), p. 121.

[59] Brotherly and patriotic evenings took the place of the *Stahlhelm*'s beer busts, and there were Sunday hikes and encampments. The external appearances of *Jungdo* were meant to be simple and to deemphasize differences of age and status. Unlike the *Stahlhelm*, the *Jungdo* uniform had no insignia of rank and, in keeping with the modest middle-class origins of most members, there were no cavalry or motorized units. Even the *Jungdo* cross was much less ornate than the traditional flag displays of *Stahlhelm* and other veterans' groups.

[60] We have some evidence from that period of the socio-economic composition of *Jungdo*, which can be compared with that of the less bourgeois Nazis and the "reactionary" *Stahlhelm*. See Kessler, *Der*

itself chiefly with a gallant defense of President von Hindenburg, who had then developed into a fortress of republican legality against the plans and plots of Hitler, Hugenberg, and Duesterberg, and with the development of a voluntary labor service to get the unemployed off the street.[61]

In this fashion, whole generations of Weimar youth had been politically mobilized without developing a democratic political consciousness. Not a few of these millions of innocents mistook the *Fuehrer* for the political Messiah. The Weimar youth should also be seen in the context of the

---

Jungdeutsche Orden, p. 91 and, for the *Stahlhelm*, Theodor Duesterberg, *Der Stahlhelm und Hitler* (Wolfenbuettel: Verlagsanstalt, 1949), p. 122. *Jungdo* was evidently much more of an "old middle class" movement than was the NSDAP, but not as closely tied to the "reactionary" old industrial and upper-class interests as the *Stahlhelm*, for which testimony before the Nuremberg Tribunal suggested a percentage of 25-30 percent of workers. The following partial comparison gives an inkling of the relationships involved:

	Jungdo (Halver)	NSDAP 1933	Stahlhelm (Baden) 1934
Blue collar	20.9%	32.1%	} 42%
White collar	11.0	20.6	
Teachers	4.4 }	13.0	21
Civil servants	4.4		
Farmers	23.3	10.7	7
Small Business	20.9		22
Professions	4.1 }	20.2	7 (Profess.)
Entrepreneurs	11.0		only
Others	—	3.4	1
	100.00%	100.00%	100.00%

[61] By January of 1933, the voluntary labor service (FAD) involved 400 *Stahlhelm* camps with 20,000 men, 350 *Jungdo* camps with 25,000, 130 open *Reichsbanner* camps with 12,000 men, and about 26,000 men with other organizations. Mahraun's Grand Plan of 1932 proposed to create a million new farms to give employment to four million persons, and another program to create three and a half million jobs in industry, commerce, and administration, as well as a compulsory labor service to absorb 80,000 young adults. Hornung, *Jungdo*, pp. 111-119.

70

demographic trends of the period. There were high birth rates in the years until 1915, when the war cut them in half; the war generation was itself reduced by deaths. The Weimar republic thus had large numbers of eighteen to thirty-year-olds, especially those born between 1902 and 1914, in the years up to the height of the Depression in 1932. The large number of politically mobilized youths and young adults were present for the outbreaks of massive unemployment and the fighting of 1930-1932 which very likely drove many young men into the stormtroopers and other paramilitary organizations of the day.

The Young Plan Campaign

Whether the KPD recognized it or not, a mighty right-wing coalition for the conquest of power had been underway since 1929. Since 1928, the antirepublican, conservative German Nationalists (DNVP) had been under the chairmanship of Alfred Hugenberg, who had been one of the founders of the PanGerman League of 1890, and now controlled a large number of German newspapers through his Economic Association. Hugenberg's ultranationalistic course had split the party, but it also opened unprecedented opportunities for a united antirepublican campaign by the various organizations of the radical right. In mid-1929, after considerable haggling, a committee consisting of Duesterberg, Hugenberg, Hitler, and others was formed under the chairmanship of Seldte to organize a joint campaign for an initiative against the Young Plan of Reparations, which to many people symbolized the republican government's "policy of fulfillment" of the demands of the victors of World War I and of the "enslavement" for many years to come of the German people to "international capital." And, as Seldte put it in a speech in the Berlin Sportpalast, "we consider this initiative campaign a device for creating a popular nationalist movement."[62]

[62] Quoted by Berghahn, *Stahlhelm*, pp. 129-130.

The initiative received enough votes to qualify for a referendum in December of 1929. The campaign began with a great deal of unrelated drama.[63] In October Stresemann died and, at about the same time, the *Stahlhelm* of Westphalia was suppressed by the Prussian minister of the interior, Albert Grzesinski, because of its large military maneuvers at Langenberg and because of various *Stahlhelm* statements that placed in a dubious light the organization's quasi-military role in border protection, military sports training, and popular military education (*Wehrerziehung*). The action was meant to obviate Allied protests against this form of illegal rearmament, but it also raised issues comparing the *Stahlhelm* with the partisan paramilitary organizations of the Red Front and *Reichsbanner*.

The referendum against the Young Plan failed, although the combined vote was a respectable 13.8 percent. The unholy alliance of *Stahlhelm*, DNVP, and NSDAP soon fell apart again, after it had helped the Nazis to break through the barriers that had hitherto kept them in a fringe position. Being associated with the respectable, financially puissant Hugenberg and the huge and prestigious *Stahlhelm* gave the NSDAP a new respectability that opened many bourgeois doors and helped it to attract new members. By comparison, the *Stahlhelm* could hardly claim the Young Plan campaign as a victory. Its patron saint, von Hindenburg, signed the Young Plan agreement, and clearly hinted at his disapproval of the *Stahlhelm's* associates in the campaign.

At this time, the *Stahlhelm* still viewed the relatively small NSDAP with benevolent condescension, even though the latter would not even permit its members simultaneous membership in the *Stahlhelm* or any other right-wing group.

[63] The Reichstag elections of 1928 signaled a painful defeat of the conservative-bourgeois majority (DNVP, DVP, DDP, Center, BVP), which slipped from 55.8 percent of the vote to 43.6 percent. This change ushered in all kinds of unrest and uncertainty in these parties and among other bourgeois groups. The SPD and KPD, on the one hand, and such new right-wing parties as the *Wirtschaftspartei* and the *Landvolk*, on the other, gained at the expense of the losers of 1928.

Stahlhelm membership in 1930 has been estimated between 400,000 and 500,000, including the *Jungstahlhelm*, while the Nazis had 116,000 members in December of 1929, and had grown little during the preceding years. The arrogant Hitler was not the most agreeable ally, in any case, as he attacked the German bourgeoisie as "the cowardly, characterless pimps of Marxism," and treated even such modest democratic ventures as an initiative campaign to change the Weimar constitution with the utmost contempt. Hitler's unrestrained political radicalism made the *Stahlhelm* look like a marching-and-chowder society that lacked the will to power.

The Road to Harzburg

The 1930 elections, at which the NSDAP scored its first landslide, gave new direction also to the *Stahlhelm* and the DNVP, which hoped to revive their dormant alliance with Hitler of the Young Plan campaign of 1929. A huge Frontsoldiers' Day rally of 140,000 *Stahlhelmers* in Koblenz on the Rhine attempted to make clear the continuing might of the *Stahlhelm* in spite of the Nazi victory over the DNVP. A year later, another Frontsoldiers' Day in Breslau (Wroclaw), with 100,000 in attendance, deliberately provoked Poland, as the one of 1930 had provoked France. At the same time, the organization launched its initiative to dissolve the Prussian diet in order to destroy its republican legislative majority. The *Stahlhelm* had still found it useful to vie for the support of von Hindenburg and, when it suited its short-range needs, even of Chancellor Bruening. But toward the end of 1931, Seldte and Duesterberg were in determined opposition to the Bruening government, and many *Stahlhelm* leaders and regional organizations were disinclined to back von Hindenburg for another term. At Hugenberg's instigation, moreover, they agreed to bring their *Stahlhelm* contingents, together with the stormtroopers, to Harzburg for a grand rally of the extreme right on October 11, 1931. As it turned out, the *Stahlhelm* leaders

73

did not hit it off very well with the cagey Austrian, who came late and refused to salute the *Stahlhelm* columns from the reviewing platform. There was little agreement on basic policies and procedures. But the outside world now saw a united right wing ready to storm the ramparts of "the system."[64]

The *Stahlhelm* had further problems of its own that restricted its freedom of action with regard to the growing NSDAP. Considerable numbers of members were leaving the fold for the brown shirts. The Depression had begun to hit the financial resources of the organization, as well-to-do supporters came upon hard times and economic enterprises of the organization went bankrupt. Subscriptions for the *Stahlhelm* newspaper were dropping. The *Stahlhelm* toyed with the thought of a more direct involvement in electoral politics, presumably in league with Hugenberg, but in the end it shied away from abandoning its traditional posture "above the parties." In the meantime, the *Reichswehr* had begun to take an interest again in the burgeoning paramilitary organizations during a time of mass unemployment: There was growing apprehension of the partisan armies of the SA and *Reichsbanner* in case of civil unrest. So the army decided to channel funds into military sports, and especially into *Stahlhelm* encampments, which, it was hoped, might keep the paramilitaries off the street and out of politics.

The presidential elections of March and early April 1932, when Duesterberg was a candidate on the first ballot, were the *Stahlhelm's* last fling in electoral politics. There were bitter diatribes between the *Stahlhelm* and the NSDAP. In

[64] There had also been rivalry and friction between the SA and the *Stahlhelm* at Harzburg and later, when the latter complained that the SA was luring away its members. Hitler may well have been afraid that once more, as in 1923, the NSDAP might become so deeply involved with the nationalists and veterans' organizations as to become a prisoner of their actions and failures. Berghahn, *Stahlhelm*, pp. 181-188. At this point even Duesterberg began to have serious doubt about the wisdom of joining with Hitler. See Duesterberg, *Der Stahlhelm und Hitler*, pp. 14-33.

the end von Hindenburg won reelection as the republican candidate, while the chief challenger, Hitler, assembled an astounding 36.8 percent of the vote with *Stahlhelm* support on the second ballot, a result approximating the Nazi vote in the *Reichstag* elections the following July. The *Stahlhelm* welcomed the opportunity to get rid of the hated Bruening, and even defended the SA against the *SA-Verbot* that Defense and Interior Minister Groener had meanwhile imposed. Von Hindenburg appears to have given the *Stahlhelm* assurances, through General von Schleicher, that it would not be similarly suppressed as long as it kept to the less political functions of military sports and voluntary labor service.[65] Thus the *Stahlhelm* by May of 1932 was in full retreat from its brief engagement in electoral politics, and concentrated once more on its traditional quasi-military functions.[66] It was encouraged in this by von Papen and the many *Reichswehr* officers who themselves were *Stahlhelm* members, and who were quite ready to use the organization as a military reserve in case of a domestic uprising.

The *Stahlhelm*'s retreat from politics in 1932 did not imply that it had no favorites or enemies. It now strongly favored von Papen over von Schleicher, and had among its bitter enemies the Nazi propagandists, who had a field day with the "reactionary *Stahlhelm*" and the newly revealed Jewish descent of Duesterberg: the leader of the *voelkisch* wing of the *Stahlhelm* had suddenly discovered that he had a Jewish grandfather, and came to experience in his own

[65] Berghahn, *Stahlhelm*, pp. 221-225. The *Stahlhelm*'s offer to provide border protection in the east also fitted well into von Schleicher's plans for a *Reichswehr* enlarged by the millions of paramilitary members of SA, *Stahlhelm*, Kyffhaeuser Veterans, and *Reichsbanner*, who would provide military sports and education for German youth as well as a reserve and pool of recruitment for active service.

[66] The *Stahlhelm* leaders, who in 1931 had vocally demanded a share of the power of the state and were still fishing for cabinet posts when Groener resigned in May of 1932, had changed their tune by July. As Seldte put it at the Frontsoldiers Day of September 1932 before 200,000 veterans: "We don't want the power in the state; we just want a powerful state." *Der Stahlhelm*, September 11, 1932, pp. 6-7.

person the awesome force of the antisemitic prejudice of the entire German right.[67] Physical clashes and attacks by stormtroopers on *Stahlhelmers* had been common since the presidential elections, although they lacked the size and intensity of the SA clashes with the left. They continued until the final demise of the *Stahlhelm* in 1933.

The Crisis of July 20, 1932

Where was the mighty *Reichsbanner*, the republican paramilitary organization, in the final years of the republic, when the other three private armies were getting ready to storm the ramparts? What were its chances and opportunities to stop the onslaught from the right? The *Reichsbanner* had been aware of the growing power of the Nazis for some time, as its principal antagonists in street violence had shifted from the Red Front and *Stahlhelm* to the brown stormtroopers.[68] After the Nazis' electoral landslide, a great surge of new recruits poured into the organization as the SPD, the trade unions, and the workers' sports associations recognized the renewed threat from the right. More than a thousand rallies and demonstrations of the *Reichsbanner* challenged the Nazis in the winter following the September 1930 elections.

More important, the *Reichsbanner* organized an elite Protective Formation (*Schufo*), which could stand up to the stormtroopers in street fighting and meeting-hall battles. *Schufo* and *Jungbanner* began to receive military training,

[67] For details, see Berghahn, *Stahlhelm*, pp. 239-243 and 246-249. This episode is revealing in its patterns of loyalty and betrayal within the circle of his close associates and friends. Duesterberg also contacted the Jewish Front Fighters League in 1932.

[68] The *Reichsbanner* casualty list reveals that in the years 1924-1928, five members each were killed by *Stahlhelmers* and stormtroopers, and three by Communists. In the following years, but before Hitler was in power, another forty-two *Reichsbanner* men were killed by Nazi stormtroopers alone, for a total of fifty. Cited by Rohe, *Reichsbanner*, p. 342.

including "military sports," transport, and communications training, although the units continued to shy away from the Prussian style of drill and goose-step marching. The leadership also insisted that they remain unarmed, even though they were trained in the use of small arms. The *Schufo* had few experienced military officers such as the right wing had in abundance. On the other hand, Prussian police officers in many localities cooperated or were in the *Schufo*, and there seemed to be an underlying assumption that, in case of civil war, the Social Democratic power structure of Prussia and other republican states would be able to supply the staff and the weapons for the tough *Schufo* army.

The *Schufo* was as close as the republican *Reichsbanner* ever came to rivaling the fighting strength of the right. Dressed in green shirts, blue cap, black breeches, and quasi-military leatherwear, its members in 1932 were variously estimated at between 250,000 and 400,000, and thus it came close to the strength of the SA. In age the members were comparable to the SA, with sixty to seventy percent below thirty, and the bulk in the postwar generation,[69] which is not to say that the *Schufo* were any less militaristic than the *Stahlhelm* veterans. In fact, the creation of elite fighting troops made for a far more accentuated leadership style and paramilitary appearance than the *Reichsbanner* had ever previously presented. The typical young *Schufo* man resembled all too closely the typical young stormtrooper, who was ready to march and fight without asking why. The rank and file of the *Schufo* was noticeably more proletarian and metropolitan than that of the SA, although it included agricultural laborers and, in some areas, even small peasants. In heavily Catholic areas, workers of the Christian trade unions predominated, and the bourgeoisie was likely to play a role only among the leadership. As a result of this heavy proletarian element, increasing numbers of unemployed made up the *Schufo*, just as they did the

[69] Rohe, *Reichsbanner*, pp. 372-375. The large *Jungbanner* made up easily for the shortfall in size.

SA and the RFB, accounting for as much as eighty to ninety percent of the membership in parts of the Ruhr area.[70]

The *Schufo* was barely a year old when the Nazis, the *Stahlhelm*, and Hugenberg's Nationalists (DNVP) formed a common front for the final assault on the republic in the spectacular meeting at Harzburg in October of 1931. Once more, the *Reichsbanner*, the SPD, and the trade unions and workers' sports groups responded by proclaiming the formation of an Iron Front of its most able-bodied men, but this time without support from the Center party, the Christian trade unions, and most former bourgeois allies.[71] A Young Front was to coordinate the youth groups of the SPD and the free trade unions. The party itself became the leading element, and its old warhorse, Otto Wels, became the Supreme Commander of the Iron Front, although the façade of suprapartisanship continued to be maintained. The black-red-gold *Reichsbanner* flag was decorated with three symbolic arrows, which stood for the SPD, the unions, and the *Reichsbanner*.[72] But the tenor of the Iron Front manifestoes and pronouncements shifted noticeably from the national republicanism of its predecessors to a stress on defense of working-class interests and on building up socialism in the teeth of the fascist menace, which presumably included the powers of the day (von Papen, von Schleicher, and Hugenberg) as much or more than the still underestimated Hitler movement.

A grand rally in the Berlin *Sportpalast* set the tone with a flaming speech of *Reichsbanner* leader Karl Hoeltermann, who displayed the new willingness of the SPD to "learn from the enemy" the skills of mass psychology and propaganda. On the advice of an exiled Russian propagandist and psychology professor, Sergei Chakhotin, a wholly new

[70] *Ibid.*, pp. 270-279.

[71] The Christian trade unions eventually created their own paramilitary group, the *Volksfront*, with the encouragement of the Iron Front.

[72] On occasion, red flags bore the three arrows, and the Iron Front participated in Red Days and SPD campaigns.

technique of emotion-arousing rallies, demonstrations, and propaganda methods was developed. Symbolic arrows were chalked over swastikas, and a wave of psychological warfare loosed against Nazi symbols, until the conservative forces of the SPD bureaucracy toned down the approach.[73] The effect of this wave of new-style propaganda is difficult to gauge except by analogy with the evident successes of similar methods in the hands of the Nazis. But there was no mistaking the obvious shift of political action from parties, interest groups, and parliaments to the constitutional dictatorship of the *Reich* President, and to the clash once more of paramilitary armies in the streets of the Weimar Republic.

The republican forces entered the electoral battles of 1932 with plenty of fighting spirit, and by no means in as desperate a mood as we might surmise in hindsight. To be sure, it was pitiful to have to rally behind the presidential candidacy of monarchist Paul von Hindenburg, an honorary *Stahlhelm* member, against candidates Hitler, Duesterberg (*Stahlhelm*), and Thaelmann (KPD). But there was an impressive display of electoral discipline on the part of the republican voters, who deserved a better pillar of legitimacy than this misguided old man. For the Iron Front and *Reichsbanner*, the occasion was one of preparation to withstand a likely Nazi coup. Historians still disagree as to whether the plans were for an uprising in case Hitler won the presidential elections, or to intercept a Nazi coup in case Hitler lost. In any case, the two civil-war armies, the *Schufo* and SA, were concentrated and poised to come to blows on March 13. But the Nazis appear to have planned only minor postelection violence, as was revealed by a police raid in Prussia a few days later.

From this moment on, Prussia and other states urged the *Reich* government to suppress the SA, and threatened to take the initiative if the *Reich* government refused. After

[73] Among other ploys, the new propaganda attempted to attach to the swastika the label of "an Indian, homosexual symbol." Rohe, *Reichsbanner*, pp. 403-411.

complex political maneuvers involving the *Reichswehr*, Defense Minister Groener, and Chancellor Bruening, the *Reich* government finally moved on April 13 to outlaw both the stormtroopers and the *Schufo*. This still left the *Reichsbanner* and Iron Front intact, while the NSDAP was kept from uniformed demonstrations and rallies. The effectiveness of such an action demonstrates the pivotal function of uniforms and formal organization, since the stormtroopers, of course, continued to serve as individuals or groups in white shirts and even shirtless, but without major violence. The *SA-Verbot* was a severe blow to their self-esteem and their propagandistic effectiveness.

Unfortunately, this was not the last word on the subject, but rather the beginning of the downfall of Bruening and *Reichswehr* Minister Groener, who were soon replaced by the unscrupulous Chancellor von Papen and his *éminence grise*, the new *Reichswehr* Minister Kurt von Schleicher. Von Papen lifted the *SA-Verbot* on June 17, called for new Reichstag elections, and plotted to overthrow the republican caretaker government of Prussia, the backbone of the republican paramilitary organization. The significance of von Papen's coup against Prussia lay precisely in the staff services and armaments that this huge state could supply to the Iron Front and *Reichsbanner* in case of an all-out right-wing assault on the republic. The crucial question remains why the Prussian caretaker government of Otto Braun and Carl Severing permitted themselves to be quietly removed from office without calling on the full power of the moderate left to forestall this long-expected coup.

There had been some preparations for this day in areas such as Hoersing's Magdeburg, where the *Reichsbanner* had contingency plans to block roads, seize the railroads, and blow up strategic bridges. Other units were only concerned with the protection of party and union buildings from fascist raids. The *Vorwaerts* building in Berlin had a radio transmitter, machine guns, and an armed guard of one hundred men of the *Reichsbanner* and the Academic Legion, which

80

consisted of students. There were also armed Socialist Workers Youth (SAJ) groups in Berlin and an effective shock troop system in Hamburg to cope with such an emergency. The *Schufo* had been reassembled when the *SA-Verbot* was rescinded, and some local units began to arm themselves. Since 1931, the trade unions had also maintained the so-called *Hammerschaften*, strong-fisted teams of workers in the major plants who would enforce a general strike against management resistance or Communist interference if necessary. Mass unemployment and depressed union morale, however, made this a less reliable weapon than it had been in 1920. Finally, the republicans hoped that the railroad unions would be able to sabotage the troop and supply transports of the enemy and facilitate their own. All of this republican defense stood more or less ready for the call from the SPD that never came. Old *Reichsbanner* men cried and threw down their SPD membership books when the crisis passed without organized resistance.[74]

There is considerable doubt, of course, whether instantaneous resistance on that fateful July 20 would have been sufficient against the German army (*Reichswehr*), the *Stahlhelm*, and the stormtroopers. President von Hindenburg, whose signature authorized von Papen's coup, was known to shy away from the risk of open civil war, and he might have been moved to withdraw the coup by a determined show of resistance throughout Germany. On the other hand, the likely participation of the Communists in such resistance might have given the situation a very different appearance in the eyes of the president and of the republican governments of the south. Conceivably, open resistance might have led to a military dictatorship, as in 1923, which would also have forestalled the eventual Nazi takeover. The most promising strategy, historians agree, would have been to impress upon von Hindenburg the possible

[74] See esp. Erich Matthias, "Die Sozialdemokratische Partei Deutschlands," in Matthias and Morsey, *Das Ende der Parteien*, pp. 124-141.

consequences of his high-handed action, and thus to dissuade him from supporting von Papen's plans.[75]

In any event, the outcome knocked the best weapon out of the hands of the republican forces and, as we know from hindsight, sealed the fate of the republic. At the time, this was not entirely clear to the Iron Front, which grimly continued to drill and train. In fact, leading republican circles even on the eve of Hitler's takeover still tended to consider him less a menace than the *Reichswehr* or the "reactionary capitalists" in the government. The Iron Front and *Reichsbanner* offered their services as border protection troops to the *Reichswehr*, and engaged in some surprising nationalistic contacts, including a scheme of forming an antifascist coalition with the *Stahlhelm's* Duesterberg and the Young German Order, and with other militant young bourgeois groups. But the Iron Front and *Reichsbanner* found themselves powerless, in fact, to stop Hitler after they had lost access to the power of the Prussian state.[76] Turbulent protest rallies and a final massive Iron Front demonstration in Berlin *Tiergarten* in mid-February 1933 only served to set up the targets for the murderous manhunts that set in from that date.

The End of the Stahlhelm

Once von Hindenburg had let the enemy into the gates of the republic he was sworn to defend, the paramilitaries of the *Reichsbanner* and of the Communists were easy to rout. They could expect no consideration from the Nazis. But what about the conservative and paramilitary allies of the NSDAP, who in spite of recurrent frictions came around to a new coalition with it in the winter of 1932-1933? The illu-

---

[75] See Rohe, *Reichsbanner*, pp. 426-437, and Bracher, *Die Aufloesung der Weimarer Republik*, pp. 597-600.

[76] Rohe, *Reichsbanner*, pp. 438-461. As the author points out, the republicans at first even mistook Alfred Hugenberg for a bigger menace than Chancellor Hitler himself.

sions of the DNVP leaders and others of containing Hitler in a DNVP-dominated cabinet are well known, but the motives of the *Stahlhelm* leaders and the subsequent fate of their organization are far less clear. Ironically, it was the erstwhile bourgeois moderate, Franz Seldte, who was most eager to rush into a government headed by Adolf Hitler, while Duesterberg's resistance could be overcome only by arranging that Hitler personally apologize for any ethnic slurs made against him by Nazi propaganda. The process was accelerated by rumors of an impending *Reichswehr* putsch of von Schleicher and General von Hammerstein.[77]

The inauguration of the new cabinet of Hitler, von Papen, Hugenberg, and Seldte was followed by enthusiastic torchlight parades in which *Stahlhelmers* joined the SA and SS *en masse.* But the honeymoon had hardly begun when new causes of friction arose. Duesterberg compensated for his earlier acquiescence by his critical observations on the details of the Nazi takeover, and by modest countermeasures until his fall in April of 1933. During the March elections he called a *Stahlhelm* alert in anticipation of the stormtroopers' "night of the long knives," though ostensibly they were to ward off a left-wing insurrection. When an auxiliary police was to be formed of SA and SS, the *Stahlhelm* insisted that *Stahlhelmers* be involved in it too, so as not to make it a purely partisan affair. During the March elections, the *Stahlhelm* and DNVP also ran a separate Black-White-and-Red Fighting Front. Nevertheless, the *Stahlhelm* took part in all the regional takeovers of governmental bodies, and most of its members looked up to Hitler as the leader of the "national revolution." Even Duesterberg was soon mouthing the Nazi slogan, "Germany awake." *Stahlhelm* men participated in most of the early Nazi campaigns to round up

[77] This is an extremely simplified version of the complex negotiations at hand. See esp. Vogelsang, *Reichswehr, Staat und NSDAP,* pp. 377-398. Duesterberg's resistance was hardly motivated by an aversion to the *voelkisch* dictatorship of the Third *Reich,* which he had been advocating for more than a decade.

83

opponents of the regime, although they may not have been involved in the terror of the Berlin jails and the first make-shift concentration camps of the Third *Reich*.[78]

By the end of April 1933, the *Stahlhelm* was fighting a desperate rearguard action to save its autonomy and a semblance of equality with the SA among the minions of the Third *Reich*. Duesterberg was dropped, and Seldte, now the "dictatorial *Fuehrer*" of the *Stahlhelm*, took his organization into the Nazi movement under the supreme leadership of Hitler himself. There continued to be local instances of harassment, and clashes such as the violent suppression by the stormtroopers of an alleged *Stahlhelm* putsch in Brunswick in March. This was brought on by a local *Stahlhelm* offer to accept 150 *Reichsbanner* members into the organization. The resulting crowds of *Reichsbanner* applicants were assaulted and arrested by the SS and auxiliary police, along with the Brunswick *Stahlhelm* leaders, a reported 1,350 persons in all. Twenty-one of the hundreds of victims of stormtrooper brutality had to be hospitalized. The postwar trial of the local minister of the interior, Dietrich Klagges, clearly revealed that the allegation of a putsch had been largely a pretext to vent his hostility on the *Stahlhelm*.

SA Chief Ernst Roehm had every reason to hate the *Stahlhelm*, which had widely publicized his homosexuality during the presidential campaign of Duesterberg. *Stahlhelm* membership, oddly enough, had increased to a million in the few months since January 1933,[79] but in June the Nazis

[78] *Stahlhelm* leaders were invited to visit concentration camps such as Dachau, and certainly must have been aware of the end results of the manhunts in which they participated. See, for example, Berghahn, *Stahlhelm*, p. 254n.

[79] Some of the influx had come from the *Reichsbanner* and the Red Front. The *Stahlhelm* had had about 245,000 members at the beginning of 1931, and 327,000 a year later, not counting another 100,000 of *Jungstahlhelm* members (1930), and an unknown number of the Scharnhorst Youth. The majority of the membership was concentrated in Central Germany, East and West Prussia, Silesia, Brandenburg, Pomerania, and Hanover.

84

simply transferred all those between eighteen and thirty-five years to the SA, and joined the Scharnhorst League to the Hitler Youth, leaving Seldte with only the real veterans over thirty-five. There was a great deal of grumbling against this measure and some resignations, but Seldte chose to grovel and hope for the best. By the end of 1933, Roehm began to take over the thirty-six- to forty-five-year-old *Stahlhelmers* as SA Reserve I, and, by March of 1934, the rest of the *Stahlhelm* was reorganized as the National Socialist German Frontsoldiers League (NSDFB). The old frontsoldiers were outraged at having to exchange their field grey uniforms for brown shirts, and even more at the final breaking up of their organization. When prominent *Reichswehr* generals were murdered in the great SA purge of June 1934, along with Roehm and other SA leaders, Seldte once more chose to grovel, and sent Hitler a congratulatory telegram.[80] But the totalitarian state could suffer a hint of *Stahlhelm* autonomy as little as it could tolerate an autonomous SA. Six months later, the *Stahlhelm* leaders found themselves under *Gestapo* surveillance again because of their allegedly revolutionary or subversive intentions.[81]

They had no friends left. Their old patron, President von Hindenburg, had died in 1934, and the *Reichswehr* was no longer willing to give the *Stahlhelm* any support or special function. The reintroduction of general conscription in 1935, according to Hitler, also made superfluous the *Stahlhelm* function of upholding the traditions of the old army. Preparing for a real war now took the place of "playing sol-

[80] See Wolfgang Sauer, "Die Mobilmachung der Gewalt," in Karl D. Bracher, Wolfgang Sauer, and Gerhard Schulz, *Die national-sozialistische Machtergreifung* (Cologne: Westdeutscher Verlag, 1960), pp. 887-888, 891-892, and 961-963. The victims of the purge included von Schleicher, Gustav von Kahr, Gregor Strasser, and very nearly Duesterberg.

[81] Among other things, the Nazis claimed that the NSDFB was popularly known as the NS-KPD. See Berghahn, *Stahlhelm*, pp. 267-271 and 279-282. A number of *Stahlhelm* leaders later played significant roles in the opposition to Hitler and the repeated attempts to assassinate him.

85

diers." By the end of 1935, the NSDFB (*Stahlhelm*) was dissolved. Franz Seldte, who had joined the NSDAP in April of 1933, had offered his resignation and had made a plea to permit him and other *Stahlhelm* leaders an honorable retirement. Hitler refused, and thus condemned him to the dishonorable fate of serving in the Nazi cabinet until the bitter end.

The Stormtroopers and the Other Groups

We have gone into this detail about the other major paramilitary organizations for several reasons. One was to show the breadth of the paramilitary phenomenon of the Weimar Republic. It was not unusual for a young veteran or member of the postwar generation to join and spend much of his free time with one of these private armies. Joining the brown stormtroopers differed only in that the Nazi movement at first was small and exotic in some settings. Being the only stormtrooper in a village, or only one of a handful in a large industrial firm was eccentric, but being with the SA in a big city like Munich in 1923 or Berlin in 1929 was not.

Another reason was to show how much these paramilitary organizations had in common. The strong veterans' element and the preference for military ranks, organization, and uniforms in all of them created a psychological climate that differed from one group to another only in the overtones of frequently shallow ideological beliefs. The *Reichsbanner*, and even the Red Front, exhibited by their quasi-military attitudes an inherent militarism that could hardly be overcome by the pacifistic and civilian strains in their parent organizations, as witnessed by the rivalry between the SAJ and the *Jungbanner*. The left-wing paramilitary groups generally were a right-wing influence within their parent organizations, just as the *Stahlhelm*, *Jungdo*, and the SA brought their "frontsoldiers' socialism" into the profoundly unsocialistic DNVP, DDP, and NSDAP.

As we have seen, the paramilitary organizations had a

number of interests in common, including military sports and voluntary labor service, not to mention arming themselves whenever their struggle became acute. General von Schleicher and other *Reichswehr* figures even believed from time to time that all of the paramilitary organizations except the Red Front could be made to serve the needs of the truncated *Reichswehr* for popular military and physical education, and for recruitment for border protection in the east.[82] Similar *Reichswehr* interests had pressed the *Stahlhelm* and other veterans' groups into Freecorps service against left-wing insurgents in the early years of the republic. The paramilitary groups also shared in varying degrees elements of Youth Movement culture and its degeneration into the authoritarian cult of the *Fuehrer* and of the homoerotic *Maennerbund*, as well as its profound "antibourgeois affect." There seemed to be no going back to the prewar bourgeois society. The Youth Movement and the impact of the war experience had seemingly shattered in this generation the normal instincts that impel human beings to live together with jobs and family in an orderly world.[83]

A third reason for describing the other paramilitary organizations was to show the importance of competition and rivalry in the genesis and growth of any one group. The presence of well-organized Communist paramilitaries was an obvious spur to right-wing and *Reichsbanner* organization, and vice versa. Communist and *Reichsbanner* raids and interference with Nazi rallies and propaganda were plausible reasons for the Nazis to develop a powerful stormtrooper organization. Nazi rivalry in the early thirties with the *Stahlhelm* and *Jungdo* played a similar role, although the casualty records of the stormtroopers and *Stahlhelm*

---

[82] The unwillingness of Hitler to lend "his stormtroopers" to the needs of "the system" is significant here, but should not obscure the fact that many SA men in the east, and also in the occupied areas of the west, did in fact serve in defense organizations of various sorts.

[83] See especially Curt Hotzel, "Der antibuergerliche Affekt," in Hotzel, ed., *Deutscher Aufstand: Die Revolution des Nachkriegs* (Stuttgart: Kohlhammer, 1934), pp. 345-355.

clearly show the vast preponderance of Communist antagonists. It was the Communists and, to a lesser degree, the *Reichsbanner* and Iron Front, who were the principal foil for the Nazi thrust. Without the left-wing enemy to clash with, the Nazis could hardly have mounted a plausible campaign to rationalize their own existence. The Nazi campaign to "conquer Berlin" is the classic example of the strategic value of having a red enemy to overcome.

The fourth and final reason for depicting the stormtroopers against the background of the other organizations lies in the extent to which the SA gained recruits from them. Since the Nazi movement before 1924 was limited mostly to Bavaria, and was in size no match for them until about 1930, it was to be expected that much of its strength in the "fighting years" would come from converts from the large existing paramilitary groups.

Let us take a closer look at some of these converts and their motives in changing over to the SA. There are frequent references to former Communists who joined the SA in the literature. Less frequent, though by no means unknown, were converts from the *Reichsbanner*, including the large numbers who joined the *Stahlhelm* after Hitler's ascent to power, and were taken over as part of the SA Reserve I late in 1933. One out of every twenty stormtroopers of the Abel Collection (which underrepresents those joining after 1930) was an earlier convert from the left. During the revolutionary years of 1919 to 1922, seven Abel respondents were already with the KPD, seven with the USPD, and twelve with the majority SPD. During the upheaval of 1922 to 1924, ten were with the Red Hundreds, the KPD, or the Red Front, and fourteen with the SPD or a socialist trade union. Two were with the *Reichsbanner* during the following years, 1925 to 1928, and four with the KPD prior to joining the Nazi party. Many left and republican paramilitaries, to speak with Goethe's *Faust*, had "two souls alas, in my breast."

The converts often expressed their reasons for the switch in revealing words. A few examples of men with two souls, one nationalist and one socialist, may suffice. A commercial apprentice born in 1911 (no. 61) ran away from home when he was young. He returned and, on a vacation job, met "all kinds of rabble," as well as some Communist organizers who talked him into joining the KPD. "We thought of ourselves as noble," he comments, although he never quite felt ready to communicate with a blue-collar worker. He read Ernst Toller's *Maschinenstuermer* and *Massenmensch.* His father was a nationalist who had encouraged him, at the age of fifteen, to join the nationalist *Marinejugend.* His teachers, according to the respondent, were Social Democrats: "They taught us to think, but never to make a serious commitment."

Another case is a teacher's son, born in 1895 (no. 493), who came upon hard times after the war. On being discharged from the service, he first served with the Freecorps-like Border Protection in Poland, then with the police in Stettin. He tried his hand at running a grocery store in Berlin and failed. He wrote:

> As a result of this impoverishment and crisis I became a Communist and had important functions as an organizer and propaganda supervisor. I also was a leader of the Red Front. I quit the party in 1929 because I could no longer agree with the orders from the Soviet Union. I attended every rally [of other parties] and became more and more dissatisfied with myself and the world till I went to an NSDAP rally. But I was still suspicious and not to be persuaded soon to join a party again. Yet on election nights the old fighting spirit would seize me again and so I went back to battle my comrades of today.

When a Nazi leader offered him the leadership of an NSDAP local, he decided to accept it, even though he expected a good deal of personal hostility from his former Communist comrades. They called him names, but refrained from physical attacks. He recruited other ex-Communists and, "shoulder to shoulder with our good old SA, we cleaned out the red pig sty."

89

A young merchant marine man and construction worker (no. 492, born 1907) who became unemployed in 1928 is another example: "I, therefore, because of unemployment, joined the KPD and now the political battle got started." In 1930, a friend persuaded him to attend a Nazi rally and soon he was talked into joining the stormtroopers. When his fellow workers saw him in the brown uniform, the following encounter ensued at work:

> When I showed up at my place of work the next morn-ing, I was received with the International and cries of "*Nazi verrecke!*" But they left me alone when I gave no answer and just laughed. After our breakfast break I had to listen to a KPD member who tried to "learn" me the goals of the party. When he noticed I was paying no heed, he started to whistle the International and I began to sing the Horst Wessel song. Suddenly there were five, six men around me telling me to shut up, and a fellow-worker held his shovel under my nose and said he'd bash in my Nazi mouth. . . . I still told him, he too would see the light some day and march with the SA. . . . [A month later] he came with me to a party meeting and became a stormtrooper himself. When the others on the construc-tion site found out, another four men joined the SA.

Considering that the KPD and SA were mortal enemies, the respondent had every reason to fear for his life. The Nazi "hall of fame" of casualties of the fighting years lists a num-ber of cases of ex-Communist stormtroopers who were sought out by their erstwhile comrades for special atten-tion.[84]

A fourth ex-Communist was the young son of a furniture factory owner (no. 466, born 1905) who worked in a central German town among members of the Red Hundreds in 1922.

> I had never been interested in politics until then . . . but soon I fell for their Communist proselytizing and be-

[84] See, for example, Hans Weberstedt and Kurt Langner, *Gedenk-halle fuer die Gefallenen des Dritten Reiches* (Munich: Eherverlag, 1935).

came a fellow-fighter of the Red Hundreds without understanding the real purpose and idea of the Communists. . . . In another town I experienced the first street
battle when we Red Hundreds tried to break up a German Day celebration. To our surprise we were beaten and
had to flee. That day I saw the first *Voelkisch* Hundreds
with a blood-red swastika banner and a picture of Hitler
with pine branches around it. Their courage and flair cast
a spell on me.

In those days, the NSDAP put the Jewish question in
the foreground. I began to read *voelkisch* literature and
particularly Theodor Fritsch's *Handbook of the Jewish
Question.* Then I joined the *Voelkisch* Hundreds and thus
the wonderful and bitter hours began in my life which
I would never have wanted to miss.

The respondent spent his eighteenth birthday in jail for
distributing *voelkisch* literature at the time of the Hitler
putsch of 1923. Back with the movement in 1926, he attended one inspiring rally after another, and had an opportunity to meet Goebbels and the *Fuehrer* in person. He
viewed their cause as a fight of the old Germanic tribes
against the Jews and "inferior races." Once he reported
violence, but not his own. At a monster rally in 1928 in the
Berlin *Sportspalast*, he reported, the police lost control over
the crowds and even shot at the stormtroopers when the
latter tried to "defend themselves against *Reichsbanner* and
Communist assailants." Twenty-nine stormtroopers were injured. The respondent ornamented his account with ringing
phrases, but said very little about his own activity, except
that he was once a bodyguard of Goebbels during a speaking tour. He held a fairly high SS office for one of his age.

Most of the converts from the left exhibited two characteristics. One is that they were not typical socialistic proletarians, but had either a bourgeois component in their family or a strong nationalistic or religious element in their
upbringing. The other characteristic was an antisemitic prejudice, which appears to have been a major reason for Social-

ists or Communists to convert to the NSDAP. These cases of ex-Communists who became fervent Nazis also illustrate the interchangeability of extremist movements. For the young in particular, changing from the Red Front to the brown shirt appears to have been no more unusual or consequential than a change of juvenile gang membership in a big city. The smell of battle and the fighting comradeship held the same promise in either camp. The anecdote is not so farfetched that recounts the boasting of a group of brawny new SA recruits in a "red" village near Munich in 1933. They bragged that they had been following the red flag even before there was a swastika in its middle.

Converts from the Right

For every convert from the left, the stormtroopers picked up six or more from the right wing. More than half of the stormtroopers of the Abel Collection who belonged to an organization during the upheaval of 1919-1921, for example, were in a Freecorps (including Oberland and the Ehrhardt Brigade), the *Einwohnerwehr*, or a veterans' group. This was particularly true of respondents who later held a rank in the SA. Notorious SA killers such as Edmund Heines, Rudolf Hoess of Auschwitz, and Martin Bormann were graduates of the Freecorps whose members committed the bulk of some four hundred politically motivated right-wing murders in the first three years of the republic.[85] Another one-fifth of the Abel stormtroopers who belonged to an organization at that time were with various *voelkisch* groups, such as the *Schutz-und-Trutzbund*, the *Deutsch-Soziale Partei* (DSP), or the early NSDAP. During the renewed upsurge of 1922, 1923, and 1924, nearly half were with the early NSDAP, the *Deutschvoelkische Freiheitsbewegung*,

[85] See esp. the detailed account of Emil J. Gumbel, *Vom Fememord zur Reichskanzlei* (Heidelberg: Lambert Schneider, 1962), pp. 25-52. The author also found that nearly all the right-wing killers remained free, whereas nearly all the thirty-eight known left-wing murderers were punished severely.

Nazi fronts like *Frontbann,* or other *voelkisch* groups, while only about a third were with veterans' groups like *Stahlhelm* or the antioccupation underground in the Rhineland. Nearly one-third of the Abel stormtroopers active in 1919 to 1924 were involved in political violence, including Freecorps actions, and another one-fifth each were involved in demonstrations and electioneering.[86]

In the quiet years of the republic, 1925 to 1928, while the Nazi movement began to build up a national organization, most of the later stormtroopers who were not already with the NSDAP tended to be in the *Stahlhelm* or in other bourgeois organizations such as *Wehrwolf* or *Jungdo.* Again, the stories of Abel respondents who eventually switched from the *Stahlhelm* or other bourgeois organizations tell a great deal about how the *Stahlhelm* or other groups differed from the NSDAP. Quite a few of them were farmers or agricultural officials in the northeast, who in 1929 or 1930 came from the DNVP via the *Stahlhelm* to the Nazis. Their conversion was a result of the agricultural crisis, which radicalized many a farmer and weaned him from conservatism.[87] Others came from *Wehrwolf, Jungdo,* or other *voelkisch* groups.[88]

Typical of many converts from *Stahlhelm* are comments such as "there was a very different revolutionary spirit among these young [Nazi] people as compared to the

[86] Nearly half (158) of the 337 Abel stormtroopers thus received their initiation in political violence and activism. It should be noted however, that the Abel Collection underrepresents the 89 percent of the SA and SS membership that joined only after the 1930 elections. Only 36.6 percent of the Abel stormtroopers joined after that date. SA men joining after mid-1931, and especially those joining after the presidential elections of March/April 1932, are the most underrepresented.

[87] See Abel cases nos. 236, 504, 507, 511, and 516.

[88] See nos. 374 and 517. Another enthusiastic *Wehrwolf* member (no. 306, born 1904) relates that "the leader of the *Wehrwolf* in the neighboring town was a Freecorps veteran and old Hitler man who [in 1925] took almost his entire group into the Hitler movement." The respondent and some friends also joined at that time.

93

Stahlhelm" (no. 77, born 1895) or complaints about the *Stahlhelm's* snobbery and lack of a feeling of community. One young Boy Scout who had already gone through several Youth Movement groups wrote, "I did not like the *Stahlhelm* anyway because there was no spirit of comradeship . . . and there were class distinctions there."[89] The most likely facilitators of conversion from the *Stahlhelm* or Youth Movement were a dose of "socialism," or awareness of the plight of the working classes, and *voelkisch* anti-semitism.

The Clash of the Private Armies

Red Front, *Reichsbanner*, *Stahlhelm*, and SA thus were almost interchangeable, and yet they clashed with deadly effect time and again in the political battles of the last years of the Weimar Republic. The conflict even reached down into families and tore them apart. As one respondent (no. 53, born 1903) related of his experiences in a family of divided loyalties:

Already when I was with the *Stahlhelm*, there was trouble with my parents and brothers. My parents and one brother were with the Center party and four other brothers were with the *Reichsbanner*. Since I was a drum major for the *Stahlhelm*, and later for the NSDAP, and one of my brothers a drum major for the *Reichsbanner*, the black-white-and-red insignia were leaning in one corner of my parents' home and the black-red-and-gold ones in another corner. Yet my brown shirt and his *Reichsbanner* jacket hung peacefully side by side in the closet. With such contrasting political views, it was not always peaceful at home. Sometimes physical clashes were unavoidable because I was not about to give up my Nazi membership since I believed Hitler to be Germany's salvation. This circumstance made me unhappy at home since I

[89] See no. 250, born 1908. For greater detail, see also Merkl, *Political Violence*, pp. 230-235.

94

realized I could never convert my parents and brothers to my view. They were reinforced in their opinion by a large number of relatives, all of the opposite camp.

Police reports to the Prussian diet for 1930 give an inkling of the general, intense level of political activity as well as of the importance of Berlin in the Nazi struggle for power. In that year alone, the police in Prussia had to be present at 23,946 open-air rallies and demonstrations involving about 25 million participants, and at 34,742 indoor meetings with 13.5 million participants, probably including many of the monster rallies of the NSDAP. The Nazis and Communists, in any case, were involved in nearly 90 percent of the rallies and demonstrations that required police intervention, and in all but four percent of the disruptions they were, in fact, the disrupters. The *Stahlhelm, Reichsbanner,* and *Jungdo* or *Wehrwolf* accounted for the rest.[90] The Berlin chief of police Albert Grzesinski, chillingly described the sudden escalation of violence between the Nazis and the Communists there in the fall of 1930: "Ordinary brawls had given way to murderous attacks. Knives, blackjacks, and revolvers had replaced political argument. Terror was rampant. Carefully prepared alibis helped the terrorists on both sides to escape conviction."[91]

For this purpose, both extremist parties apparently organized four-man squads of "hit-men" who would operate in districts of the city where none of them was known. Grisly death threats were communicated to the victims, including police officers. Grzesinski estimated that there were about twenty such squads in operation, but none of them was ever caught. In response, the Social Democratic chief of police, over republican protests, revived the old Prussian "protective custody" from a mid-nineteenth century statute that permitted arrests without a court warrant. He badgered the

[90] *Sammlung der Drucksachen des Preussischen Landtags,* 3. Wahlperiode (June 8, 1928), pp. 6053-6055.

[91] Albert C. Grzesinski, *Inside Germany* (New York: Dutton, 1939), p. 130.

Prussian diet into passing a series of special emergency laws in March and October of 1931. During a wave of terror in May of the same year, twenty-nine persons were murdered —twelve Communists, six Nazis, one *Stahlhelmer*, two Social Democrats, four policemen, and four of unknown political allegiance—including nine by Nazi assailants and thirteen by Communists. The KPD finally disavowed the use of "individual terror" by the end of that murderous year. Grzesinski also describes some of the SA and KPD hangouts, including one SA tavern where police found two life-sized puppets with the features of himself and of the Prussian minister of the interior, Carl Severing, their heads punctured with bullet holes from target practice by the young toughs. Most of the stormtroopers arrested in Berlin were under twenty years of age, generally between seventeen and twenty. As the chief of police put it, they were "no longer adherents of a political creed—just gangsters . . . , well-schooled in the methods which were to find their culmination in concentration camps and prison dungeons of the Third *Reich*."[92]

The Nazi efforts to memorialize their own casualties, however dubious in some details, substantially bear out the impression of large-scale political mayhem throughout the republic. One Nazi source even offers statistics on the number of policemen allegedly killed by the Communists between 1918 and 1933: 216, of whom the bulk died in 1919 (21), 1920 (105), 1921 (42), and 1923 (17). Another 1,972 policemen are said to have been injured by Communists, this time also including large numbers injured in 1929 (145), 1930 (274), 1931 (332), and 1932 (304). The same source claims 387 dead and 43,000 injured Nazis, not counting those killed during the Nazi manhunts of 1933, when some of the victims were waiting for their Nazi captors gun in hand.[93] The list of the dead follows:

[92] Grzesinski, *Inside Germany*, pp. 131-134. The author's count of riots and casualties in Prussia for the period of June 1 to July 20, 1932, is 461 political riots, with 82 killed and 400 seriously wounded.
[93] Will Decker, *Kreuze am Wege zur Freiheit* (Leipzig: Koehler &

1923	23, including 17 in the beer-hall putsch.
1924-1929	30, including 10 by Communists and 5 by "Marxists" or the *Reichsbanner*.
1930	17, including 8 by Communists and 5 by "Marxists" or the *Reichsbanner*.
1931	42, including 29 by Communists and 9 by "Marxists" or the *Reichsbanner*; also one by a policeman and one by an SA dissident of the Stennes group.
1932	84, including 58 by Communists and 15 by the Iron Front or "Marxists"; also 4 by the police, 2 by Center party members, one by his own father, and one by his brother.
1933 (January-March)	33, including 16 by Communists and 7 by "Marxists" or the *Reichsbanner*; also 2 by the police.[94]

Of the Nazi casualties since 1930, ninety-six died of gunshot and forty of stab wounds, according to this source, which seems to confirm Grzesinski's assertion that the partisan struggle had escalated from fist fights to murderous weapons. In Berlin alone, thirty-seven Nazis were killed, most of them after the 1930 elections. The information is somewhat incomplete and flawed, but probably not far from the truth.

Amelang, 1935), p. 96. The total number of dead Nazis named by the author falls far short of 387. Only 229, in fact, are listed prior to April of 1933, after which he lists another 14 names. No mention is made, furthermore, of policemen killed or injured by Nazis, an occurrence not uncommon in newspaper reports.

[94] Decker, *Kreuze*, pp. 109-132. Any information culled from such sources, of course, is likely to be unreliable and impressionistic as to occupation and status, and sometimes even as to age, not to mention with regard to any description of the assailants.

The large proportion of Nazis allegedly killed by Communists may have been inflated for political reasons. But it is not implausible, considering the Nazi approach of constantly provoking violent clashes in Communist strongholds for the sake of the publicity.

Another Nazi source, which includes fifteen *Stahlhelm* casualties, mostly of the years 1923-1929, also lists the occupations and dates of birth of most of the casualties. We can use this as an approximate description of the average age and occupation of the most violent elements among the Nazi stormtroopers and *Stahlhelm* converts. Only a little more than one-fourth of the casualties belonged to the war and prewar generations. Of the nearly three-fourths in the postwar generation (born 1902 or later), four-fifths were born after 1905 and over one-third in 1910 or later. Their ages at death averaged around twenty-four years with about half of the casualties concentrated between the ages of eighteen and twenty-five. As far as one can determine their occupations, the dead stormtroopers were far more proletarian than were the stormtroopers of the Abel Collection or the NSDAP at large, or even than the German population at the time (Table II-3).[95] Their working-class members, however,

[95] These occupational and status categories are not very satisfactory to the social statistician, although they may help to establish a rough sense of the proportions involved. According to the official statistics, the general population was composed of 46.3% workers, 12.4% white-collar, 9.6% business and professions, 20.7% farmers, and 6.2% others, as of 1933. *Statistisches Jahrbuch für das Deutsche Reich 1935*, Berlin, 1935. Michael H. Kater, "Quantifizierung und NS-Geschichte. Methodologische Überlegungen über Grenzen und Möglichkeiten einer EDV-Analyse der NSDAP-Sozialstruktur," *Geschichte und Gesellschaft*, 3 (1977), 453-484, has examined the new entries in the NSDAP catalog of the Berlin Document Center and, while analyzing their social composition, discussed the difficulties of definition and conceptual problems of the German social statistics. *Ibid.*, pp. 465-472. In the process, he also addressed himself to the controversial definition of the "lower-middle class" component of the pre-1932 NSDAP which, depending on the inclusiveness of the definition, can vary from a good third to three-fourths of the new entries into the party: a hard core composed of handicraft masters (4.3%), nonacademic professions

TABLE II-3   Occupations of Abel Stormtroopers, Nazi Casualties, and the NSDAP (percent)

	Abel SA	Casualties	NSDAP 1933
Skilled and unskilled workers	38.5	56.8	32.1
White collar, retail clerks	21.3	10.9	20.6
Business and professions (including students)	12.3	25.0	20.2
Civil service	13.2	3.2	13.0
Farmers	9.3	3.6	10.7
Others	5.4	.5	3.4
Totals	100.00	100.0	100.0

were chiefly composed of skilled workers and those in service occupations, such as chauffeurs, cooks, waiters, and messengers. They were quite different from the industrial workers of the SPD or KPD. Equally striking is the large share of small businessmen, university students, and the professions as compared to the underrepresentation of white-collar and civil service personnel, two very prominent elements in the Nazi party. Farmers, too, are underrepresented here, but this may merely reflect the urban nature of most of the conflict.[90]

This, then, was the profile of political violence in the Weimar Republic, and of stormtrooper violence in this context. The contagion started on the left, but soon huge forces on the right were ready to do battle with the republic itself. Hundreds of political assassinations and open civil war

---

(3.9%), lower white-collar (10.6%), lower civil servants (4.5%), and small business (11.4%) can be augmented with farmers (11.7%) or, most inclusively, with skilled workers and dependent handicraft (24.2%).

[96] The casualties are reported region by region and with somewhat unsystematic accounts of age, occupation, and occasion in NSDAP, *Ruhmeshalle der SA, SS und HJ, des früheren Stahlhelm und der für das Dritte Reich gefallenen Parteigenossen*, Fuerstenwalde: Militär-verlag, no date. In a speech, Seldte named a figure of three hundred *Stahlhelm* casualties during the entire republican era. Duesterberg, *Der Stahlhelm und Hitler*, p. 103.

marked the early years of the republic, 1919 to 1922. The Weimar republic very nearly went under in the year 1923 from the combined assault of the French occupation and the revolutionary right, not to mention the Communist dreams of "a German October revolution." Even during the quiet years, 1924 to 1928, huge paramilitary armies were rising once more behind a façade of normal democratic politics, pitting the defenders of the republic against the declarations of hatred by the *Stahlhelm* and the KPD, and against the alienated millions of organized veterans and Weimar youth. The fury of the final battle among the militant camps had thus been prepared for years on a massive scale.

The Nazis and their violent stormtroopers became a major and growing force in this struggle only from about 1929, when large numbers of converts, especially from the right, swelled the ranks of what had been a violent fringe group. Under the circumstances of accelerating mass unemployment and political crisis, their violent assault on the equally violent Communists and the *Reichsbanner*/Iron Front drew violent elements throughout German society into the vortex, much as a magnetic field rearranges metal filings, profoundly changing the character of Weimar politics. At the center of this storm, Nazi and Communist killer squads and demented militants, especially youth of the lower classes, were murdering each other in cold blood. Except for the youngest stormtroopers, whose behavior will have to be explained separately, the violent stormtroopers were mostly the violence-prone of the other organizations whose years of militancy culminated in the Nazi "fighting years." In this fashion, the political culture of violence of the entire republican period and its violent struggles, and even the war itself, contributed to the violence of the final showdown. More important still, it determined much of the character of the totalitarian regime to follow, a regime that miraculously dissolved the militant street violence of the private armies only to refocus it on the hapless victims of persecution and concentration camps, where the most violent streetfighters became the guards.

100

Chips off the Old Block

No one who witnessed it will forget the first outburst in August, 1914. Propaganda had nothing to do with it. . . . It was something without parallel in the history of the German people. Spontaneously the 67 million Germans rose as one man. A wave of enthusiasm, carrying everything before it, swept aside all differences of political creed, class, religion, age. . . . This feeling of national unity came from the conviction of the essential righteousness of Germany's cause and of the defensive nature of her struggle.

Herbert Rosinski, The German Army, p. 132.

It is not easy in this antimilitaristic age to imagine the aura surrounding even a minor professional military career in imperial Germany. Marlene Dietrich still sings the old marching song

Wenn die Soldaten durch die Stadt marschieren,
Öffnen die Mädchen die Fenster und die Türen. . . .[1]

Uniforms and drums and fifes indeed impressed not only the girls but also many a young fellow tired of his humdrum apprenticeship to a trade. One of the Abel respondents, a locksmith born in 1873 of working-class parents (no. 27), relates how he reenlisted after the draft: "The love for a

---

[1] "When the soldiers come marching through town, the girls open up their windows and doors."

soldier's calling made me become a professional military man. . . . After seven years I was promoted to sergeant and after nine to sergeant, 1st class. . . . During these years I dutifully attended the first two grades of the school for non-commissioned officers and voluntarily went for further semesters of training." Many young men of that generation similarly went through years of subofficer training without setting their sights any higher than this. A person of the lowest social origins could enter this training program. After twelve years of service below the rank of commissioned officer, moreover, he was entitled to a civil service career at a low or medium level. Many of the Abel respondents followed this route and ended up as minor officials of the Imperial Railroads or the Postal and Telegraph Service. Some became grade school teachers, and thus may have carried their drill sergeant's ways from one "school of the nation" into the other.

All of these military or civil servants among the Abel Nazis felt a strong attachment to the empire and its social order, which broke down in the defeat of 1918. The fall of "their *Kaiser* and empire" frequently politicized these people, even without necessarily making monarchists of them. But most of them also felt a seething resentment of the imperial class society's barriers, which would not permit a sergeant to be the social equal of an officer or reserve officer, or to attain that rank. If they were elementary schoolteachers or lower civil servants, they were equally resentful of the university-trained gymnasium teachers or higher civil servants, who would not "accept" them, either. This mixture of seething social resentments of prewar class barriers, together with the politicized patriotism of old soldiers and civil servants, explain much of the prewar legacy in the Nazi party. Add the *Fronterlebnis*, the war experience in the front-line trenches with its overtones of egalitarian solidarity in the face of enemy and death, and the *voelkisch* ideas and groups spanning the prewar and postwar periods—the message of the past to the Nazi movement is complete. Much of the ardent motive force behind the Nazi party, especially during the early years of the republic, was fueled by such chips off the old block of the empire.

The motives that propelled the NSDAP and the storm-troopers during the "fighting years" tended to fall into two complexes related either to the empire and the war or to the gathering political and economic storm that broke ten years after the Great War. The watershed for both issues and generations was 1924, when the war-related turbulence came to an end, even though such problems as the French occupation of the Rhineland and the questions of Weimar foreign policy and of reparations continued. The history of the Nazi movement fits this periodization well, although it would be a mistake simply to consider the pre-1924 activities as strictly empire- and war-related, and those of the reconstructed NSDAP after 1924 as propelled only by the motives of the struggle for power and the Great Depression. The empire- and war-related motives of the earlier period culminated in the crisis of the defeat, and in the revolutionary and counterrevolutionary sentiments following it. These reactions were widely shared, moreover, by other organizations and parties outside the fledgling NSDAP. After the Nazi party was reorganized in 1925, there continued to be nationalist and *voelkisch* groups that shared at least some of the beliefs we associate with the NSDAP. But the sheer size of the movement after 1930 and its extremely effective recruitment of *Stahlhelm*, *Jungdo*, and other elements clearly pointed toward the day when all organizations of kindred beliefs were dissolved and taken over by the Third *Reich*, and even the literary spokesmen of the "conservative revolution" were coopted or silenced.

The Reichswehr and the SA

The history of the SA, as distinct from that of the NSDAP, also fits this division, if in a peculiar way, beginning with the entry of *Reichswehr* Captain Ernst Roehm in the new (NS) DAP in the fall of 1919. A staff officer descended from Bavarian civil servants, Roehm had been with the

Freecorps von Epp during the "liberation" of Munich from the Soldiers and Workers Councils. He and Hitler brought with them many "fellow-fighters of the *Reichswehr*."[2] Among the 193 entries in the membership list of that period, no fewer than four officers, eight sergeants, twelve soldiers, and a number of university students barely out of the service can be found. At the time he joined in 1919, Hitler himself was an information officer of the *Reichswehr*, which sent him to look over the tiny new Nazi party, as the *Reichswehr* had been monitoring many right-wing fringe groups at the time. Close relations to the *Reichswehr* and to the Free-corps von Epp, Ehrhardt, and Oberland dominated the life of the fledgling party for years.[3] In this atmosphere, the SA evolved quite naturally. At the first meeting-hall brawl at the Munich *Hofbräuhaus* on February 24, 1920, the speaker, Hitler, found that his audience had been packed with left-wing opponents. As he reported, there was heckling, violent clashes, and finally, "a handful of war comrades and other adherents" fought off the disrupters.[4] According to one account, armed veterans and bullies attacked the interlopers with sticks, rubber truncheons, horse whips, and pistol shots. All this, of course, stands in marked contrast to the freedom of the SA after 1925 from anyone but the party.

From that moment on Nazi goon squads began to raid left-wing meetings until the Munich SPD organized its own

[2] Ernst Roehm, *Geschichte eines Hochverraeters*, 2nd ed. (Munich: Eher, 1930), p. 107. Hitler himself still belonged to the *Reichswehr* until March 1920.

[3] Heinrich Bennecke, *Hitler und die SA* (Munich: Olzog, 1962), pp. 23-24. Only four of the officers and sergeant were still active in the *Reichswehr* at the time. Bennecke himself joined the SA in 1922 and later rose to a responsible position in it. The *Reichswehr* was very pleased with the frequent rallies and the patriotic speeches of its protégé Hitler in the years 1919-1920.

[4] Adolf Hitler, *Mein Kampf* (New York: Reynal & Hitchcock, 1939), p. 405. Later accounts speak of the November 1921 rally as the hour of birth of the SA, when there were a mere "forty-six fighting off eight hundred enemies." See Hitler's foreword to *Das Braune Heer. Leben, Kampf und Sieg der SA and SS* (Berlin: Zeitgeschichte, 1932), p. XI.

guard.[5] In November of 1921, after another big battle in the *Hofbräuhaus*, the early *Ordnertruppe Saalschutz* and the first "Hundreds" received the name *Sturmabteilung* (SA). Throughout this period, veterans and even active soldiers played the dominant role in the SA, which grew as rival paramilitary organizations such as the huge *Einwohnerwehr* of Bavaria dissolved. High SA officers like the First SA Leader Hans Ulrich Klintzsch were on loan from and paid by the Marine Brigade Ehrhardt—which casts doubt on whether the SA was really under Hitler's control, even though he had taken over the party in mid-1921 and, following this coup, reorganized the SA.[6]

There was an obvious gap between what Hitler wanted the SA to be in those years and what Roehm and others made of it. Hitler's conception appears to have been a partisan instrument suitable for propaganda and for terror, for spreading the faith as well as for "the conquest of the streets." The propaganda function implied strong ideological convictions, a proselytizing fervor, a knowledge of effective propaganda techniques, and the sheer impact of uniformed marchers on the public. This crusade also required the determined use of force to protect the party's speakers and meetings, to disrupt rival speakers and meetings, and on occasion to engage in full-scale battles with paramilitary organizations of the left. Members of the SA were supposed to be the most active party members, but not really a separate, autonomous, military organization. With their windbreaks, ski-style caps, swastika armbands, and canes, the stormtroopers soon showed their mettle as Hitler's political soldiers and fighters of the faith in an episode that later SA histories liked to embellish. In 1922, Hitler had been invited by the *Schutz-und-Trutzbund* to attend a German Day in

[5] Wilhelm Hoegner, *Der schwierige Aussenseiter* (Munich: Isar, 1959), pp. 18-19.

[6] Bennecke, *Hitler und die SA*, pp. 27-29. Bennecke also tells of an entire howitzer company that belonged to the SA and participated in many battles. The nonveterans appear to have been even then predominantly very young men, too young to have served in the war.

Social Democratic Coburg with "a few friends." He brought along eight Hundreds of the SA with flags and a military band in a special train, and they proceeded to march in formation with their flags, against the will of their hosts, who had cleared their activities with the city government. There were clashes in the street and nocturnal encounters, and in the end the Nazis claimed to have "broken the red terror" in Coburg.[7] They subsequently carried out similar actions in Landshut and other Lower Bavarian towns, in order to "overcome the red terror systematically" and in a fashion reminiscent of Mussolini's raids of 1921-1922.

Hitler undoubtedly considered the SA also as an instrument for a revolutionary takeover and as the police and army of a future Nazi regime, but these functions were curiously miscarried during the early years. Hitler himself expressed his desire to keep the SA different from the typical kind of *Wehrverband* such as *Stahlhelm, Reichsflagge*, and *Oberland*. But Roehm and Ehrhardt's officers-on-loan made it into a *Reichswehr* reserve, trained by the *Reichswehr* and organized with artillery and even cavalry units along *Reichswehr* lines. Early in 1923, Hermann Goering was called in by Hitler to take the command away from the army officers, and a special body guard for Hitler was formed, which came from different sources from the *Reichswehr* elements, chiefly workers and craftsmen. But it was too late. Hitler was unable to disentangle himself sufficiently from the military-nationalist junta in Bavaria during that turbulent year to make more than one token effort to seize power by himself: the abortive beer-hall putsch.[8] It was not until much later, if ever, that he could

[7] This incident followed their first major demonstration to go beyond their guard functions: a nationalist rally protesting the 1922 Law for the Protection of the Republic. See *Deutschland Erwacht, Werden, Kampf und Sieg der NSDAP* (Hamburg: Cigaretten-Bilderdienst, 1933), pp. 17-19.

[8] The nominal head of the putsch was General Erich Ludendorff. See also Heinz Hoehne, *Der Orden under dem Totenkopf. Die Geschichte des SS* (Hamburg: Spiegel; and Guetersloh: Mohn, 1967), pp. 23-24. On the general question of the character of the pre-1924

realize completely his idea of the SA as the armed fist of the party.

Knowledge of these external constraints can be combined profitably with a quantitative assessment of the internal legacy of the war on the members of the SA and NSDAP during the fighting years. We need to know how much of this military element (which was overwhelming in the early years) was present among the Nazis of 1932, and what it meant to them fourteen years after the end of the war. By the same token, we can look into the importance to the members of other prewar and wartime experiences as they themselves relate them in their autobiographical statements. For this purpose, we need to start with some basic statistics about the distribution of age and other variables in the pre-1933 NSDAP, and among the SA and SS in order to assess the proportions in which the relevant views and experiences may have occurred among their members. Views that were widely held and were obviously important to the membership can then be considered to have been important elements of the organizational purpose of the SA and NSDAP, and as reasons for joining them.

Three Nazi Generations

To come back to the two complexes of issues, the best way to separate them is to define the generational groups in the party. The war generation is easy to set off from the postwar generation by the last age cohort to be drafted into World War I, those born in 1901. According to the official party statistics, exactly one-third of the Nazis who had joined by January 1933 were actually veterans.[9] Of the two-

---

SA, see Wolfgang Sauer, "Die Mobilmachung der Gewalt," in Karl D. Bracher, Wolfgang Sauer, and Gerhard Schulz, *Die national-sozialistische Machtergreifung* (Cologne: Westdeutscher Verlag, 1960), pp. 830-837.

[9] NSDAP, *Parteistatistik 1935* (Reichsorganisationsleiter, 1935), i, 236-237. By 1933, the percentage was somewhat lower than before

thirds who were not, the vast majority—almost exactly one-half of the total membership—had been too young to serve in the war. The rest were either too old or had managed to avoid the draft for other reasons. The official party statistics give no information on the number of professional soldiers or former officers in the party or in the SA, nor even of the number of veterans in the SA. However, we can get a rough idea of these proportions from the Abel Nazis and, better yet, make an assessment of how important the war was in their motives of joining the party or SA, or both.

About half of the 581 Abel Nazis were veterans, and one-third of these had already served a stint in the peacetime imperial army, not counting 43 professional officers of various grades. Four-fifths of those who did not serve were too young to have been drafted by 1918. We can regard the difference between the official party statistics of 1933 and the Abel figures (which have a pre-September 1930 bias) as a key to what might have been true of the party and SA in January of 1933: the ratio of postwar to war/prewar membership was 1:1 in the 1933 statistics, and 2:3 in the Abel file. By augmenting the postwar generation Abel figures by one-fourth or deducting one-sixth from the war/prewar generation figures, we can obtain a reasonable estimate of the proportions in the NSDAP.[10] We shall refer to these approximate proportions henceforth as the "corrected Abel figures," and take them to represent the party as of January 1933, immediately prior to Hitler's appointment as chancellor. Thus more than one-fourth of the veterans in the NSDAP may have been in the peacetime imperial army,

the 1930 elections, when 36.6 percent were veterans. Between 1930 and 1933, the party also became slightly younger, with about 6 percent more under thirty.

[10] The exact ratio is 38.7 percent postwar generation to 51.3 percent war/prewar generation in 1933 and 39.5 percent in the Abel file. The suggested factors of correction still omit the likely possibility that during the rapid expansion of 1930/1933 the NSDAP may have tapped entirely new groups unrepresented it in before 1930. This caveat applies particularly to occupational and geographic groupings.

one-eighth pre-1933 Nazis. Another one out of ten was an enthusiastic volunteer. And one out of every sixteen was a professional soldier or ex-officer, for a total of 28.3 percent with a strongly militaristic background. This figure represents the most palpable war experience of the "front generation" that was knocking at the gates of power in 1930-1933.

Were the SA and SS more heavily of the front generation than the NSDAP? In corrected Abel figures, the postwar generation among the SA and SS amounted to two-thirds, and the war/prewar generation to only one-third (NSDAP, one-half). Among the SS, the older generation was only one-fifth of the total. Only one-twelfth (NSDAP, one-eighth) of the SA/SS was in the prewar army, only one-fifth (NSDAP, one-third) was constituted of real veterans, and only one-fourteenth (NSDAP, one-tenth) of volunteers. On the other hand, of the mostly lower and middle-echelon leaders of the SA and SS in the fighting years, more than two-fifths were of the older generation, and more than one-third of them were veterans (Table III-1). A thoughtful comparison, in other words, shows the SA and SS to be much younger than the party at large, as is to be expected. At the same time, the military element, and especially the prewar veterans and professional soldiers, occupy a signif-

TABLE III-1   Military Elements of Pre-1933 NSDAP SA/SS, and SA/SS Leaders Compared (percent)

	NSDAP	*SA/SS*	*SA/SS Leaders*
Share of war/prewar generation	60.0*	32.2	39.1
Peacetime army	14.5	8.3	9.7
1914/1918 volunteers	11.3	6.2	7.1
All veterans	53.0*	34.4	38.6
Professional military, ex-officers	7.7	4.6	5.5

* According to the official party statistics, the share of the war and prewar generation was 47.3 percent and of the veterans 34.1 percent. The table figures are from the Abel file.

icantly larger share of the party than of the stormtroopers or of their lower-level leadership, despite the earlier heavy recruitment of army and Freecorps officers to lead the SA.[11] The effect of the frontsoldiers' generation on the fully grown party appears to have been more in the transmission of superpatriotic beliefs than as teachers or perpetrators of violence.

Critical observers of our method may raise several objections at this point. They could say, for instance, that we have ignored the likely impact of the war on youngsters who grew up during that period, and who came to identify strongly with the war effort without reaching the draft age. Or they could raise doubts as to whether we can take for granted that a person who had been a soldier had to be a fire-breathing nationalist, militarist, or revanchist—or that a professional military man would be of this description. After all, soldiers are drafted whether they like it or not, and many of them may have been less than enthusiastic about the war effort. These are all legitimate objections, and we shall attempt to come to grips with the questions they raise.

As for the vicarious enthusiasm of youngsters during the war, there is indeed an age cohort born between 1902 and 1905 that strongly reflects the impact of the war. These people often had fathers, uncles, older brothers, or friends in the war, with whose imagined exploits they tended to identify, quite likely following the official war propaganda

---

[11] These figures can be compared with those of the KPD rank and file and leadership of 1927, that is before the rapid deterioration of the party set in. The 143,000 KPD members of 1927 included 12.3 percent of the postwar generation, but altogether 31.8 percent aged thirty or younger; 87.7 percent belonged to the war and prewar generation, with the vast majority probably having been actually in the war. Of the leadership, according to a sample of 504 of 550 1924-1929 functionaries, 93 percent belonged to the war and prewar generation, but 29 percent were thirty or younger. Only a few of them report service in World War I, including a few officers. Hermann Weber, *Die Wandlung des deutschen Kommunismus* (Frankfurt: EVA, 1969), II, 26 and passim.

with rapt attention and perhaps marking the great battles on maps on the walls of their homes or classrooms. One Abel respondent (no. 15) describes his attitude:

> I was thirteen when the war broke out. My eighteen-year-old brother volunteered and had to report to Friedrichsfeld for training. The following Sunday I walked the sixteen miles to Friedrichsfeld with friends of my own age to visit him and become acquainted with a soldier's life. . . . We used to gobble up the war news in the paper and celebrate solemnly all the victories, as there was no school on days of major victories. At school everybody strove to get mail from soldiers at the front and so we often wrote to all our friends and relatives at the front and asked for war souvenirs. . . . I always hoped that the war would last so long that I would be old enough to fight.

Three years later, however, this respondent showed strong signs of disaffection and resentment toward the government, especially when he heard that "they used the draft to punish people," that is, by drafting malcontents. There were indeed many—as many as one-third—of the postwar generation in the party whose early enthusiasm turned sour when hunger, death, and shortages followed after the early years of the war. The total share of this age group in the pre-1933 NSDAP was about one-seventh and, in the SA and SS, it was at least one-third. But it is not clear that a pattern of early war enthusiasm and later disaffection gives us much of a clue as to whether the war experience had an effect lasting the fourteen years of the republic, or what this effect might have been.

To be sure, the vicarious young war enthusiasts also included substantial numbers who exhibited attitudes more clearly pointing in the Nazi direction. Some were full of hostility for "draft-dodgers, Jews, and subversives." Others again seem to have sustained their positive attitude, as one of them, born in 1905 (no. 66) describes the onset of the war:

111

A terrific time began for us boys. Everyone turned soldier and we plundered kitchen and cellar in order to give presents to the departing troops. Then came the first victories. One victory celebration followed the other. But gradually things calmed down. Young as we were, we realized war was not a game of soldiers. Air raids day and night brought the war closer and closer. . . . Then came the collapse. For us boys who had been soldiers with body and soul, a great deal collapsed.

It is easy to imagine how these youngsters might have grown up to be superpatriotic activists ready to march and fight for any one of the many nationalistic organizations or parties.

As for the veterans, the vast majority of those who later became Abel respondents showed a sustained enthusiasm that often earned them decorations or promotions. This was especially true of the older cohorts, those born before 1894, whereas the younger veterans were more likely to show the emotional impact of their experience. One out of five specifically mentioned the egalitarian experience of comradeship in the trenches, which set aside all class and status distinctions in the face of death. The others were divided among the hostile bitter-enders, those eloquently relating their *Fronterlebnis*—the experience of death and gore in the great patriotic struggle against hostile encirclement—and those whose commitment was mute and to be sensed only between the lines. The *Fronterlebnis* obviously left a deep imprint on their lives and characters, marking them off as the "front generation" from both younger and older men, including respondents who had served in the war only in their mature years. As one Catholic respondent (no. 8) put it:

My old world broke asunder in my experiences. The world of the trenches instead opened itself to me. Had I once been a loner, here I found brothers. Germany's sons stood shoulder to shoulder in heated battles aiming

112

their rifles at the common enemy. We lay together in the bunkers, exchanging our life stories, sharing our possessions. We got to understand one another. . . . In battle we tied up each others' wounds. Who would ever question authentic German-ness (*Volkstum*), or how much education you had, or whether you were a Protestant or a Catholic?

The overwhelming nature of the events seemed to obscure all the petty divisions of German society. It should be noted that the Nazi party had no monopoly on the *Fronterlebnis*, which patterned men of all German parties at the time. However, soldiers and their sons and younger brothers at home in left-wing families very likely did not translate their *Fronterlebnis* into a political right-wing message.

The war invalids and prisoners of war bore the heaviest burden of all the survivors of the lost war, for they had their commitment to the national cause indelibly branded onto their bodies. When the same sacrifices that had once been called patriotic or even heroic began to encounter scorn and derision after the war, they must have found it psychologically impossible to retreat from their national commitment.

The Shock of the Defeat

If the *Fronterlebnis* had been a profound, formative experience, the impact of the defeat and of the political changes that were taking place was worse. It often was a real cultural shock to the returning soldiers, especially those of the prewar generation (born before 1894), who had developed an idealized picture of what it was like back at home. They were particularly shocked by the disparagement of military honor that took the form of physical attacks on the flag, the uniform, or on officers' insignia by hostile mobs. They simply could not understand the vast wave of internationalism and pacifism that was sweeping the land. The ignominious flight of the *Kaiser*, the downfall of the monarchy and of the traditional institutions of the German empire left their sense of legitimacy deeply shaken. The new rulers of Weimar society and politics, the red (Socialist), black (Catholic Center), and Democratic politicians, and the aggressive world of Weimar business and the press, all frequently seen as taken over by Jews and Catholics, were not accepted as legitimate authority. Germany's defeat in the war appeared to them to be the result of a "stab in the back" by the "Marxists" and the Spartacus movement. They also tended to blame the inept leadership of the *Kaiser* and his high command, the weakness of the civilians, and the trickery of President Wilson and his allies, especially the French. The "revolution," on the other hand, was attributed mostly to the new Weimar parties (SPD, DDP, and Center), the real red revolutionaries, or to an unspecified rabble in the streets.

An outsider can hardly imagine the severity of the trauma of defeat and revolution on the eager volunteers of 1914-1915 who had gone out into the great slaughter with patriotic songs on their lips and boundless enthusiasm in their hearts.[12] On their return, after four years of absurd, molelike existence in the badly shored-up trenches, among decaying bodies and amidst incessant cannonades, they felt like strangers in their own land, and often complained bitterly of the shocking social or moral disintegration or the lack of order and discipline that had set in back home. Their shattering war experience at a relatively young age brought them very close to the reactions of many a grizzled imperial officer or civil servant.

The reaction of the front generation is well represented by a building contractor's son from Munich, born in 1893 (no. 55), who served throughout the war and sustained major injuries. He reports on his return in 1918:

The sad pictures of red rule we saw while marching

[12] For a moving account of the culture shock of the war among British officers and soldiers, see Paul Fussell, *The Great War and Modern Memory* (New York: Oxford University Press, 1976).

back deeply depressed us frontline soldiers. We just could not and would not understand that this was the upshot of four-and-a-half years of our struggle. . . . The homeland had become so alien and un-German to me and I felt a longing and desire for a new order which, on the basis of the *Fronterlebnis,* would resurrect the tormented fatherland in better and wonderful ways.

His feelings led him into the early NSDAP in Munich, although he was rather cryptic about the extent of his involvement. Older respondents, and sepecially military-civil servants of the empire, often related their theme of moral and social disintegration to their antisemitic prejudice. A Prussian civil servant, born in 1885 (no. 28), told how as an officer he was ready for the call to the last resistance with pistol and hand grenade in September 1918. When no such call was issued, he took his "regular (*ordnungsmaessige*) vacation" in East Prussia, but was back in time for the fateful day when "mobs with Jewish-looking girls tore off the insignia on officers' uniforms." Physically aggressive against Marxist workers and allegedly Jewish strangers, he was also in close touch with the military unit that murdered the Spartacist leaders Karl Liebknecht and Rosa Luxemburg, with the Kapp putsch, and with Ludendorff and Hitler in 1923. His constant burrowing in the bureaucratic molehills of the Weimar Republic evidently found the support of the DNVP, militant veterans, and patriotic civil service groups. His rabid antisemitism is nearly matched by his venom against the Catholic church and the Marxist leaders. Other officers in their fifties spoke of "the moral disintegration at home and . . . the human meanness, cowardice, and cravenness" of the changeover from the old society to the new: "I can still feel the nausea rising in me today when I think of it" (no. 132).

The complaint of social or moral disintegration in some of the more irrational Abel stories takes a decided turn toward accusations of sexual dissoluteness and revelry, as in the description of the allegedly gypsy-like appearance of

115

red demonstrators in 1918: "they ambled along with the music of shawms, accompanied by girls with red scarves, singing away." The respondent from whose vita this phrase is quoted was a disciple of Ahlwardt, a dismissed school principal who had founded an antisemitic association before the war.[13] After the war he made the rounds of *voelkisch* action groups, and was involved in the vigilante *Einwohnerwehr* and the Kapp putsch. His violent antisemitism was matched by his aggressiveness toward alleged Communists. He reports having once "poured water on a demonstration of Communist women in the dark below his window in order to sober them up." Another frequent image of the "red gypsy caravan" is an Antonioniesque vision of shouting or singing young people in the back of speeding trucks festooned with red banners, dragging the imperial flag through the dust.[14] Another picture is that of returning soldiers dancing in drunken intoxication, or people living it up, forgetful of the fatherland (no. 133). All of these tales, of course, are significant not as reports of actual events but as expressions of subjective experiences in the minds of the early Nazis.

We can interpret this curious kind of sex-related alienation as a regression to childhood problems of establishing stable relationships to the sex roles of father, mother, and

[13] There are pictures of red demonstrations with such musical instruments. See also the account of Ahlwardt's career in Peter G. J. Pulzer, *The Rise of Political Anti-Semitism in Germany and Austria* (New York: Wiley, 1964), pp. 112-116 and the sources quoted there.

[14] A variation on the theme is of the Communist leader "Liebknecht, the Jew, riding on the running board of a cab with the red flag, shouting, gesticulating, and preaching hatred. . . . Red soldiers, drunk and with red armbands, looting," which was offered as a Berlin scene in November 1918 by no. 24. The writer is an antisemitic clerk who in 1933 briefly ran the concentration camp Oranienburg for political prisoners. He also adds stories of a lot of ex-convicts, and examples of fraudulent, corrupt deals, innocents being murdered, and big-time operators feasting to his description of postwar decadence. "Honest work was punished and the corrupt became rich. Cafes with whores as waitresses appeared everywhere."

son in the family, from which there are important linkages to prejudice against sexually potent stereotypes of Jews, gypsies, Latins, or blacks.[15] The theme of complaints about a lack of discipline and order, on the other hand, relates to difficulties of establishing a stable relationship to paternal authority and its substitutes during latency and adolescence. The discipline-and-order people of the Abel Collection tended to be solely of the war generation, and to be relatively free of antisemitism. On the other hand, their reaction to the great collapse had a distinctly militarizing effect, sending them off to join the *Einwohnerwehr* vigilantes and Freecorps in large numbers. These two groups of alienates, the antisemitic/moral disintegration group and the law-and-order group, each made up about one-fifth of the stormtroopers of the 1930s, judging from the Abel *vitae*. Another two-fifths gave no indication of cultural shock, presumably because they were too young to have experienced the collapse consciously.[16] The rest were the respondents who complained about the disparagement of the old flag, military insignia, and other traditional trappings. These people tended heavily toward the cult of leadership, expecting deliverance from a man on horseback, while expressing hostility and contempt for the old leadership of the empire. Here are a few examples: "Everything sacrosanct to a German soldier was stepped upon. I still remember painfully the day they took away my sabre and insignia," an officer reports (no. 274). "I was amazed at how the leading circles allowed themselves without a fight to be thrown out of the saddle. . . . Everything in the fatherland had begun to stagger. I was particularly demoralized when General Groener told the *Kaiser* the oath of loyalty sworn by all the soldiers and civil servants was a

[15] See also Gordon W. Allport, *The Nature of Prejudice* (Garden City, N.Y.: Doubleday/Anchor, 1958), pp. 349-355.

[16] Considering the large influx of very young people in the SA of the 1930s, the younger age suggests that this group may have amounted to nearly half of the stormtroopers of 1933.

117

mere idea. This cost me my innermost countenance." The respondent promptly joined a Freecorps and went to fight in Upper Silesia.

Another respondent (no. 199) combined the psychological wound of a war invalid, having lost his left leg, with the hurt he felt at the assault on other soldiers' insignia:

> The hour of the birth of national socialism was in the *Fronterlebnis* and only by understanding the *Fronterlebnis* can one understand national socialism. . . . When the revolution broke out on November 9, 1918, I was in the hospital in Trier. I still thank my stars for sparing me the experience of witnessing the shame and humiliation inflicted in the streets upon wounded comrades by these subhuman animals (*vertiertes Untermenschentum*). I shall never forget the scene when a comrade without an arm came into the room and threw himself on his bed crying. The red rabble, which had never heard a bullet whistle, had assaulted him and torn off all his insignia and medals. We screamed with rage. For this kind of Germany we had sacrificed our blood and our health, and braved all the torments of hell and of a world of enemies for years.

His sense of outrage soon brought him into the *Stahlhelm* and into conflict with the Weimar leadership. He especially disliked the leftwing parties

> because they failed to accord the front soldiers, and especially the war invalids, the respect and honor which are unquestionably their due, for they are the first citizens of the state. It was solely the fault of the SPD that a large part of the populace even came to despise the war invalids. You often got the answer thrown into your face: if you hadn't been so stupid and [had] stayed home like me, man, you would still have your leg today. The Socialists even gave me dirty looks because I always wore the ribbon of my Iron Cross in the lapel.

118

Antisemitism, 1918-1919

One-third of the Abel respondents and almost as many stormtroopers report a sudden outbreak of virulent anti-semitism under the impact of the cultural shock of 1918-1919, or of personal crises more or less associated with it.[17] Like the other expressions of cultural shock, this *Judenkoller* is not to be taken as a reflection of specific concrete events, but rather as a statement about the subjective, violent rupture in the continuity of the respondents' mental life. Great inner tensions, but not always a pronounced prejudice, may have been present for years prior to the sudden outbreak. "Coming out" as a raving antisemite released the tensions and focused them on the object of the displacement. Afterwards the restored balance may have been rationalized with a reinterpretation of the respondent's life, which may have taken the form of a personal anecdote by which the respondent explained his prejudice to himself and to others. The content of these alleged episodes usually involved primary relationships, implicating good faith, personal honesty, decency, sexual probity, or parent-child relations rather than the broader stereotypes of conspiracy or grand economic manipulations.

The *Judenkoller* group was composed overwhelmingly of members of the war and especially the prewar generations and, therefore, they experienced the outbreak mostly at a mature age of thirty-five or older. Many were professional soldiers or business or professional people, in other words, particularly vulnerable to the collapse and the red scare of 1918-1919. Quite a few belonged to the generation of

[17] If we count those who tell anecdotes of alleged encounters with Jews (which cannot be dated as easily as the reported outbreak), nearly two-fifths of the war and prewar generation and one-third of the presumably younger stormtroopers fell into this category. The correction factor makes each proportion about one-third. The SA leadership was somewhat lower in respondents reporting *Judenkoller*. The difficulties of dating the outbreak with precision from an autobiographical statement suggests caution in naming precise figures.

Germans who had migrated from the countryside to the city before the turn of the century, while others tended to be from families in social decline. Surprisingly often they report having had a freewheeling childhood, roaming through the countryside with little parental restraint. Their parents' politics was generally nationalistic or militaristic rather than *voelkisch*, although antisemitic parents were not unusual in this group.

Some of these antisemitic respondents are physically so aggressive that we need not be in the least surprised at the direction taken by the Third *Reich*. A high Prussian civil servant born in 1885 (no. 28), was so outraged by defeat and revolution that he went from one rally of the left to another to heckle and harass prominent Socialists, republicans, and revolutionaries of the time. In November 1918 he attempted to call a mass meeting against the revolution, and subsequently he founded innumerable nationalistic organizations for civil servants, officers, and Catholics, mostly as fringe groups of the DNVP. His aggressive hatreds included not only Marxists, "the *Reichstag*, the red headquarters," the "treasonous and godless Social Democrats," but also the Center party and the Catholic church—that "imperialist world power"—and the Democrats, "all Jews." His antisemitism he described as "an instinctive aversion against the Jewish race," which in 1919 turned into a mania. He relates, "Whenever a Jew was carrying on impertinently on the elevated or on the train and would not accept my scolding without further impertinence, I threatened to throw him off the moving train . . . if he did not shut up immediately." This sociopathic civil servant also threatened Marxist workers with a gun and with his boot during the Kapp putsch, according to his own account. In less violent accounts, the mania often ushered in a voracious hunger for antisemitic and anti-Masonic literature. A locksmith born in 1889 (no. 273), who was a peacetime soldier and in the war as well, took the German defeat and the "revolution" very hard:

The partisan squabbles took an even greater hold of the people. The Jews had laid such a foundation and they had managed to prepare all this inner corruption behind the facades. Wherever you looked, wherever you went to talk to people, you found Jews in the leading positions.

And so I was seized by such a tremendous hatred that once . . . at a war invalids' meeting, I launched into the open struggle against the Jews without realizing in my innermost [being] the consequences to which their regime was to take us. I began to search. I bought books that threw some light on the Jewish way of life and their goals. I studied Freemasonry and discovered that, according to the documents handed down, this terrible war had long been prepared and planned. Although they tried to tell us that the war was our fault, I suddenly realized that it was all a game of intrigues, a net of lies without equal in world history.

The *Judenkoller* here turned into paranoid delusions of global conspiracy. The respondent was unemployed for years and very lonely until, in 1932, he joined the brown movement, where he developed a peculiar fixation on the martyrs and casualties of the struggle. There is a certain plausibility about outbreaks of the *Judenkoller* among military-civil servants under the impact of defeat and revolution, or among small businessmen when economic crisis struck. Few people are mentally so stable that one cannot picture them going through a breakdown in which "my hatred against the Jews grew by leaps and bounds, and I became certain that the Jews are Germany's misfortune" (no. 523, born 1886).

Joining the Counterrevolution

From these varying views and reactions sprang specific involvements with counterrevolutionary organizations and activities. The youthful victory watchers (born 1902-1905) reacted with strong emotions, and the enthusiastic young soldiers were the most likely to be involved in actual combat with the red insurgents; some were even on their side. A young victory watcher among the Abel Nazis, born in 1903 (no. 174), related his feelings at the end of the war:

> The war was over. . . . Our troops came home, but the sights they saw were disgusting. Very young boys, degenerate deserters, and prostitutes tore the insignia off our best frontline soldiers and spat on their field-grey uniforms, shouting something about liberty, equality and fraternity. . . . In Berlin, violent battles raged around the Imperial buildings. . . . Defenseless people and wounded soldiers were bestially murdered. That was the liberty these heroes from back of the front were talking about. . . . For the first time a searing hatred rose in me against these subhumans who were stepping on everything pure and clean with their feet. Well, at least I knew I did not want to have anything to do with those people, even though I was still rather young.

This young man touched on all the themes of shock at the defeat and the "revolution," without having personally witnessed much of anything. Some very young victory watchers joined the Freecorps, including Ernst von Salomon and Reinhard Heydrich.[18] Typifying the involvement of the front generation is the account of a shell-shocked soldier (no. 21) about his return from the front:

> At war's end we returned in a march of twenty-eight days to Duesseldorf. Here the first red gangs were going to assault and rob me and my comrades. They did not overcome our resistance and we went on to Remscheid where we were stopped once more. The Red Guards there demanded our pistols and luggage. An old frontline fighter . . . took out his army pistol and knocked off a

[18] Von Salomon was involved in the assassinaton of Weimar leaders. Heydrich later became Himmler's right-hand man and chief of the SD.

Red Guard. We were with another four comrades who also fired some shots. I hit one of the red scoundrels over the head with my crutch and he collapsed right away. We abandoned our things and jumped on the moving train back in the direction of Duesseldorf. There was no thinking now of going home.

The young respondent (born in 1900) instead of returned to his unit and soon joined a Freecorps operation in the demilitarized Ruhr area against the insurgents of the extreme left. Battles raged with artillery on both sides, and he relates,

We took lots of prisoners whom we at first brought to Wesel to lock them up in the citadel. But soon we began to shoot them directly after their capture because there were too many enemies and we could not spare any of our men. They were miserable, accursed scoundrels; traitors who wanted nothing but cowardly to stab the fatherland in the back and to build a new *Reich* like the one in the Soviet Union.

The respondent went on to tell of a nighttime assault by the insurgents that cost his troops eighteen dead and many wounded before they took "bloody revenge" the next day. There can be little doubt but that to a battle-hardened soldier, this fratricide was not much different from shooting at Tommies, *poilous*, or Ivans. And, as the egregious rationalizations seem to indicate, he may have hated them even more than his wartime enemies.

If the Abel Collection is any guide, nearly half of the Nazis and stormtroopers of 1933 blamed the revolutionary activities, more or less correctly, on the Spartacist multineers, or on "international Bolshevism." One-fourth (or one-fifth of the SA) instead blamed them on the Jews, or deliberately confused the legal takeover of the Weimar parties with "the revolution." As Annelise Thimme has pointed out, the entire right wing felt a great compulsion to dramatize the alleged "revolution" in order to rationalize the internal weakness of the old regime in the face of its collapse.[19] One out of six of the Abel respondents joined a Freecorps, *Einwohnerwehr*, defense association, or a militant veterans group like the *Stahlhelm* during the years 1919-1921. One out of ten joined a *voelkisch* group such as the early NSDAP;[20] another one in ten went, respectively, to the conservative-bourgeois (DNVP, *Jungdo*), republican, and radical left-wing groups.

There is an account of this last kind of group by a militant, unemployed worker born in 1894 (no. 125) who had been in the SPD and the Free Unions since 1911: "I welcomed the ninth of November 1918 in the belief that the German worker had won out. Only weeks later in Berlin I saw that the contrary had occurred. I witnessed how the workers and comrades were bashing in each other's heads while SPD, USPD and Spartacus were wrangling over jobs." He left the SPD in protest and briefly joined the KPD, when he encountered an officer friend of his on his way to join a Freecorps in the east. The respondent followed him and joined the Iron Brigade (Freecorps) in the Baltic area. On his return in 1922 he married a girl who voted for the DNVP the same year, while he still voted for the Independent Socialists (USPD). He began to spurn the parties of the left, and gravitated to the red flag with the swastika, which may well have responded to his need to overcome the political ambiguities in his life. He proudly reported that after spending five years as the only Nazi among two hundred Marxists, his fellow-workers almost unanimously elected him a works councillor in 1933.

Another respondent of this description was an enthusiastic victory-watcher born in 1901 (no. 15), who had received a Christian upbringing from his mother. His father, a skilled worker, died early. Toward the end of the war, he became

[19] See Annelise Thimme, *Die Flucht in den Mythos: Die deutschnationale Volkspartei und die Niederlage von 1918* (Goettingen: Vandenhoeck & Ruprecht, 1969).

[20] Prominent among them were the *Schutz-und-Trutzbund*, the *Deutsch-soziale Partei*, and the Munich NSDAP.

124

disaffected, but not enough not to resent the armistice conditions and the indignities visited upon the returning troops. The respondent joined a Communist union to which most of his fellow-workers belonged, and quickly became involved in the civil war tensions of 1920:

> The constant strikes and unrest caused the police to be reinforced with very young and nervous *Reichswehr* soldiers. They tended to view any larger group of workers coming out of the mines or waiting at the intersections or streetcar stops as trouble-makers and brutally drove them apart. Thus hatred awoke for the *Reichswehr* and it was intensified by means of leaflets to great heat. Hence, when the Ruhr uprising broke out, nearly all the workers participated and armed themselves. The first step was disarming the police.

The clashes with Freecorps units, the red snipers, the looting of the dead, and the mistreatment of captured Freecorps fighters changed his mind: "Then I had enough of Communism and its struggle for human rights, for I saw how the decent worker was fighting in Lippe while the rabble behind the lines and in town terrorized the people. That was also where the leaders and functionaries of the KPD were playing the big man." The respondent, with many others, then left the Communists for the SPD. It took years for him to overcome his aversion to the NSDAP.[21]

21 There are other political wanderers between the two worlds, such as no. 148, a worker born in 1900 who had difficulty holding down a job after the war, and who ended up with the Duesseldorf police. The Ruhr uprising must have been hard on him, too, for he wrote: "I was so turned off by the doings of our rulers that I resigned in November 1920. I would rather be a miner than to be punished in place of the November criminals. And, since all parties I knew in 1921 except the KPD were for the shameful peace of Versailles [*sic*] I joined the KPD. In the summer of 1931, however, I realized that Communism and its ideas were the greatest crime against the German people." He still worked a while against the KPD from within until the party forced him to resign. See also no. 399, a truck driver who claimed to have joined the KPD in 1929 because his wife was deceiv-

Respondents who blamed the "revolution" on the Spartakists were the most deeply involved in counterrevolutionary activity. They not only expressed strong feelings toward the insurgents, but joined the Kapp putsch and various Freecorps and vigilante organizations to fight the insurgents from the extreme left. Their reaction was shared by the respondents who blamed the "revolution" on the Jews. The latter group, however, tended to belong to *voelkisch* action groups, including the early Nazi party, while the anti-Spartacists heavily belonged to groups like the *Stahlhelm* and conservative opposition groups ranging from *Jungdo* to the DNVP. The Kapp putschists and their sympathizers among the Abel Nazis tended to be of the prewar generation (born before 1894), while the Freecorps fighters were clustered in the war generation. By occupation, both groups were mostly military-civil servants or white-collar employees, including retail clerks. In addition, the Freecorps members often were university students and blue-collar workers.

If the first turbulent years of the republic permit us to speak of a counterrevolution, mostly in the sense of opposition to the revolutionaries of the far left, the years 1922-1924 distinctly changed the direction of the right-wing opposition from the USPD and KPD to the republic itself. The attitudes of the Abel respondents of these years are distinctly less oriented toward the war experience than among the Freecorps fighters of 1919-1921. About two-fifths of the Abel Nazis and nearly two-thirds (in corrected figures) of the stormtroopers of 1933 were politically involved during the turbulent year of 1923. One-sixth were either in other political parties and another sixth claimed to have participated in or sympathized with Hitler's beer-hall putsch. One in twelve was with a militant veterans group like the *Stahlhelm,* and one in eight was in one of the other *voelkisch*

---

ing him with other men and because he had encountered injustice at work and hypocrisy in the SPD.

parties or embroiled with the French occupation of the Rhineland.

By this time, many of the old members of the dissolved Freecorps and *Einwohnerwehr* had already found their way to the *Stahlhelm* or the *voelkisch* parties, including the fledgling NSDAP, which in late 1922 had absorbed many of the former members of the dissolved *Deutsch-soziale Partei* and the outlawed *Schutz-und-Trutzbund*. However, much as the brown converts from the Freecorps, the *Einwohnerwehr*, and the Kapp putschists may have helped to build up the NSDAP in those years, many of them did not simply rejoin the reconstructed party of 1925, but stayed away until the Nazi bandwagon got underway in 1930-1931, or even later. The *voelkisch* group members, by comparison, were far more committed to the cause and ready to rejoin Hitler as soon as he got out of prison and refounded the party. Their numbers in the Abel Collection, in fact, included such a high proportion of respondents who claimed to have been the first in their town or area to join that it seems fair to regard them as the dragon seed of the full-fledged movement of the 1930s.

When Hitler's first bid for power failed with the beer-hall putsch of November 1923, and he was imprisoned, the NSDAP had fifty-five thousand members and the SA no more than two thousand, which was a negligible force in comparison to the size and armaments of the Bavarian *Oberland* or *Reichsflagge* paramilitary organizations, with which the SA had become linked earlier in the year.[22] His

[22] Estimates of the number of Nazi sympathizers go into the hundreds of thousands and, in spite of the outlawing of the NSDAP in Prussia and several other German states, the party had begun to establish local branches all over Germany. The NSDAP had grown prodigiously in just one year prior to the putsch, benefiting from the nationalist reaction to the French invasion as well as from the general right-wing ferment in the bourgeoisie. The SA may also have drawn on the rising numbers of the unemployed. See also Georg Franz-Willing, *Krisenjahr der Hitlerbewegung 1923* (Preussisch-Oldendorf: Schuetz, 1975), pp. 172, 199-252.

putsch and token march in front of the *Feldherrnhalle* in Munich was a far cry from Mussolini's successful March on Rome the previous October, or of the Anatolian successes of Kemal Ataturk, who had also opposed the conditions of peace dictated by the victorious allies. The leadership of the nationalistic opposition in right-wing Bavaria in 1923 clearly remained in the hands of the military-conservative junta there, which wanted to make Bavaria into a German Anatolia, a "cell of order" to help bring back the health of the diseased German body politic. Nevertheless, Hitler profited from his beer-hall debacle, even in defeat. His trial for high treason made him known throughout Germany and provided him with a platform to deliver his propaganda. Furthermore, the disorganized right-wing forces had acquitted themselves very poorly of their opportunity to overthrow the republic, whereas he had at least put up a show of defiance that cost the movement a number of dead and wounded. What better way was there to show commitment to the cause of right-wing insurrection than to create martyrs, even though the police was only acting on the orders of the similarly antirepublican Bavarian government?

Experiences Abroad and Overseas

The era before and after World War I was characterized by intense nationalistic feeling and a sense of ethnic identity that verged on an identification with race. The war tended to aggravate these sentiments wherever different nationalities confronted each other, and painfully separated many existing links between people of different nations. The Nazi party had a surprisingly large number of leaders who had been born abroad or who had extensive experience living abroad: Rudolf Hess, Walther Darré, Alfred Rosenberg, and Joachim Ribbentrop, for example; so many, in fact, that social scientists have repeatedly called attention to this feature as a possible explanation of Nazi character.[23] The

[23] The study of Daniel Lerner, Ithiel de Sola Pool, and George K.

Abel Collection, too, has many examples that show the possible connection between foreign experiences and the superpatriotism of the Nazis. Quite typical are two men, both born in 1886 (nos. 70 and 161), who went abroad to get ahead, one as a teacher to Turkish Adrianople, the other as a university assistant to St. Petersburg. The assistant fled from the incipient Russian revolution into what to him looked like its German counterpart. When the Nazis held their first rally in his Communist-dominated area, he fell for them.[24] The other man bravely overcame his homesickness in Turkish Bulgaria by making a fetish of the smallest mementoes from home. His encounter with the national pride of the restive peoples of the Balkans reinforced his own ideas of blood and race, and brought out a swashbuckling militarism. Expelled from Bulgaria at the end of the war, he settled in West Prussia only to be expelled once more when the Poles took over. Passing through the DNVP and the *Stahlhelm*, neither of which was mindful enough of the true *Volksgemeinschaft* for him, he eventually became a Nazi.

A Swiss-German respondent (no. 381) who fought in the German army found himself and his family humiliated, detained, and boycotted when he returned to Switzerland in 1919. He came to hold office in a German Protective Association there and eventually returned to Germany a superpatriot. There are also some who resided for a while in the United States (nos. 366, 539, and 557), including one who

---

Schueller pointed out that half of the "propagandists" and a fourth of the "administrators" drawn from the *Fuehrerlexikon* of 1934 were persons of foreign contacts, including 7 percent and 4.6 percent, respectively, who had been born abroad. Harold D. Lasswell and Daniel Lerner, *World Revolutionary Elites* (Cambridge: MIT Press, 1966).

[24] See also the two German-Russian aristocrats (nos. 90 and 123) who felt outsiders when Russia was at war with Germany and then, after fighting with the Whites against the Bolsheviks, fled to Germany to lead the lonely life of a refugee lecturing to German right-wing groups about Bolshevism. The Nazi party finally welcomed them in its comradely embrace.

founded a Nazi group in New Jersey in the early thirties. His reaction to America is worth quoting, since it mirrors an attitude that can produce intense nationalism during a foreign sojourn. Obviously, not every German immigrant reacts as he did:

> Here I glimpsed a different world. Everything we already scorned as old and inadequate such as the Bismarckian social security system had not even arrived in New York, and the masses were not even talking about it. I was also disturbed about the attitude of the Americans toward us Germans. Whereas we looked at them as the honorable, soldierly enemy of the war, they regarded us as pariahs. Well-schooled as I was, I came to feel sorry for the Americans, for they had been brainwashed by *alien elements* (italics in original). . . . They learned to see everything through spectacles of arrogance, "from above" as it were . . . an arrogance which stems from alien inoculation. . . . I also suffered from the degeneration of German-American circles I had approached unsuccessfully—the same "democratic" arrogance—and behind it the grinning face from Syria. Life was made intolerable for me and my German wife. . . . I traveled to many countries and peoples but none could compare with the civilization we were struggling for back home.

He returned late in 1932.

There are quite a few German colonists in the Abel Collection who were born in the early 1880s and volunteered to serve in Southwest Africa against the uprising of Herreros and Hottentots (nos. 304, 320, 368, and 388). Some of them served there under the same General von Epp who in 1919 led the Freecorps that bloodily put down the Soldiers and Workers Council of Munich, or under his equivalent in Hamburg, von Lettow-Vorbeck. Their attitudes of swashbuckling adventure led them directly into *voelkisch* action groups such as the *Schutz-und-Trutzbund* or to the early Nazi party. They viewed the victorious British as "destroyers of our peaceful homeland" and the French occupiers as "black beasts raping German girls." Their "indelible hatred" for the enemy nations of the war was easily transferred to the Weimar leaders, the "parliamentary clique of criminals," and to the Socialists and Communists. Some of the colonials, a dozen years older, were high military officers in Tsin-tao (China) or Africa (nos. 132 and 235). They reacted with the same vituperation toward all the enemies of the Kaiser's regime, foreign and domestic, with the further reinforcement of old prewar hatreds and phobias.

There were also internal colonists (nos. 313, 407, 414, 427, and 436) whose fathers had followed the governmental encouragement to move to Metz in the Alsace or Prussian-ruled Poznan. The sons grew up just as the fruit of the parents' labors was wiped out by the end of the war and by expulsion from areas that were no longer German. Their youth was often spent with ethnic friction or distrust of the "politically unreliable" natives. The expulsion was brutal, and was often preceded by violent clashes. Many immediately joined Border Protection (Grenzschutz) units in the east or joined voelkisch action groups or the Nazi party while still teenagers.

Another significant group comprised the German ethnics from Austria or from the disputed borders in the east among Poles and Czechs. The border Germans are comparable in age to the internal colonists of the collection, and their situation requires an understanding of the dynamics of ethnic friction in Austria, Czechoslovakia, and Poland at that time. As one respondent relates with a subtle sense of class, sex, and ethnicity (no. 47), "in Graz it was always considered a shame for a Christian girl to dance with a Jewish boy, or for a university-educated men to be caught with a Jewess." The respondent interprets this as a defense of the Germans in Austria against the intermingling of the "races." He came to the Nazis not for ideological reasons, he admits, however, but because his father involved him in vigilante military training with the Einwohnerwehr from the age of eleven, and because of a freely admitted "lust for brawling." Other Austrians and Sudeten Germans grew

131

up with a burning desire to join the German nation, to them the epitome of a desirable identity among many flawed choices. Adolf Hitler himself was born in Austria and became a German citizen only in 1931. Many were well aware of Austrian antisemites such as Mayor Lueger or Schoenerer, or became involved with the German National Socialist Workers Association of Czechoslovakia (nos. 33 and 69).[25] Others were temporarily in the Communist, Independent Socialist, or Social Democratic party at the same time that they expressed bitterness about "the alien Czechs taking over our homeland" and joined Sudeten German defensive organizations (nos. 400 and 475).

The Polish border area respondents are more articulate about the ethnic dynamics of their situation. Some begin their tale with sincere expressions of the belief that they thought they were surrounded almost only by loyal Germans, until the unrest of 1918 taught them how many Poles all around them were awaiting self-determination. Then the politicking began with a wave of mutual distrust, and German hatred for anyone who sympathized even moderately with Polish demands, or who threatened to divide German solidarity with Marxist slogans of class struggle. Public officials who cooperated with the decreed plebiscites and cessions of territories in the Weimar government or among local officials (nos. 63, 65, 168, and 258) were vilified. The intensity of these ethnic-patriotic, antirepublican feelings may well account for the early wave of Nazi support along the borders of East and West Prussia and Lower Silesia in 1930.[26]

[25] See also Andrew Whiteside, "Austria," in Hans Rogger and Eugen Weber, eds., *The European Right* (Berkeley and Los Angeles: University of California Press, 1965), pp. 312-334.

[26] See Alfred Milatz, *Wähler und Wahlen in der Weimarer Republik* (Bonn: Bundeszentrale fuer politische Bildung, 1965), map 10. The NSDAP polled over 20 percent in these areas at a time when only Schleswig-Holstein, South Hanover-Brunswick, and the Palatinate were anywhere close to this level.

The Occupation of the Rhineland

The Franco-Belgian invasion of the Rhineland in 1923 and the subsequent occupation up until 1929 (some areas were freed in 1925; others had been occupied from the end of the war) had a similar effect of awakening ethnic friction and rekindling the hatreds of the past war. The late historian Koppel S. Pinson described the German reaction thus: "German public opinion was only united all the more in an orgy of nationalistic frenzy. . . . A flood of propaganda was let loose, both in Germany and throughout the world, charging the French with carrying out a policy of terror, brutality, rape, destruction, abuse of justice, sadism, and willful creation of starvation and disease."[27] Much of this right-wing propaganda campaign may have exaggerated French harshness and the deeds of the patriotic underground. Nevertheless, the actual conflict and the emotions generated on the German side seem to have played a major role in motivating the progress of many of the Abel respondents toward the Nazi movement. The French encouragement of separatism also contributed to the hard feelings on the German side. In this, the antioccupation struggle bears some resemblance

[27] *Modern Germany, Its History and Civilization*, 2nd ed. (New York: Macmillan, 1966), pp. 430-431. See also P. Wentzke, *Ruhrkampf, Einbruch und Abwehr im rheinisch-westfaelischen Industriegebiet*, 2 vols. (Berlin, 1930-1932). More recently, an East German literature on the Ruhr invasion has been added to the large existing literature that stresses the Communist fight against the mine owners and other collaborators with the French occupation. See, for example, Heinz Koeller, *Kampfbuendnis an der Seine, Ruhr, und Spree* (Berlin: Ruetten & Loening, 1963), or Manfred Uhlemann, *Arbeiterjugend gegen Cuno und Poincaré, das Jahr 1923* (Berlin: Neues Leben, 1960). See also the exaggerated account of Gauleiter Josef Grohe, *Der politische Kampf im Rheinland nach dem ersten Weltkrieg* (Bonn: Universitaetsdruckerei, 1941), or the book by Hans Spethmann, *Der Ruhrkampf 1923-1925* (Berlin: Hobbing, 1933), which has on its cover a picture of a greedy French capitalist in coattails and proletarian German Michael standing on top of the Ruhr industrial area.

133

to the uses of the Young Plan campaign of 1929 by which the right wing succeeded in mobilizing hundreds of thousands who later joined the Nazi surge into power.

The most immediate effect of the foreign occupation was to spur political interest and patriotic feelings. "The invasion [of the Ruhr] mobilized my political instincts," wrote a judge (no. 89) who was only sixteen then. A shoemaker and pacifistic Socialist, born in 1888 (no. 114), related that "I came to feel the rifle butt of the French and became patriotic again." Some respondents under the pressure developed a regular anti-Communist choleric outbreak, a *Bolschewikenkoller*. The events had a strong impact on youth. "The separatists and the occupation really taught me a patriotic outlook," reported a young itinerant artist (no. 424), who was fifteen in 1923. A schoolteacher, born in 1880 (no. 186), lived in the area left of the Rhine and commented on the misbehavior of the French long before 1923: "I was saying already then that we should build a monument to the French, particularly to Clemenceau and Poincaré, and to their allies for their chicanery, for they managed with their torments to make genuine Germans out of us, just Germans and no longer Prussians, Bavarians, Hessians, etc. Even people of Socialist or Communist persuasion agreed with me on that."

After the French occupation took over the mines and railroads and the Weimar government responded with a campaign of passive resistance, much of the bitter confrontation occurred at work, and especially in public employment. A Saar miner in the Abel Collection, born in 1879 (no. 334), related his visceral reaction to the French takeover of his place of employment:

We miners had to suffer particularly from the coming of the French to the Saar because all the mines passed into their direct ownership. The French mining officials expressed their Germanophobia and desire for revenge from the war toward us mine workers. Hatred and bitterness built up in my innards day after day against these alien elements and drove me physically and mentally to the end of endurance. I just could not bear the thought that these creatures were laying hands on our things and bodies. I could not go on letting these alien tyrants dominate me and decided to leave the mine.

He soon fell sick and had to be pensioned off to the little forest village where he was born. Many military-civil servants responded to the French overlords even more bitterly. The many respondents expelled by the occupation to the other side of the Rhine fell into two categories. Some participated in the passive resistance policy and suffered expulsion on a few hours' notice, while their belongings were confiscated. These were particularly federal officials such as railroad officials of all ranks and their families. Others were expelled for various hostile actions, often of a personal, spiteful sort, or committed with political intent. Sometimes the political and the personal elements are hard to separate. One bank clerk and *voelkisch* activist, born in 1897 (no. 438), was expelled with his family for a "violation of respect" toward a French captain. Little imagination is required to guess that his disrespectful action, which he did not describe, probably grew from his strong beliefs and activist temper. He may also have acquired a reputation with the occupation as a political trouble-maker and may have been deliberately provoked into a confrontation. Another respondent, born in 1902 (no. 443), told of "a physical collision" with a French occupation soldier "who insulted my honor." The respondent ran all the way to Saxony to escape the consequences of this confrontation. Another popular complaint concerned the restrictions the occupation placed no the singing of patriotic songs and on the wearing of insignia of patriotic organizations, such as black-white-red ribbons or the swastika of Captain Ehrhardt's Navy Brigade. Quite a few of the Abel Nazis engaged in violence against the occupation or the separatists, ranging from childish pranks to bombings and shootings.[28]

[28] See Merkl, *Political Violence*, pp. 190-206. The persons residing

Finally, there are unabashed racial animosities and fears on display in many instances. "The yellow and black hordes of France were raging through our Palatinate," writes a young miner from the Saar (no. 448). Another respondent relates how "Siamese, Senegalese, and Arabs made themselves the masters of our homeland." He told luridly of a brother who suffered a knife wound while defending his wife against assault (no. 183). A young civil engineer (no. 198), born in 1906, discussed the coming of the French to the town of Langen on the heels of the German retreat with a sharp eye for French prejudice, as well:

> The last German troops had not been gone for half a day, when French officers rode into town and marked the occupation boundaries. Shortly thereafter our town was heavily occupied. All private houses had to accept billets. Blacks, Moroccans, and Arabs were put up in schools and public buildings. . . . We had our fun with the colored colonial troops. They were so stupid you could show them an old newspaper in place of a valid pass at the checkpoints. But it was dangerous at night for women and girls. Rape and miscegenation were unfortunately frequent.[29]

It is remarkable that the American literature on the early Nazi party gives so little indication of the significance of the antioccupation struggle in the west.[30] The struggle against the occupation and the separatists appears to have been a major recruiting vehicle for the NSDAP in the areas concerned, just as the *Deutsch-Soziale Partei* (DSP), the

---

in the occupied areas were overrepresented in the Abel Collection. Among them, one in eight was involved in violent underground activities, and one in five was either punished or jailed, one in five was expelled, and another one-fifth was involved in passive resistance or nonviolent demonstrations.

[29] See also nos. 24, 30, 54, 57, 111, 335, 384, and 415.

[30] The Nazi literature has not ignored the role of the struggle against the occupation in the west nor of the border struggles in the east. See, for example, Will Decker, *Kreuze am Wege zur Freiheit* (Leipzig: Koehler & Amelang, 1935), pp. 75-81.

Schutz-und-Trutzbund, and various militant organizations such as *Oberland* and *Wehrwolf* or the Black *Reichswehr,* a conglomerate of militant and veterans' organizations in eastern and central Germany, became primary recruiting vehicles in their respective territories during those crucial years. Only the beer-hall putsch debacle seems to have retarded the coming together of a potent nationwide Nazi movement in the mid-1920s.

How widely shared were the experiences abroad, at the borders, and with the French occupation among the Nazis of the 1930s? If the Abel Collection is any guide, as many as one-third of the party members may have been influenced by these experiences of ethnic conflict. Nearly one-third of these were respondents who resided in the occupied areas, and reported friction with and hatred for the French occupation and the separatists.[31] There can be no doubt that Nazis outside the occupied area, other nationalists, and practically the entire German public shared the sense of outrage at the French invasion of 1923. In 1929, there were huge nonpartisan rallies all over the country to celebrate the final exodus of the French. The antioccupation activists tended to be rather young and less well-educated than the rest of the Abel Nazis. They were also far more often involved in political violence in the early period and, consequently, included a high proportion of people who graduated from their antiseparatist vigilante group (*Landesschutz*) or Freecorps to the SA. As a result of their intense superpatriotism, frequent cases of *Judenkoller,* and early engagement in political violence, in fact, they tended to join the NSDAP and SA in droves at a time when the party was hardly growing, in the years from 1925 to 1927.

The next largest group of these Nazis motivated to join the party by ethnic patriotism was composed of the border Germans on the east, who amounted to an equally large

[31] Since these cases are overrepresented, we have reduced the figures without changing the internal proportions among those affected by the occupation in different ways. About half of them report only strong feelings rather than active involvement or punishments.

segment of the NSDAP, but were less prominent among the stormtroopers and stormtrooper leaders than was the antioccupation group. The border Germans' experiences of expulsion or conflict with other nationals surprisingly seem to have given them less of a motivation to join Hitler, one of their number, than did the struggle against the French and the separatists in the west. The colonists and respondents with foreign contacts other than those of the war, finally, make up a relatively small segment of the party and, because of their higher age, an even smaller share of the SA. But this is not to deny the significance of the link between foreign contact and Nazi xenophobia.

A Lower-Middle-Class Revolt?

Among the motive forces of the pre-1933 Nazi party must be included the dynamics of German society. We have already encountered a glimpse of this in the imperial drill sergeants who, after many years of a successful career still could not become officers, or the grade-school teachers who were looked down upon by their university-trained *Gymnasium* colleagues. Not a few of the drill sergeants actually were made officers on the battlefields of World War I, only to be deprived of the fruits of their longing by the Treaty of Versailles, which limited the number of soldiers and officers in such a way as to leave them no future. Even teachers faced a critical shortage of jobs as large numbers of teachers from the lost territories and abroad were given preference, for example, over the new crop graduating from the Teachers' Colleges. There were plenty of other social predicaments of upward mobility in German society.

The social drama of the Abel biographies opened upon the seemingly tranquil and stable stage of prewar imperial society. Walter Rathenau, the economic genius of the war and later foreign minister of the republic, painted a telling picture from his grand bourgeois vatange point in his prewar essays:

The *Kaiser* was surrounded by his self-effacing, adoring court, which regarded matters of state as the family affairs of the Highest Family and kept all annoyance from him. The court was enclosed by the whole stratum of the landed military and bureaucratic aristocracy. They owned Prussia, which they had created, and they were linked with the Crown by mutual interests. . . . This layer of society in turn was besieged by the plutocratic bourgeoisie, which craved admittance at any price and was ready to defend everything, accept responsibility for everything. . . . Outside, however, there were the people: The rural populace, tenacious beyond comparison and devoted to the leadership of the country nobility, the church, the drill sergeant, and the local prefect (*Landrat*); the urban populace, nimble, disrespectful, and yet easily impressed, transported and consumed by the rush of making a living and living it up. On the sidelines, the resentful working class, spiteful for being spited, living for the future and rejecting the present on principle.[32]

There is more than a hint of social tension in Rathenau's picture of prewar society, especially in the pose of the working classes.

It has long been a popular game to speculate on the manifold social and economic conflicts of imperial society, and to relate them to the motivations of the Nazi movement. One of the most obvious explanations has centered on the Marxist theory of economically derived class struggle between the proletariat and the capitalist bourgeoisie. In its most simplistic form it sees the Nazi party as a movement of the class struggle *au rebourse*, that is, by the capitalists and their lackeys against the revolutionary labor movement. The bourgeoisie, the lower middle class, and backward or demoralized parts of the proletariat presumably made up the capitalist army against the industrial workers. Since

[32] Quoted in Harry Graf Kessler, *Walter Rathenau, sein Leben und sein Werk* (Wiesbaden: Rheinische Verlagsanstalt, 1962), pp. 53-54.

the movement was hardly in their economic interest, the lower middle classes were said to participate for fear of "proletarization," while the *Lumpenproletariat* did so for lack of proletarian class-consciousness. Since the theory failed to account for the prominent role of veterans, professional military men, civil servants, alienated youth, and peasants in the Nazi movement, and for the anticapitalist strains of Nazi thought, a Marxist interpretation usually requires non-Marxist additions to give it plausibility. The charisma of the leader, the "uprootedness" of youth, soldiers, and peasants, or the "inborn resentments" of the lower middle class have often been used to buttress this weak line of argument.[33] The work of Max Horkheimer and Theodor W. Adorno then deemphasized class, while stressing the psychological nature of the "new authoritarianism" of fascist movements.[34]

To this should be added certain theories of social development commonly known under the labels of mass society or anomie. The development of society from the familiar rural or small-town *Gemeinschaft* (community) to impersonal large cities in which only the cash nexus and centralized bureaucracy manipulate human interactions is said to have brought on social disorganization, a weakening of primary links, and individual alienation and disorientation. The atomized mass society of uncommunicative individuals without a sense of identity then is said to tend toward the

[33] The writings of Franz Neumann, Max Scheler, Werner Sombart, and Erich Fromm, each in its own way, can serve as an example of the linkage between a class-based and a psychological analysis of fascism. Inasmuch as a strictly economic interpretation does violence to historical fact, especially before the arrival of the "economic society" of capitalist development, such a linkage constitutes, of course, a giant step toward realism.

[34] By the new authoritarianism they meant an ambivalence toward authority figures resulting from the decline of traditional authority in society and the family. See Horkheimer's *Autoritaet und Familie* (Paris, 1936) and Adorno's *The Authoritarian Personality* (New York: Harper, 1950).

formation of mobs and extremist movements.[35] The psychology of neoauthoritarianism and the alleged qualities of the "mass man" can, of course, also be linked to one another to give the nebulous mass man more empirical substance, although he certainly need not be authoritarian. A class interpretation and the mass society analysis of fascism can be at variance. On the one hand, there are writers like Ortega y Gassett who have elitist fears of a "revolt of the masses" against traditional elites. Others such as Hannah Arendt stress the *déclassé* nature of mass society and of fascist movements.[36] In either case, class and status are swallowed up by the mass and thus rendered ineffective as factors of social motivation.

In the case of Germany, these differences of interpretation become poignant indeed. Was the Nazi revolt really a class revolt, say of the bourgeoisie and its allies, against the rising labor movement, and did it result in a dictatorship of the capitalist or bourgeois class? Was it a revolt of the lower middle classes against a society dominated by big business and organized labor? Was it an example of the revolt of the masses over traditional elites, which resulted in a dictatorship of mass men over the homogenized mass society? How can these sweeping abstractions be brought down to an empirical level suitable for our purposes? Much of the social dynamic of fascist movements may indeed be universal among industrialized societies. But what was it that made the Nazi movement so enormously attractive to vast numbers of Germans after the First World War, thereby sealing the fate of Germany's first try at parliamentary democracy? Was it the perverse ambition and the "resentments" of the lower middle class?

To give an example of the inherent ambiguity of the lower-middle-class experience, we may consider the fol-

[35] See especially William Kornhauser, *The Politics of Mass Society* (London: Routledge & Kegan Paul, 1960).

[36] See especially Arendt, *The Origins of Totalitarianism*, new ed. (New York: Harcourt, Brace, 1966).

lowing true experience. In the 1880s, having done his service with the elite First Guard Regiment in Potsdam, Jan T., a farmhand from Holstein, migrated to the big city of Hamburg and took a job as a lorry driver. He was thrifty and soon was able to get married and buy his own cellar tavern. Later he owned and ran a store selling fish, beer, and groceries, with which his growing son Ernst soon had to help. Ernst's mother was pious and politically conservative. Following his father around on purchasing errands, the son soon became aware of grinding poverty and of Socialist and trade union agitation; meanwhile he was learning to appreciate German literature and history at school. A typical career of the suspect, Nazi-bound lower middle class? Yes and no. It was a typical lower-middle-class career, but the son became Ernst Thaelmann of the KPD. The ambiguity obviously lies not only in our readiness to jump to conclusions, but in the choices lying before people in this situation.

Let us take a close look at the social motivations of the members of the pre-1933 SA and NSDAP in the context of the most salient social crises and conflicts experienced by identifiable social groups. Rather than using the large, unempircially defined classes of economic interest of Marxist interpretation, let us look for empirically identifiable social classes and status groups. Such groups are social communities of sorts, share social self-images and other attitudes, and tend to pass them from generation to generation. Each such class or group undergoes its own process of modernization and social mobilization, including, possibly, its dissolution into a larger social community.[37] Thus, the various groups of the German bourgeoisie formed at a certain point in history and underwent their own crises

[37] On the concept of "social mobilization" see Karl W. Deutsch, "Social Mobilization and Political Development," *American Political Science Review*, 55 (1961), 493-514. The concept of social mobilization as currently used refers to the process by which immobile, particularly rural, populations are motivated to seek a better life elsewhere or to advance socially by means of political organization and action.

and evolutions during the period in question, including their great moral crises of 1918 and the early 1930s. Except for the German equivalent of the working-class Tories, most working-class groups were well-consolidated and conscious of their goals prior to their moral crisis of 1914 and the subsequent history of fateful splits and schisms. As may be recalled from our discussion of the KPD, their biggest split turned up all kinds of unassimilated groups. The German peasants and farmers, finally, had barely begun to develop a sense of identity in the 1920s, after many years during which social mobilization among them chiefly denoted the departure of young farmers from the countryside and from the social class and status of the peasantry to membership in the working and middle classes.[38] Many of these rural migrants to the cities very likely continued to vote for the conservative or liberal parties of their rural past.

The Nazi movement appears to have recruited itself from a variety of groups motivated by the social dynamics of prewar or postwar society. Their social crisis sometimes stemmed from their unhappy in-between state between the major class communities, as was the case with the urban migrants, the new white-collar workers, or the displaced handicraft groups who had not found their way into the bourgeoisie or the working classes. Or it was the result of the impact of the German defeat in World War I on professional military men, civil servants, and countless others affected by foreign occupation or the cession of their homeland to other countries. The economic stagnation and recurrent crises of the Weimar economy tended to aggravate the

[38] On the social mobilization of the rural population, see especially Frieda Wunderlich, *Farm Labor in Germany, 1810-1945* (Princeton: Princeton University Press, 1961). On the development of a class consciousness, see for example Alois Hundhammer, *Die landwirtschaftliche Berufsvertretung in Bayern* (Munich: Pfeiffer, 1926); Karl Heller, "Der Bund der Landwirte (Landbund) und seine Politik," Ph.D. dissertation, Wuerzburg University, 1936; or Wilhelm Mattes, *Die bayerischen Bauernräte* (Stuttgart: Cotta, 1921).

143

problems of these groups. In the former case, such processes of change as rural-urban migration or upward social mobility and decline as dimensions of social experience became very important, inasmuch as they often involved being caught between the antagonistic major social classes. The sergeant whose career left him stranded between the classes; the rural-urban migrant or upwardly mobile person who never completely arrived, and could not go back again, either; the working-class Tory who tenaciously clung to the conservative (DNVP or BVP) or liberal (DVP or Center) parties of his rural antecedents until they abandoned him at the onset of the Depression;[39] the person uprooted by expulsion from occupied or ceded territory; the middle-class daughter who took employment and found herself ostracized by the traditional prejudices of the bourgeoisie—these are typical examples of the social dynamics that tended to make many of the Abel respondents "marginal," frustrated, and available for Nazi recruitment, just as Adolf Hitler himself was a good example of the in-between status and of a stranded military career.

Migration and Stagnation

The great social drama of the prewar generation of the Abel Nazis (born before 1894) was the migration from the countryside to the cities, and from the farm to a different occupation in the city. In the period from 1871 to 1890, the share of the German population in rural communes under two thousand inhabitants dropped from 63.9 percent to 53 percent, while the number of cities over one hundred thousand rose from eight to twenty-six, and the population in them from 4.8 percent to 12.1 percent of the total. By 1925 there

[39] See for example the forthcoming book of Richard F. Hamilton on the metropolitan voters, *The Bases of National Socialism: The Electoral Support for Hitler, 1924-1932*, and the description by Konrad Heiden of the predicament of the small-time officers in the Weimar Republic in *Der Führer* (Boston: Houghton Mifflin, 1944), pp. 28-29.

144

were forty-five such big cities, and they comprised 26.7 percent of the population, while the rural population had declined to 35.7 percent.[40] This migration was accelerated through the severe agricultural crisis beginning in 1876, and aggravated by a general state of economic depression from 1873 into the 1890s that tended to push the lower bourgeoisie, especially, into the arms of social-conservative and anti-Socialist sentiments.[41]

Against this background, basic information about the proportion of rural-urban migrants among the Abel Nazis and about the changes in occupation between the respondents and their fathers is obviously relevant. It serves to correct, in particular, the common stereotypes of a static lower middle class and of a static class society unmoved by the drama of upward mobility and urbanization. Of the respondents who supply this information (about two-thirds), fewer than half never moved from where they were born. Almost one-third was quite mobile among cities, and more than a fifth (22.2 percent) were rural-urban migrants. Most of these migrants were of the prewar generation and upwardly mobile. Nearly three-fourths had farmers, agricultural laborers, or artisans for fathers. Their occupations tended to be in the military or civil service, or business and the professions. This conjures up a mental image of an older generation of Nazis whose life experience was based on an at least initially successful departure from their rural past. Many of them chose the public service or the "old middle class" way of small entrepreneurship or professional skills as their road up and out of the countryside.

[40] The definition of rural area here differs from that of Kater in "Quantifizierung und NS-Geschichte," where communes under 10,000 are considered rural. German standard statistics apply the term rural only to communes under 2,000. *Statistik des Deutschen Reiches*, N.F., vol. 68, Die Volkszählung am 1. Dezember 1890, and *Statistisches Jahrbuch 1926*, pp. 6-7.

[41] See especially Hans Rosenberg, *Grosse Depression und Bismarckzeit* (Berlin: DeGruyter, 1967), pp. 38-39.

A later generation of Nazis was made up of the less successful families, the "losers of the industrial revolution," both the immobile and the perhaps aimlessly mobile. Both of these groups had far smaller numbers who were upwardly mobile (one-third) and a larger share of families in social decline (15 to 20 percent), a feature that probably rose with the onset of mass unemployment in 1929. The highly mobile among cities tended to be blue or white-collar workers, and to have the largest number of unemployed between 1928 and 1933, nearly one-half. Their fathers were mostly independent and professional people, military-civil servants, or workers. Disproportionate numbers of this group were with the SA or SS, and not just in the party. The families in economic decline that were so typical of the mobile group had a high rate of unemployment and bankruptcies not only in 1928 to 1933, but already during the earlier years of the Weimar Republic. The spatially immobile group that is closest to the lower-middle-class stereotype heavily belonged to the war generation, and was presumably the most influenced by the war.[42] Contrary to the stereotype, a large part of this group that never moved lived in a metropolitan area to begin with,[43] but there were also many in rural areas (one-fourth). Three-fifths of their fathers were farmers, businessmen, or artisans, as we would expect, but one-fifth were laborers. They suffered little economic difficulty during the republic, but they also did not go in much for careers that promised social advancement, such as the military, the civil service, or white-collar occupations. The evidence from the Abel file, in other words, presents us with at least three

[42] The migrants were equally divided between the war and prewar generations. The mobile group was relatively young, although the immobile group had about as large a share of the very youngest (13 percent), who were born in 1909 or later as did those mobile among cities.

[43] In the Abel Collection, respondents from Berlin are overrepresented. Having been born in the big city was not incompatible with retaining the political outlook of their rural or small-town parents.

groups of strikingly different social motivations in place of the stereotype of the rebellious, static lower middle class.

Do these arbitrary groupings according to spatial mobility have any bearing on the political behavior of the respondents? Yes; they bring out considerable differences. Generally speaking, the immobile tended to be among the very first in their area to join the NSDAP, in contrast to the other two groups. They liked to refer to the enemy as subhuman, "rodents," or immoral and venal. As for their attitude toward the Nazi party after they had joined, the immobile and the rural-urban migrants both stressed the classlessness of the party and the joys of fighting for a utopian goal as the features that attracted them the most. The highly mobile, on the other hand, tended to describe the political struggle itself as the aspect from which they derived exhilaration and a sense of integration of their personalities. Both the rural-urban migrants and the mobile also often looked forward to concrete economic rewards, such as being reinstated in their jobs. The immobile and the rural-urban migrants seemed to have been the most involved in actual political violence, while the highly mobile tended more toward proselytizing and demonstrations.

The extremism of the immobile, who are presumably well rooted and at home in their environment, seemed to come to an earlier and more self-confident expression than that of the other groups. The split attitudes of these people toward authority mirrored the options open to a political dissenter short of moving away: either he used the police to control his antagonists or, failing this, he had to discredit the legitimate authorities altogether. The rural-urban migrants resembled the immobile in many respects, but seemed to possess a lower self-confidence and breaking-point, characterized by the frequency of paranoid fears and *Judenkoller* that reflected, perhaps, the trauma of their initial migration. The highly mobile were very different from both in their exhilaration at the struggle. The seeming paradox between this love of struggle and the fact of their actually lower involvement in political violence can be

147

explained by their more detached attitude toward involvement. Their fundamental political orientation was introverted and directed toward the self rather than toward changing the community in which they happened to be living at the time. Identification with the struggle and nonviolent participation in demonstrations, electioneering, or proselytizing was quite sufficient as a quasi-realistic backdrop for their self-image. They felt no great urge to grace the list of martyrs for some transient local cause. If "the system" became too unbearable or "the establishment" too repressive, they could always move on again. There are interesting parallels with the large numbers of transient youth in the American movements of revolutionary dissent of recent years, moving from one locale of confrontation to another. There is every likelihood that the myth of the violent "outside agitator" or "out-of-town crazy" might be exploded if social scientists would design a parallel study to compare the violent activities and attitudes of the immobile and the highly mobile of "the movement" in America.

Occupation and upward Mobility

The lower-middle-class thesis and the thesis of fascism as a bourgeois counterrevolution against the advancing working class hinge, among other things, on whether the Nazi movement had a "revolutionary" or "reactionary" character, and on an analysis of the significance of its occupational composition. Its revolutionary character is obvious from the attitudes and violence of its members, unless one insists on tying the word "revolution" exclusively to a Marxist interpretation of social development. It was an utterly radical, populist crusade to capture power not only from the republican elite but also, with a vengeance, from those the Nazis liked to call "the reactionaries." Many of the latter were pushed aside, humiliated, or even killed after 1933, as in the great purge of June 1934. Others cravenly sought to jump on the bandwagon or were coopted on Hitler's terms. Even the mighty *Reichswehr* and German industry were

148

soon cowering at the feet of the *voelkisch* dictatorship, which was not only oppressing workers and the leaders of the organized working class, but everyone who would not knuckle under.

As for the occupational analysis, the weakest point in both the conventional lower-middle-class thesis and in that of the bourgeois counterrevolution appears to be their empirical demonstration. It is not difficult to define and explain the social motivations of the "old middle class" of shopkeepers, independent artisans, and other small businessmen who were once the mainstay of the Liberal (in France, Radical) parties of the nineteenth century, until they began to feel outflanked by big business and bureaucracy on the one hand and organized labor movements on the other. We can also add the independent professions, although the motivations of the German university students in this category are hardly exhausted by their prospective economic status. These groups of the old middle classes, however, only account for one out of seven of the Abel sample, or one out of six of the Nazi party statistics of 1933. Of the latter, nearly half were artisans and two-fifths small businessmen and shopkeepers.[44]

The conventional middle-class theory adds to this old middle the "new middle classes" of white-collar workers and the civil service, two groups that were also overrepresented in the Nazi party as compared to the total population. The white-collar employees, mostly retail clerks and other commercial employees, made up a good one-fifth of the Nazi

[44] *Parteistatistik 1935*, i, 70. The precise percentages are 44.8 percent artisans, 39.5 percent small businessmen, and 15.7 percent professions in this component. The students are lumped together with high-school students, a category about half as large as that of the professions in 1933. The Abel file has one-third artisans, two-fifths small businessmen, and a good one-fourth from the professions and students in this old middle-class component. But see also the greater detail given by Kater, "Quantifizierung und NS-Geschichte," pp. 464-465, where the academically trained are counted as upper or upper-middle, while skilled workers and dependent artisans may be working-class. *Ibid.*, p. 477.

party and one-sixth of the Abel file, which shows nearly two-thirds of them to be either upwardly mobile or in social decline.[45] This should not surprise anyone, as there was practically no white-collar stratum to speak of among the generation of the fathers of these Nazis. Sociologists customarily determine social class, among other things, with the help of the father's occupation (Table III-2), since this tends to determine a person's starting condition.

TABLE III-2   Occupation of Abel Respondents' Fathers

	Number	Percent
Military-civil servants	95	20.3
Independent businessmen	63	13.6
Professions, artists, students	10	2.1
Artisans, dependent or independent	89	19.1
Workers, skilled or unskilled	87	18.6
White-collar employees	—	—
Farmers	98	21.0
Farm laborers, domestic servants	9	1.9
Others	16	3.4
Total	467	100.00

The Abel Nazis also include a substantial number (one-fourth to one-third) of deprived childhoods on marginal farms, in large families, in poverty, or without a father. If the Abel Collection is any guide, the social origins of the Nazi movement were quite different from the distribution customarily hypothesized.[46] Except for the overrepresentation of the military-civil servants and underrepresentation of farmers, the fathers' occupations are quite representative of the German population, say, in the 1880s. This

[45] Of those in the Abel file, 44.5 percent moved to the middle class from their parents' lower status, and 17 percent moved down from a higher status. See Merkl, *Political Violence*, p. 73.

[46] See Seymour M. Lipset, *Political Man* (Garden City, N.Y.: Doubleday/Anchor, 1960), pp. 146-147. The overrepresentation of the independents, the white-collar employees, and the civil servants is shown also in *Parteistatistik*, ı, 58.

prominent role of the military-civil servants, the close link between the military and the civil service under the empire[47] and the fact that they were sheltered from the economic marketplace, where the old and new middle class suffered, persuaded us to question the inclusion of the professional military and the civil service in the "lower-middle-class thesis." The civil servants had no economic reasons to fear either big business or big labor, and could hardly be said to hate the interventionistic state. Their motivations were purely political, often *voelkisch*, and hardly class-related.

The inclusion of farmers is another dubious feature of the old middle-class thesis, and this not only because they too were relatively isolated from the clash of big business and big labor. In spite of the Nazi-*voelkisch* sloganeering about "blood and soil," or of farmers being the "true Germans," farmers were often underrepresented among the party members (though not among the Nazi voters), which undercuts any argument based on the overrepresentation of "lower-middle-class" strata. They were only one-eighth of the party, although one-fifth of the German population. The official party statistics of 1935 designate nearly half of the farmers as "hereditary owners" and the rest as "farmers and leaseholders." Their composition in the Abel file, however, does not conform to the image of the freeholder. Fewer than one-third of the Abel farm respondents owned a farm. The bulk were dependent farmers (especially family helpers in families where the farmer himself was not a Nazi), farm laborers, or agricultural managers or apprentice managers, such as Heinrich Himmler once was. Their motivation, too, was more likely political, in particular *voelkisch*, than determined by economic class.

The largest Nazi element by far comprised blue-collar

[47] This argument covers only the old civil servants who identified with the imperial establishment, not the new civil servants hired under the republic, which for the first time included Social Democrats, left-wing liberals, and minorities. There are hardly any new civil servants in the Abel file.

workers, but perhaps workers somewhat different from those of the SPD or KPD. Close to one-third of the Nazis were workers in January 1933, and of these nearly two-thirds were skilled workers, including one-fifth metal workers, according to the official party statistics. However, the Abel file reveals these skilled workers to be mostly dependent artisans in smaller shops, and foremen.[48] Only one out of six Nazi workers was in a larger factory. The party statistics also suggest one-fifth to have been unskilled laborers and one-eighth agricultural workers.[49] It is not clear whether the usual gaggle of Nazi domestic servants, taxi drivers, or apprentices was included among workers or "others" in the official party statistics. The large number of working-class unemployed in the NSDAP during the 1930s, moreover, can only be estimated at about one-third of the Nazi workers. In big cities the proportion must have been much higher, perhaps as much as one-half to two-thirds of the entire party in some localities.

If we compare these rough statistics with those of the SPD and KPD of the same period, we find, of course, far larger over-all proportions of working-class members in these two workers' parties. There were also far larger pro-

[48] The Abel percentages of this component are 15.5% industrial workers, 29.7% dependent artisans, 5.8% foremen, 12.2% unskilled, and 21.3% unemployed, the rest being miners, domestics, apprentices, or unclassifiable but proletarian. Kater's count is 14.2% unskilled and 24.2% skilled or dependent artisans for a total share of 41.1% workers among the new entries of 1925-1932.

[49] *Parteistatistik*, I, 72. Miners, too, are present as about one in thirty Nazi workers. The reliability of the official party statistics is sometimes questioned, especially with regard to the occupational categories, which the NSDAP may either have intentionally misrepresented or distorted for lack of sociological expertise. The German census categories were a poor model. However, it makes little sense to compare partial sums, such as the 34,000 workers of 1930, to the total of the dubious membership numbers issued—that is, 300,000 by that time—rather than to the actual enrollment of 1930, namely 129,000. The turnover was high and the membership numbers misleading. See Albrecht Tyrell, ed., *Führer Befiehl . . . , Selbstzeugnisse aus der Kampfzeit der NSDAP* (Duesseldorf: Droste, 1969), p. 379.

portions of industrial workers in the SPD and of unemployed workers in the KPD.[50] Still, such a large proportion of blue-collar workers in the Nazi party, obviously not just *Lumpen* proletarians, makes the lower-middle-class thesis rather doubtful. Nearly one-half of the Nazi workers, by the way, were also upwardly or downwardly mobile, but the majority of them simply remained at the level of their fathers, unlike the white-collar Nazis (one-third). Of the farm respondents, two-thirds were socially immobile. On balance, then, the thesis of the middle-class revolt, or of the bourgeois counterrevolution, seems badly in need of revision. There were some points of socio-economic concentration, to be sure, but otherwise the Nazi party presented the picture of a varied "catch-all" or "people's party" rather than of a "class party," a catch-all party dominated by military-civil servants and white and blue-collar elements. The term class party is certainly inappropriate for this movement which had succeeded in catching the voters of Protestant liberal and conservative middle-class parties during a crisis of faith.[51]

The Social Dynamics behind the Stormtroopers

The stormtroopers did not completely share the social characteristics and motives of the NSDAP members, who in 1933 ranged in age from callow youths to men and women in their seventies.[52] In the party, the war and prewar gen-

---

[50] See above, p. 152.

[51] See especially Theodor Geiger, *Die soziale Schichtung des deutschen Volkes* (Stuttgart: Enke, 1932), pp. 108-109, who comments on "the complex and confusing middle whose sophisticated analysis increased the impression of complexity, especially when we attempt to summarize its mental and ideological state. Geiger also questions the internal cohesion of the middle-class elements in the rising Nazi vote.

[52] For an example of the motives of a woman in her seventies, see Merkl, *Political Violence*, pp. 122-123. Stormtroopers over 40 were rare in 1933. Only about one sixth of the SA/SS members and leaders, in corrected Abel figures, were of that age as compared to nearly one third of the party. *Parteistatistik 1935*, i, 167-168.

153

eration was the dominant element, even though it amounted only to half of the membership. Their socially derived
motives of frustrated upward mobility, migration, and social decline, therefore, were not equally at work among the
young stormtroopers. Let us compare the NSDAP and SA/
SS with regard to some of the patterns of mobility and occupation we discussed above. The SA/SS had only a negligible portion of the upwardly mobile rural-urban migrants
(one-ninth) in the city. The most typical stormtroopers appear to have been the blue and white-collar respondents,
who were highly mobile among German cities (two-fifths).
Many of them were from families in social decline. The
highly mobile were also the most salient group among the
stormtrooper captains, who were frequently in social decline or had never attempted to rise above the station of
their fathers. In many cases of SA/SS members and leaders,
in fact, their fathers had died (possibly in the war) or lost
their livelihood during the childhood or adolescence of the
respondent.[53] Nearly one-third grew up in poverty, and another one-sixth as half-orphans. Nearly two-thirds of them
became unemployed or bankrupt in the republican years.[54]
The socially declining and highly mobile stormtroopers, finally, had the highest unemployment rate in the 1930s.

A second large group among the stormtroopers was composed of those who had never moved from where they were
born. These included substantial numbers in the small town
and rural areas, as well as many big-city residents who were
upwardly mobile from the urban working class to a white-
collar or civil-service status. This group very likely included

[53] This was true of one-fourth of the members and nearly two-
fifths of the SA/SS leaders. Disproportionate numbers of them also
report having had a strict or disciplinarian upbringing, especially
among the stormtrooper leaders.

[54] The unemployment figure is an estimate, based on corrected Abel
figures, and is heavily weighted by the economic casualties of the
depression. These hard-times elements among the SA/SS form a
strong contrast to the surge of the upper-middle-class vote in 1932
for the NSDAP, as determined by Hamilton, "Bases of National Socialism" (unpublished ms.), chapters 3-8.

154

a number of farm respondents and small business and professional people, as well as the white and blue-collar workers. Comparing the occupations of party members and the SA/SS of the Abel file (Table III-3), including the middle-

TABLE III-3   NSDAP, KPD, and SA/SS Occupations Compared

	Blue Collar	White Collar	Independent	Civil Service	Farmers	Others	Total
NSDAP 1933	31.5	21.0	17.6	6.7	12.6	10.6	100.0
Abel NSDAP	27.1	18.7	13.6	19.9	8.2	12.5	100.0
Abel SA/SS	38.5	21.3	12.3	13.2	9.3	5.4	100.0
SA/SS leaders	39.0	17.2	12.8	14.4	12.2	4.4	100.0
KPD leaders 1929	63.0	11.0	17.5	4.0	2.0	2.5	100.0

NOTE: The 1933 NSDAP statistics are from *Parteistatistik*, I, 70. The "others" category includes especially housewives, pensionists, and university students (which in the Abel count are included among the independents). The students generally amounted to no more than one percent. Kater's count, however, gives them 3.1 percent. "Quantifizierung und NS-Geschichte," pp. 464-465.

echelon leadership, we find that the stormtroopers appear more often to have been proletarians, white-collar workers, farmers, and perhaps military-civil servants than were the NSDAP at large. The occupational information in the Abel file is often vague and not easy to classify, and we cannot be sure how the Depression modified it in the end. Comparing the SA/SS leadership to the KPD functionaries of the period 1924-1929,[55] the outstanding differences appear to lie in the larger proletarian share of the KPD, on the one hand, and the many more military-civil servants and farmers of the

[55] The SA/SS leadership of the Abel Collection consists of lower and middle echelons. Of the 63 percent workers of the KPD functionaries, 49.5 percent were skilled and more than half of these metalworkers. The information on the KPD functionaries is in part difficult to fit in because Hermann Weber has such categories as "persons with completed secondary but not completed university education, professional revolutionaries." *Die Wandlung*, II, 27-28. We counted them with the university students as "independents," which may not be the best choice.

SA/SS, on the other. In any event, it would seem simplistic to insist that the storm troopers were a predominantly bourgeois or lower-middle-class movement motivated by that economic class interest.

If we look at the occupations of the fathers of the stormtroopers as a clue to their early tracking, we find blue-collar workers, military-civil servants, and farmers among the dominant elements.

A breakdown according to the level of education, finally, is in Europe one of the most reliable tools to measure social status (Table III-4). The educational level of the storm-

TABLE III-4 Educational Levels of Abel NSDAP, SA/SS, KPD, and KPD Leaders

	Abel NSDAP	Abel SA/SS	SA/SS Leaders	KPD Leaders	KPD
Primary only	22.9	21.9	21.8	75.0	95.0
Primary & trade training	42.2	43.4	45.2		
Some secondary	8.0	7.2	6.5	2.0	4.0
Secondary completed (*Mittlere Reife*)	14.5	15.9	16.5		
Abitur, university	12.4	11.6	10.0	23.0	1.0
Totals	100.0	100.0	100.0	100.0	100.0

troopers, it turns out, is remarkably close to that of the NSDAP, and even the stormtrooper captains differ only in minor ways. The KPD, on the other hand, appears to have had an obviously lower level of education overall, although its functionaries included a far larger contingent of the well-educated.[56] The most obvious difference between the two was the comparative strength of the secondary levels in the Nazi and SA/SS groups. But, again, this hardly appears to be strong enough evidence to call them a middle-class move-

[56] Weber, *Die Wandlung*, pp. 27-29. The occupations of the KPD at large in 1927 were 40 percent skilled and nearly 30 percent unskilled workers, 10 percent artisans, and the rest white-collar.

ment except relative to the "workers-and-intellectuals" image of the KPD.

There appear to be no easy answers to the basic question of construing a "social purpose" of the Nazi movement, let alone a "class purpose."[57] Perhaps the solution lies in

[57] The detailed occupational analysis of the Nazi party has long been a bone of contention, owing to the vagueness of the available information and, perhaps, the unwillingness of most researchers to be rigorous enough in their analysis of the murky mysteries of German occupational categories. See the thoughtful discussion by Michael H. Kater, "Zur Soziographie der fruehen NSDAP," *Vierteljahreshefte fuer Zeitgeschichte,* 19 (April 1971), 125-137. The author presents a breakdown for 4,624 NSDAP members of 1923, which consisted of 19.7% workers, 12.9% white collar, 7.2% military-civil servants, 20% artisans, 19.3% business and professions, 10.4% farmers, and 10.5% others, differentiated by community size and north and south Germany. See also the remarks about the same period of Harold J. Gordon, *Hitler and the Beerhall Putsch,* pp. 71-86, and Kater's articles, "Ansaetze zu einer Soziologie der SA bis zur Roehmkrise," in Ulrich Engelhardt et al., eds., *Soziale Bewegung und politische Verfassung* (Stuttgart: Industrielle Welt, 1976), pp. 798-831, and "Sozialer Wandel in der NSDAP im Zuge der nationalsozialistischen Machtergreifung" in Wolfgang Schieder, ed., *Faschismus als soziale Bewegung* (Hamburg: Hoffmann & Campe, 1976), pp. 25-67. In "Quantifizierung und NS-Geschichte," pp. 465-472, Kater came to grips with the inherent difficulties of the German census categories and suggested alternative, very detailed lists of working-class, lower-middle-class, and upper-middle-class occupational and status groups. His distinctions at least permit the differences of interpretation to be discussed on a factual basis. Nevertheless, his sample of 18,940 "new entries" still leaves questions as to the gaps in the Berlin Document Center file, and as to possible variations in turnover among the occupational groups. Of the total sample, 2339 (12.8 percent are new entries of the 1925-1932 period. He also presents tabular material on the distribution and fluctuations of his new entries over rural, small-town, and urban areas, which shows the marked decline of the share of metropolitan areas in the years 1928-1932. Unfortunately, Kater here defines "rural" as a community size of 10,000 and under, and "small town" as communities populated by 10,000 to 100,000. It may be debatable whether the customary cut-off point between the two should be as low as 2,000, but there can be no doubt but that the upper limit is much too high. The 1925 census called communities from 2,000 to 5,000 "rural towns," and those from 5,000 to 20,000

157

looking instead for the political purposes freely expressed by
many Nazis at the time. The chips off the old block are little more than erratic pieces of a puzzle that will not lend
itself to any single grand reconstruction. The legacy of the
war, the border struggles and occupation, and the counterrevolutionary stirrings all supply only partial answers, which
stop far short of making the Nazi movement of the 1930s
simply a revanchist movement. The theses of the bourgeois
counterrevolution or the lower-middle-class revolt likewise
fall short of explaining more than a small minority of the
motives of the leaders and followers, not the mention those
of the voters of the movement at this time.[58] Each social
group, it seems, requires a separate explanation based on its
own situations and options. No grand causal theory can tie
them all into a meaningful unity.

At this point we do well to remember that human beings
in society are not merely the passive objects of underlying
"causes" in the sense in which physical objects such as billiard balls on the green cloth may be pushed around by outside forces. Humans are free to form a political will, to join
with the like-minded, and to intend political meanings as
no physical object ever can. Our search for causes can only

"small towns," *Statistisches Jahrbuch für das Deutsche Reich 1926*
(Berlin: Hobbing, 1926), pp. 26-27. Current regional planning usage
would call a community of about 10,000 (including surrounding
areas) a *Kleinzentrum*, and one of 75,000 a *Mittelzentrum*. See, for
example, Bayerisches Staatsministerium für Landesentwicklung und
Umweltfragen, *Zentrale Orte und Nahbereiche in Bayern* (Munich,
1972), pp. 23-33.

[58] Voting trends in the Weimar republic have been studied almost
exclusively from ecological data that are rarely detailed enough to
reveal the crucial shifts from one group to another. A consensus has
established itself, nevertheless, according to which the big Nazi landslides of 1930 and 1932 were heavily nonmetropolitan and Protestant.
In the big cities, however, there were also important shifts from the
conservative and liberal parties, which Richard Hamilton has pin-
pointed as probably coming from upper-middle-class districts and
from the non-Socialist "Tory" working-class voters rather than disproportionately from the lower middle class. *Bases of National Socialism*, chapters 3-8.

find "influences," such as the socialization of the persons concerned may have indicated or their selective perception may have singled out as threatening or attractive. With the Nazi movement in particular, any search for "causes" runs the risk of ignoring the political nature of one of the most politicized movements of this century.

The Making of Stormtroopers

What we need are not a hundred or two hundred daring conspirators but hundreds and hundreds of thousands of fanatical fighters for our faith . . . to work with gigantic mass demonstrations . . . conquering the streets. We have to make Marxism understand that National Socialism is going to be the next master of the streets, just as it is going to be the master of the German state some day.

Adolf Hitler in 1926[1]

WITH the collapse of the beer-hall putsch and Hitler's imprisonment, his career as a politician had reached its nadir. Even after his trial and release, he was still under the threat of deportation, and was forbidden to speak in public for years throughout most German states. The government was likely to watch his moves, and especially any revived paramilitary organization of his, with profound suspicion. And his authority as a leader of the *voelkisch* forces, in spite of the publicity resulting from his trial, was very limited outside of Bavaria and on the national level. Nevertheless, there had been signs of a considerable expansion of the *voelkisch* forces during his incarceration, which gave an

[1] Quoted from a letter to Captain Pfeffer and circulated among SA leaders on the occasion of the reestablishment of the SA in November of 1926. Heinrich Bennecke, *Hitler und die SA* (Munich: Olzog, 1962), p. 238.

160

inkling of the existing reservoir of sentiment he might exploit in the long run. The elections of May 1924, for example, mobilized nearly two million voters for von Graefe's and Ludendorff's National Socialist Freedom party, and another 333,000 for Richard Kunze's *Deutschsoziale* party. This was a respectable showing, which, however, was reduced to one-third of its glory by the end of the year and to even less when Ludendorff ran for president in 1925.[2]

Captain Roehm, who had gotten off with probation, organized *voelkisch* paramilitary groups, including remainders of the outlawed SA, with remarkable success in the *Frontbann*, which soon had more members outside of Bavaria than the movement had had before the putsch.[3] Roehm was at first authorized by the imprisoned Hitler, and was in contact with the exiled Captains Goering and Rossbach in Austria and with Ludendorff and many prominent regional figures and former Freecorps leaders in Germany. But the tension among the different leaders, especially the northern German, Ludendorff-oriented *voelkisch* groups and the southern, Hitler-oriented groups, proved too much for any attempt at union in 1924. Roehm's *Frontbann*, like the old SA, grew in the shadow of *Reichswehr* interests in a military reserve and in the maintenance of military education and training, as well as with a sidelong glance at the new paramilitary organizations of the *Reichsbanner* and the Communists.[4] Roehm evidently did not mind the politicization of his concept of *Wehrverband*, as long as he

[2] Ludendorff polled only 285,793 votes, barely over 1 percent of the total. The winner was Paul von Hindenburg, who handily defeated the republican candidate, Wilhelm Marx. Ludendorff had the belated endorsement of Hitler.

[3] *Frontbann* membership was an estimated 30,000 by September of 1924, when the Bavarian government undertook an investigation with the intent of suppressing the organization.

[4] For details see especially Andreas Werner, "SA und NSDAP," pp. 204-232, 239-248, 268-283, and, on the relations to the *Reichswehr*, pp. 245-261. The *Frontbann* was designed in three parts, a *Frontjugend* comparable to the Hitler Youth, the *Frontbann* stormtroopers, and an inactive *Frontkriegerbund* for older veterans.

believed he could keep its military and internal command equal to and separate from the political leadership he hoped to bestow on Hitler and Ludendorff. Unfortunately for Roehm, neither Hitler nor Ludendorff would accept the political leadership of the *Frontbann* in the form he envisioned. The disappointed Roehm finally tendered his resignation in May of 1925, and accepted a position in South America.[5]

Hitler had no intention of permitting the reestablishment of the SA as an autonomous *Wehrverband*, nor of sharing his resurgent authority with Roehm, Ludendorff, or anyone else. His conception of the function of the SA reverted to the partisan propaganda and protection squads of the years before the military element won the upper hand in the SA; he did not wish autonomous, ill-considered actions of the SA to get him and the whole party outlawed again. His Basic Guidelines for the Reestablishment of the NSDAP of February 26, 1925, specifically barred armed or quasi-military formations or conspiratorial groups such as *Organisation Consul* (O.C.), *Wiking* (Ehrhardt), or the Freecorps and veterans' groups from which the new SA could expect to draw many recruits. Every stormtrooper would have to join the NSDAP, and could not belong to any rival organization at the same time. The SA was to be tightly controlled by the party leadership, but not on a local or regional level. As organized by the former Freecorps leader and Westphalian Nazi *Gauleiter* Captain Franz Pfeffer von Salomon in 1926, it became a nationwide, uniformly organized partisan army whose lower units were subordinated exclusively to the central leadership of SA and party. Pfeffer also received command over the Hitler

---

[5] Werner, "SA und NSDAP," pp. 305-314. See also Historical Institute of the University of Jena, *Die bürgerlichen Parteien in Deutschland, Handbuch*, 2 vols. (Leipzig: VEB Bibliographisches Institut, 1970), II, 93-95, where the *Frontbann* is described as "civil-war formations of the *grande bourgeoisie* against the working class." Upon the dissolution of the *Frontbann*, many members joined, if not the NSDAP, the *Tannenbergbund. Ibid*, II, 668-671.

Youth (HJ), the SS, and the Nazi students. He created a rather flexible organization that combined tactical independence with central control, and encouraged the local leaders to recruit as many further members as possible. His organizational hierarchy of *Schar, Trupp, Sturm, Standarte*, and *Gausturm* turned out to be an excellent vehicle for the rapid expansion of the SA in the years 1930-1933. By this time also, the brown shirts had been introduced, according to one source, from leftover uniform shirts of the East African colonial troops. *Sturm* numbers, buttons, and insignia were given these "political soldiers," who were instructed to appear only in closed formation. At every annual NSDAP rally, furthermore, the larger units were given quasi-regimental flags (*Standarten*), which were to be displayed on special occasions.

What was the purpose of this partisan army of "political soldiers,"—the overthrow of the government? Ostensibly, it was the "conquest of the streets" from the moderate and extreme left. During the half century of the struggle of the labor movement in Germany, street demonstrations in working-class areas had become a symbol of strength and dignity, a reinforcement of working-class solidarity as well as of defiance of outside authority. With the "revolution" of 1918 and the establishment of the republic, this "control of the streets" took on even greater symbolic significance for the organized working classes. In the hands of Socialist or Communist militants, as we have seen, the control of the streets on occasion implied also political violence, disruption of the meetings of opponents, or "individual terror," that is, acts of terrorism by and against individuals. To the angry World War I veteran, Freecorps member, *Stahlhelmer*, or *Einwohnerwehr* vigilante, instances in which the revolutionary host had actually taken control called for well-organized military action to regain control by force. To Hitler and the stormtroopers, on the other hand, the object was a symbolic "struggle against Marxism," not a struggle for control over specific strongpoints. He simply pretended that the "Marxists" had taken over Germany's streets.

By grappling with the Communists and, less often, the *Reichsbanner*, the SA and SS could achieve tremendous propaganda victories in the eyes of the German bourgeoisie and the conservative right, including the non-Socialist working-class, and, at the same time, attract an endless stream of new recruits for the movement. "The first task of propaganda," according to Hitler himself, "is the recruitment of bodies for the future organization; the first task of organization is to get people to carry on the propaganda." But then he went on to add, "the second task of propaganda is the undermining of the status quo and its infiltration with a new doctrine, while the second task of organization must be the struggle for power in order to realize the doctrine completely."[6]

The "Conquest of Berlin"

The symbolic conquest of the streets had already been rehearsed in the first years of the movement, at the first SA demonstration at a patriotic rally in Munich in 1922, and again in Coburg and in other Bavarian towns. Every time, the conquest was meant not so much as a gaining of control but as a bold and sanguinary head-on confrontation, although in meeting-hall battles control for the duration of the meeting was, of course, important. In the streets, however, or at the rival group's hangout or meeting, a bold appearance and perhaps a quick confrontation was quite sufficient for propaganda purposes. They did not view big city streets as the military or the police might view them, as an object of physical control, but rather as a staging area for heroic happenings in which the bold stormtroopers had to put in an impressive appearance, no more. The heroic self-

[6] Adolf Hitler, *Mein Kampf*, p. 654. There are obvious parallels between this symbolic use of the "Marxists" as a foil for propaganda and a recruitment device, and the political use of antisemitism, as in the otherwise rather puzzling frequent charges of "Jewish terror" in Nazi propaganda. See, for example, Werner, "SA und NSDAP," pp. 43, 59.

164

image of the stormtrooper clearly emerges in spite of the bogus enemy:

SA men never give in. They answer the enemy in kind. They put up terror against terror. When the KPD assaults a comrade, the SA smash the tavern where the murderous mob is known to be. And when the police arrest them by the hundreds during a propaganda campaign and drag them off to *Alexanderplatz* [Berlin police headquarters], they smash up the hall in which they are locked up. They smash the benches, throw the telephones through the breaking windows, and tear out the waterline so that the upset police have to call the fire brigade for help.[7]

The story of the "conquest of Berlin" by the SA and SS is perhaps the clearest example of the assault on the republic by way of assaulting a bogus enemy. Some of the SA militants, especially of *Sturm* 33 (Charlottenburg), could trace their antecedents to obscure *voelkisch* groups of the early twenties, such as the *Turnerschaft* Ulrich von Hutten or the *Voelkisch* Hundreds.[8] Others could recall their association with the Freecorps Rossbach, with Julius Streicher's DSP, or the Nazi front, the Greater German Workers' party, as well as with clashes or raids by the "reds" at their earlier meetings. During the interim period after the beer-hall putsch, the *Frontbann* arrived and, in time, enrolled some 2,000 members, of whom only 450 were left at the time of the reestablishment of the SA in March of 1926. The adoption of the brown shirts at first provoked objections from right-wing veterans' groups, who found these uniforms strange.[9] Then Josef Goebbels came to

[7] Fritz Stelzner, *Schicksal SA* (Munich: Eher, 1936), p. 55.

[8] *Sturm 33 Hans Maikowski*, 9th ed. (Berlin: Deutsche Kultur-wacht, 1940), p. 15.

[9] Karl W. H. Koch, *Maenner im Braunhemd*, 2nd ed. (Berlin: Stubenrauch, 1936. The 1934 edition has the title *Das Ehrenbuch des SA* and appeared in Duesseldorf with Floeder), p. 163. See also J. K. von Engelbrechten, *Eine braune Armee entsteht* (Munich: Eher, 1937), pp. 31-39.

town from the Rhineland as the new *Gauleiter* and, from this moment, the "conquest" of Berlin began.

The opening shot was an SA march with music through Communist Neukoelln, which brought out incredible scenes, according to a Nazi source, of shrieking mobs trying to destroy the musical instruments of the SA, especially the drums, and attacking marchers. On a balcony, a man in a nightshirt with a trombone did his best to add to the cacophony. The "reds" were furious indeed about the invasion. *Gauleiter* Goebbels, "our doctor," had achieved his goal, not by any real conquest but by breaking through the curtain of silence imposed in the bourgeois press. For now the papers, especially the left-wing press, all expressed their disgust at the outrageous brownshirts. The Nazis, moreover, had a few bandaged heads and broken limbs to prove how anti-Communist they were. The publicity and the martyrs inevitably brought converts and helped to start a recruiting campaign in the factories.

Captain Pfeffer explained the rationale of the SA appearances in an SA Order of November 1926.

The only way the SA addresses the public is in closed formation . . . one of the strongest forms of propaganda. The sight of a large number of . . . uniformed and disciplined men marching in step whose unconditional will to fight is clear to see, or to guess, will impress every German deeply and speak to his heart in a more convincing and moving way than any written or spoken logic ever can.

Calm bearing and matter-of-factness underscore the impression of power, the force of the marching columns and the cause for which they are marching. The inner force of the cause makes Germans jump to conclusions about its righteousness . . . if whole groups of people in planned fashion risk body, soul, and livelihood for a cause, it simply *must* be great and true.

The SA chief added, "this emotional proof of the truth is not enhanced but disturbed and deflected by simultaneous

166

appeals to reason or by advertisement. There must be no cries of 'down with' . . . or 'long live' . . . , or posters about issues of the day, vituperation, speeches, handbills, or popular amusements accompanying the display."[10]

After a rousing first meeting-hall battle in February of 1927 (*Pharussaele*), Goebbels' flying start soon came to a halt when an incident led to the suppression of the movement for a year. The story of Protestant pastor Stucke and his heckling of Goebbels at a major rally went through all the Nazi accounts and many Abel vitae, usually with embellishments about the heckler having been "drunk," incoherent, and "a defrocked minister." In any event, pastor Stucke was roughed up and ejected, and the party and its mouthpiece Goebbels silenced for a year, but the SA continued to grow and to organize. By 1928, the first SA *Sturmlokale*, about twenty of them, had appeared in Berlin, "fortresses in the battle zone . . . offering peace and security from the enemy . . . rest from the strenuous service . . . centers of SA life because of the regular *Sturm* and *Trupp* evenings there. . . . Here the men experience what they almost always lack at home, a warm hearth, a helping hand . . . comradeship."[11] By this time, the movement had recovered its momentum. When the decree outlawing it was first lifted, the stormtroopers were still instructed to play dumb and say "I know nothing" when interrogated by the police. But at the celebration of its reestablishment, at *Kriegervereinshaus* and *Tanzsaal Koenigsbank*, a big battle ensued when the SA found one of the halls packed with RFB, Communist Youth (KJVD), and Lenin Leaguers (dissident Communists).

Following the big trade union parade of May 1, and repeatedly before the *Reichstag* elections of May 20, 1928,

[10] SA Befehl of November 3, 1926. Another SA leader and old Freecorps officer, Manfred von Killinger, in *Die SA in Wort und Bild* (Leipzig: Kittler, 1933), pp. 41 and 57, emphasized the ineffectiveness of the typical demonstrations of the left with their women and baby buggies, and men chatting, smoking, and looking around. Precision in timing and execution were vital, according to the author.

[11] Engelbrechten, *Eine braune Armee*, p. 85.

the stormtroopers again confronted the lion in its own lair. They marched through the working-class areas of Wedding amidst screaming and howling mobs. "Flowers were thrown, with the pots attached, and junk was flying through the air." But this time the SA stopped and turned to face the vast, hostile crowds. They rolled up their sleeves and took off their shoulder belts when, suddenly, the police decided to clear the streets. "Thus," according to SA historian Engelbrechten, "Communist power in Wedding was broken for the first time."[12] In reality, of course, it was not broken at all. On the contrary, the *Reichstag* elections gave the NSDAP only 39,000 votes in Berlin, as compared to 611,000 for the KPD and 815,000 for the SPD.

There followed other clashes, such as a half-hour street battle involving 100 to 150 Red Fronters near their *Sturmlokal Volksgarten* and two trucks full of SA returning from a campaign in small towns outside Berlin. Pavement stones, beer steins, fence poles, garden furniture, and flag poles served both sides until the *Volksgarten* was totally demolished, with beer gushing from the smashed counter. There were sixteen wounded, including four of the SA, according to the report of the latter. Soon after four thousand SA men marched through working-class *Lichterfelde* on their way to a monster rally at Berlin's equivalent of Madison Square Garden, the *Sportpalast*. There was an audience of ten thousand, the biggest to date, but at the end Communists and Berlin police ("the cossacks of Herr Zoergiebel," the chief of police) injured a total of twenty-three SA men.

The biggest target in Berlin was the KPD headquarters, the *Karl-Liebknechthaus*, luridly described by Engelbrechten:

> On the first floor there is the RFB guard which sleeps in the basement. . . . There are flags, many with Russian lettering on the red cloth. Mountains of leaflets and brochures, hundreds of thousands of handouts. . . . There are printing presses for *Rote Fahne*, large meeting rooms,

[12] *Ibid.*, pp. 74-78.

editorial offices, the Berlin headquarters of the KPD; on the fourth floor is the Central Committee, the highest Communist command station in Germany. Archives, newspapers . . . many in Russian. A steel mast at a corner of the building for the flag . . . the symbol of the Soviet blood dictatorship, fluttering above the armored observation platform on the roof. . . . From here, Jewish "workers" leaders conduct mass organisation and propaganda, and Jewish editors write the meanest hatesheets. Here the black list is made up with the names of Berlin Nazi leaders, SA and SS, suspected Nazi sympathizers among the police and businessmen, even of Hitler Youth boys. ; . . . Lists of SA *Sturmlokale*, Nazi party offices, Nazi garages, license numbers of Nazi cars and motorcycles. With the help of this murder file, they plan terror and murder for German Berliners and order their executions. . . . Couriers go out from here constantly to the Communist taverns and hiding places of terrorist groups.[13]

In front of this building, five SA *Sturms* once demonstrated in March 1929, without creating much of a stir.

There was also a new kind of confrontation, initiated by Communists who were evidently bent on real conquest of sorts. Three times in one week, they tried to storm the Treptow *Sturmlokal* of the SA, the second time allegedly with 180 men of the elite Liebknecht Hundreds, and under police protection. The third time, the RFB completely destroyed the SA hangout. Soon, the SA began similar raids on KPD hangouts, and continued to seek confrontations with the "reds" wherever they could be found and provoked. In one month, from mid-September to mid-October of 1929, the Berlin SA had forty seriously injured comrades and its second casualty. It was campaign time for the municipal elections, and "every member of the affiliated organizations . . . the trade union (NSBO), student, Hitler Youth, high school, and women's sections had to distribute election propaganda. They went out with their pockets full in the

[13] *Ibid.*, pp. 89-90.

morning, and came home empty by nightfall. . . . There were passionate appeals by speakers at rallies, agitators standing on the tables of taverns and inns. And everywhere the SA as protectors and chief agents of the struggle." Now they no longer needed to march through Wedding; driving through in trucks was enough to bring out a wild reaction: "Red flags in all windows, garlands, Communist banners. . . . An enormous roar greeted us; a hail of rocks, bottles, junk, full chamberpots came flying through the air. Women, in particular, were acting like crazy, jumping around and shrieking, spitting on us, showing their bare behinds. . . ." The election brought the NSDAP thirteen city council seats and 132,000 votes as compared to 1,222,000 for the "Marxist" parties.[14]

Discipline and Revolutionary Spirit

The carefully stage-managed partisan struggle of the storm-troopers was also a way of maintaining discipline and revolutionary spirit among the membership toward the day when the final struggle for power might arrive. The SA men had to exercise their fanaticism and the "spon-taneous" gestures and shouts of the big rallies, just as the recruits of the imperial army had had to exercise their goose step and clicking of the heels. Much of it was just a chan-neling of the motor instincts of physically well-trained, athletic young men whose marching feet could hardly be restrained. But in addition to this army-like militarization, there also had to be indoctrination in the political mysteries, "the idea of the Hitler movement," about which the master himself was amazingly vague. Beyond a sketchy synthesis of nationalism and non-Marxist socialism, with relatively lit-tle antisemitism, and due respect to the all-encompassing people's solidarity (*Volksgemeinschaft*), the SA men only

[14] *Ibid.*, pp. 82-84, 98-109. Although they complained about con-tinual searches for weapons, the SA obviously enjoyed plenty of police protection on many occasions.

170

1. Stormtroopers are brought in by truck for the beer-hall putsch of November 9, 1923.

2. The "struggle for Berlin": Dr. Goebbels speaking to the faithful.

3. The "struggle for Berlin": Sturmfuhrer Horst Wessel and his stormtroopers.

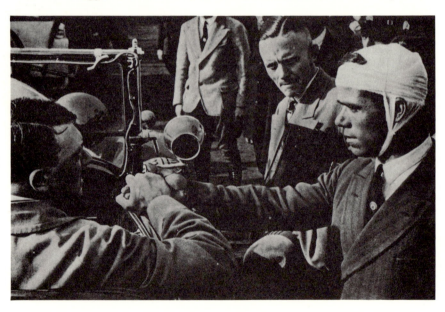

4. Adolf Hitler poses with one of the injured stormtroopers.

5

6

Kämpft gegen Hunger und Krieg.
WÄHLT THÄLMANN

8

7

5. The SA has to change to white shirts because brown shirts are banned. 1930.

6. Street fight: unidentified young ruffians surround their victim on the sidewalk while passersby scatter.

7. A Communist Red Front demonstration in physical confrontation with Berlin police.

8. An election poster of Communist leader Ernst Thaelmann.

1

9. Brunswick 1931: 100,000 SA men are said to be marching past Adolf Hitler.

10. Looking at the vast army of stormtroopers through the eyes of the leader. Dortmund, 1933.

11. Triumphant stormtroopers march through the Brandenburg Gate. Berlin, 1933.

12. Following the Pied Piper: Hitler Youth marching past HJ leader Baldur von Schirach. Nuremberg, 1933.

Opposite page:

13. SA, SS, and Stahlhelm: Stahlhelm leader Franz Seldte and Hitler, Berchtesgaden 1933.

14. Captain Ernst Rohm and his nemesis, Heinrich Himmler.

13

14

15. Communists rounded up and held at bay by stormtroopers. 1933.

16. Calling roll at concentration camp Oranienburg. 1933.

knew whatever their local leaders might tell them.[15] The fulcrum of stormtrooper ideology seems to have been, in the manner of George Orwell's *1984*, on the one hand a craven Hitler cult—love Big Brother—and on the other hand, hatred for the chosen enemy, the Marxists. It will be interesting to look, as we shall, at the beliefs of the Abel stormtroopers.

To keep the extremist temper fed, a never-ending series of hectic campaigns and activities kept the members busy. "The impetus of the young movement was immense," *Sturmfuehrer* Horst Wessel wrote in his diary. "One rally followed the other, each one crazier and stormier than the one before. Red Front (RFB) tried to break us up dozens of times, always in vain. There were street demonstrations, press campaigns, propaganda tours through the province, all creating an atmosphere of activism and high tension which could only help the movement."[16] The reader may recall the large literature on the radical right and left in the United States, which suggests that clients of all radical movements are attracted and retained only by such hectic activity, and tend to drop out as soon as the action lags. In the same manner, the putschist ex-Freecorps men, the ter-

[15] See Sauer, "Mobilmachung der Gewalt," in Karl D. Bracher, Sauer, and Gerhard Schulz, *Die nationalsozialistische Machtergreifung* (Cologne: Westdeutcher Verlag, 1960), pp. 840-842. The party members, unlike the SA fighters, had a better grounding in Nazi ideology, including antisemitism, although the extent of their ideological knowledge could hardly stand comparison with that of even the less well-educated KPD.

[16] Quoted *ibid.*, pp. 843-844. Wessel was a minister's son, born in 1908, who had been active in 1922 in *Bismarckjugend* and *Wiking*, and who had abandoned his university studies and taken a job as a construction worker on the underground project. Another typical *Sturmfuehrer* was Hans-Eberhard Maikowski, also born 1908, and evidently raised without a father. He joined the forerunners of the Hitler Youth in 1923 and the paramilitary Olympia in 1924, and then the *Frontbann* in 1925. After unsuccessful attempts to become an officer, he was unemployed from 1929 until he fled after a killing in 1931; he died early in 1933.

171

rorists of O.C., and, not least, the impatient young rebels in the youngest age groups of the SA probably had to be entertained and thrilled so they would not withdraw from the movement. Among the Abel stories there are many respondents who were deeply involved with the German radical right before 1924, but who then dropped out of politics completely until the pot of right-wing revolution began to boil again in the 1930s.

The pace of the "conquest of Berlin" accelerated dizzily with the onset of mass unemployment and the first Nazi landslide in the elections of September 1930. Physical clashes with the Communists, the *Reichsbanner*, and the Berlin police now occurred continually and at times under macabre circumstances, as at Horst Wessel's funeral, when the Communists attacked the procession and allegedly tried to seize the coffin.[17] There were official attempts at harassment and suppression, including continual police searches for weapons, occasional mass arrests, decrees suppressing Goebbels' hate sheet *Der Angriff* for periods of time, and the so-called "shirts-and-pants war" conducted by the government: a short time before the 1930 elections, brown shirts were outlawed and the SA had to switch to white shirts, which in time had to be replaced with ordinary street clothes. The police in the meantime had to supply institutional clothing to the violators and escort them home so that the clothing could be retrieved. The change to white shirts did not affect stormtroopers' activities much, although there were fears that the complete suppression of the SA would follow, since the RFB had also been outlawed. Taking away the white shirts and all other identifying marks, on the other hand, tended to confuse the stormtroopers and to reduce their combat from the massive, quasi-military

[17] Engelbrechten, *Eine braune Armee*, pp. 115-118. The besieged SA, on this occasion, called for help and received assistance from other right-wing groups as well, such as *Jungstahlhelm, Kyffhaeuserjugend*, and *Bismarckjugend*. For other stories of clashes, see *ibid.*, pp. 110-111, 123-127, 139-140, 149-158, 170-171, 174-175, 181-183, 188-191, 197-205.

scale to the small-group level, where they could still identify friend and foe.

The enormous growth and fluctuations of the Berlin SA from about 5,000 at the beginning of 1931 to 32,000 at the end of 1932 must have posed extraordinary challenges to organization and leadership—comparable, no doubt, to the difficulties of the KPD during its prolonged crisis. With well over half of the stormtroopers unemployed,[18] the dependence of the SA on financial support became crucial, and much of the haggling between the SA and the NSDAP was over questions of discounts and subsidies.[19] Apart from the SA Homes and Kitchens and SA Chief Pfeffer's economic enterprises, the Berlin SA also soon set up its first *Arbeitssturm* of unemployed comrades willing to do voluntary labor service.

The nature of the combat with the Communists also took on more characteristic forms underneath a thin veneer of major propagandistic actions, such as massive demonstrations against the pacifistic movie "All Quiet on the Western Front," or a mock debate between Goebbels and Walter Ulbricht at *Friedrichshain*, which really served to kick off a gigantic meeting-hall battle that three hundred policemen were unable to stop.[20] The accounts of the physical clashes subtly shifted emphasis again by 1931, mentioning wrestling club fighters with brass knuckles," "a selection of

[18] As Heinrich Bennecke described it, persons losing their employment first had to wait between one and three weeks, depending on their family status, then were entitled to unemployment insurance for a period up to twenty weeks, after which they could be given "crisis assistance" for another thirty-eight weeks. The payments were bare subsistence, calibrated according to a wage scale, and there was no crisis assistance for farmers, domestic servants, or persons under twenty-one. Local welfare took over at the end of crisis assistance; Bennecke, *Hitler und die SA*, pp. 167-170.

[19] See, for example, the documents on the Stennes revolt at the Munich Institute of Contemporary History, Fa 88 Hauptarchiv Fasz. 325 and 83.

[20] There were sixty injured. Engelbrechten, *Eine braune Armee*, pp. 145-148.

our best sluggers," innkeepers and *Muttchen* (motherly caretakers), or girlfriends who hid the stormtroopers' weapons at times of police searches under their skirts. There were gunshot battles, and incidents where a handful of gunslingers simply opened the door of a *Sturmlokal* of the enemy and fired away. Some SA fighters had underworld names like *Mollenkoenig, Revolverschnauze, U-boat, Schiessmueller,* and *Gummibein;* some of the *Stuerme* were called Robber *Sturm,* Murderer *Sturm,* or Dancing Guild. One of the most chilling accounts is that of a battle at Raddatz *Festsaele,* where ninety SA sluggers locked in their opponents and beat them without mercy or escape:

> Twenty-five of the best sluggers of the SA are in front of the stage, to the left a strong contingent, and to the right above the door the rest of the SA. So the Communists are in the terrible grip of fists, and hit by beer steins and legs of chairs, which almost immediately turns them to flight. While in the middle of the hall, the reds are literally being knocked down in rows, there is a desperate struggle at both [locked] emergency exits. . . . One Communist tries to crash through the window head first to open a free path for his comrades. But he did not count on the metal screen in front of the window. He falls back and the window glass severs both his ears. The other windows are too narrow. Their heads hang out while their backs are being thrashed resoundingly. The entrance has been barricaded with . . . chairs and tables so the police can't get in either. . . . The Neukoelln Communists had forty-five wounded, including eight seriously, and one of them died.[21]

Did the SA really ever "conquer" Berlin? Did they take it away from the "reds" as a result of these battles and eagerly sought confrontations? The Nazi student association took over the student government of the University of Berlin at an early point in the struggle. The Nazi vote rose prodigiously during the constant hectic demonstrations and

[21] *Ibid.,* p. 188.

street battles of 1931 and 1932.[22] And yet it never quite caught up with the Communists until the latter were suppressed after the still mysterious *Reichstag* fire. Between the July 1932 and the November elections, in fact, the Nazi vote in Berlin declined, while the KPD vote rose to unprecedented heights. Table IV-1 shows clearly that the KPD gains, at least from 1928 on, were essentially at the ex-

TABLE IV-1 Reichstag Election Returns in Berlin 1924-1933 (percent)

	1924 (I)	1924 (II)	1928	1930	1932 (I)	1932 (II)	1933
NSDAP	3.6	1.6	1.4	12.8	24.6	22.5	31.3
DNVP	21.5	22.0	15.7	11.7	6.7	8.8	9.1
DVP	6.8	4.9	4.3	2.2	0.4	0.6	0.5
DDP	8.6	10.1	6.6	4.3	1.2	1.1	1.3
Z	4.0	4.1	3.4	3.6	4.6	4.2	4.7
SPD	21.8	32.5	34.0	28.0	27.9	23.8	22.5
KPD	20.6	19.1	29.6	33.0	33.4	37.1	30.1

Source: Alfred Milatz, *Waehler und Wahlen in der Weimarer Republik* (Bonn: Bundeszentrale fuer politische Bildung, 1965), pp. 90, 93, 97, 104, 108, and 112.

pense of the SPD. As SPD voters became radicalized or unemployed, or both, they tended to vote KPD. The NSDAP, on the other hand, gained its increases in equal parts from the voters of the DNVP and of the DP and DDP. The Nazi campaign to conquer Berlin from the "reds," in other words, essentially conquered not the red voters' ample majority of 1924 (II) to 1933, but a substantial conservative-liberal following from the working, middle, and upper classes.

Stormtroopers against the Party Leadership

A short time before their great electoral triumph of 1930, the relationship between the SA and the party leadership

[22] The NSDAP staged fifteen unemployment rallies in Berlin in mid-January alone, and there were up to fifty-five rallies a day throughout Brandenburg before the presidential elections.

entered a prolonged crisis that was not resolved until after Hitler came to power, in 1934. There had been dissension in the NSDAP previously, during the difficult years of reconstruction from rather heterogeneous *voelkisch* and paramilitary elements; dissension was especially bitter between a north German left wing associated with Goebbels and Otto and Gregor Strasser, and a southern right wing linked especially with Goering, Frick, and Hitler.[23] Many SA leaders, especially in the north, were former army officers whose antibourgeois and anticapitalistic attitude and "front-soldiers' socialism" placed them on the left side of these issues. SA Chief Pfeffer represented these attitudes well in his concept of the reconstructed SA as a revolutionary army in a latent civil war. Like many former army and Freecorps officers among the SA leaders, Pfeffer had no use for party politicians, parliaments, or for the avowed course of "legality" of Adolf Hitler in the pursuit of power.[24] Nevertheless, at about the same time that the *Stahlhelm* and *Jungdo* succumbed to the temptation of wanting to be represented in the *Reichstag*, the SA leaders wanted the party to nominate at least three of them—including the eastern SA leader, Captain Stennes—for the 1930 elections. Their ostensible reason was to gain the governmental protection as well as the salaries and perquisites of the office for the SA. Hitler flatly refused, and commissioned the unhappy Pfeffer to tell his lieutenants that the growing size of the SA posed a problem for the proper proportions in the movement. Pfeffer carried out the assignment and then resigned.

With this confrontation and further refusals on the part

[23] See especially Otto-Ernst Schueddekopf, *Linke Leute von rechts* (Stuttgart: Kohlhammer, 1960), and Reinhard Kuehnl, *Die national-sozialistische Linke* (Meisenheim: Hain, 1966). Also Joseph Nyomarkay, *Charisma and Factionalism in the Nazi Party* (Minneapolis: University of Minnesota Press, 1967).

[24] The debacle of the beer-hall putsch and the repeated fears that the NSDAP would be outlawed again because of uncontrolled stormtroopers' actions persuaded Hitler again and again to insist that he would not attempt another coup. The last such instance was the *Reichswehr* officers' trial in Ulm in October of 1930.

of Adolf Hitler to receive SA delegations and messages, a number of smoldering issues came to a head all at once. There had been financial grievances in the eastern SA (OSAF-Ost) and frictions with the Gau office so acute that a mob of thirty SA men once came to beat up a certain party official who had repeatedly slighted them.[25] There was also a sense of disgust about the extravagance of the party leadership, which had acquired the palatial Brown House in Munich and proceeded to furnish it in style. The southern SA leader, Major August Schneidhuber later wrote a lengthy memorandum in which he claimed for the SA the "lion's share" of the credit for building up the movement and expressed his contempt for the incompetent but "godlike" political *Gauleiter*, as well as for the "rotten remainders of the bourgeoisie" that now came flocking to the party. His social preference, like that of the eastern SA leader, Walther Stennes, was for a "sound social base" of *Workers, Peasants, Soldiers*, as Stennes later called the periodical of his dissident organization. These ideas brought the SA leaders close to the Black Front of dissident Nazi Otto Strasser, who had left the party not too long ago. The irate SA leadership of Berlin, facing the 1930 elections, meanwhile refused to offer the usual protection to a major election rally of Goebbels and others. In fact, they threatened to break it up themselves. To make matters worse, an SS spy was found listening to an SA leaders' conference, and the SS guards in charge refused to obey an order to be discharged and replaced by an incoming SA detachment, even though the SS then was still subordinate to the SA leaders present.[26] There ensued a free-for-all between the

[25] This account follows essentially the story told by OSAF-Ost leader Walther Stennes in his memorandum, "Wie es zur Stennes-Aktion kam," Munich Institute for Contemporary History, Fa 88 Hauptarchiv Fasz. 325, and the commentary of Werner, "SA und NSDAP," pp. 477-494. Further details can be found in Albert Krebs, *Tendenzen und Gestalten der NSDAP; Erinnerungen an die Frühzeit der Partei* (Stuttgart: DVA, 1959).

[26] In November 1930, Hitler separated the SS from the SA and assigned it police functions within the movement.

SS guards and the superior SA detachment. The clash ended with an SS man calling the police to come to the rescue and arrest the SA assailants.

Hitler responded to the crisis in his characteristic manner by taking over as supreme SA chief in Pfeffer's place. He flew to Berlin, full of suspicions against Stennes and the other leaders, but anxious to conciliate the SA rank and file in the *Sturmlokale*, who idolized him. The SA welcomed his direct assumption of leadership and pledged full cooperation, believing that with him at the helm of the SA the impasse was over. But the tensions, grievances, and threats of reducing the size of the SA continued and, by the end of the year, Stennes offered to resign. His offer was countered with assurances of Hitler's full confidence. The other SA leaders also persuaded him to stay.

In the meantime, Hitler had once more chosen Captain Ernst Roehm, who had returned from Bolivia, as the new supreme SA chief. Roehm took over in January of 1931, and loosed a blizzard of communications to adjust the SA organization to the burgeoning membership. Stennes and his lieutenants were unhappy with the choice of Roehm and his homosexual clique, and frequently objected to orders "going over the heads" of the regional SA leaders to the lower echelons. He also questioned the "political proclamations," the "miserable maneuvers in the *Reichstag* (where the NSDAP now had an unexpectedly high representation of 107 seats)," the "claims of Rome,"[27] and the wasteful extravagance of the Brown House at the same time that there were so many unemployed and needy men: "The political leadership throws the money out the window while we risk our bodies for them."[28] Late in March of 1931, Roehm came to Berlin and deposed Stennes, while many of his erstwhile supporters beat a cautious retreat.

[27] An allusion to Hitler's and Bruening's Catholicism and their alleged collusion against Protestant Prussia.

[28] "Stennes-Aktion." The documents also contain reports by party agents on Stennes and his alleged desire to make the SA independent of the party.

Captain Stennes promptly founded a National Socialist Fighters Movement (NSKB), which established contact with Otto Strasser and Captain Ehrhardt. The latter, according to confidential reports, was hoping for support from dissident SA men and *Reichsbanner* men against the reactionary ties of Hitler. Ehrhardt's successor group to *Wiking* had a reported two thousand members in West Germany and Thuringia, while Stennes was credited with five to six hundred followers in Berlin, and twelve hundred more in various parts of the east and west. A considerable number of SA leaders in Pomerania were persuaded to sign a statement: "We have come to the realization that the NSDAP has abandoned the revolutionary course of true national socialism toward Germany's freedom and started on the reactionary road toward becoming just another coalition party."[29] The signers pledged allegiance to Stennes' NSKB against the "reactionary Roman spirit." By May, the new organization already claimed a strong position in Berlin, Pomerania, Mecklenburg, and Silesia, and many bridgeheads elsewhere. Stennes had good connections to important people in the DNVP, the Economics Ministry, to Goebbels and Rudolf Hess, but he got no further than other dissidents. His last confidential document was a *Gestapo* letter to Roehm, dated September 22, 1933, indicating that Stennes had been released from custody to emigrate to China.

Roehm now was left to preside over the extraordinary growth of the SA which, despite repeated utterances by Hitler, was never curbed. Just as the party locals had mushroomed from a mere 1,378 in January 1928 to 4,964 in 1930, and 11,845 at the beginning of 1932, the SA grew by leaps and bounds. From the size that Hitler thought excessive in the fall of 1930, 60,000, it tripled to 170,000 in September 1931, and quadrupled by December 1931, when there were reported to be 250,000 SA men. By late summer of 1932, there were 470,000 and, when Hitler be-

[29] Institute of Contemporary History, Fa 88 Hauptarchiv Fasz. 83.

179

came chancellor, an estimated 700,000, including the less active reserves, while the total number of party members was only 849,000. The old leadership cadres of ex-officers thus were quickly exhausted, and new men of the postwar generation almost universally took over as *Trupp-*, *Schar-*, and *Sturmfuehrer*. Roehm also founded a *Reich* Leadership School with regional branches that could train these officer recruits for his brown army.[30] There were also many new suborganizations such as the Motorized SA, which supplied the motor pool to move the stormtroopers to where they were needed.

After Hitler's takeover, the SA kept right on growing and, eventually, incorporated what was left of the *Stahlhelm*, the the Kyffhaeuser League, and other veterans' groups as SA Reserves I and II, depending on their ages. By the end of 1934, the SA including SA Reserve I had 2.17 million members, and SA Reserve II another 1.38 million, not counting the motorized NSKK and the now independent SS. Thus the SA had become the final collecting point of the entire paramilitary right wing. But only one-fourth of these SA members were also members of the NSDAP, which had no longer permitted the same helter-skelter influx of opportunists after May 1 of 1933.[31] Especially in areas where the rival paramilitary groups had not lost out to Nazi recruitment long ago, such as Baden, Wuerttemberg-Hohenzollern, Schleswig-Holstein, and Mecklenburg, the share of the SA Reserve II was more than half of the total SA. Where the *Stahlhelm* and others had lost most of their membership to the SA before 1933, as along the Polish border or in Danzig, on the other hand, and in Berlin and Duesseldorf, the original stormtroopers were strong.

[30] See Wolfgang Horn, *Führerideologie und Parteiorganisation in der NSDAP 1919-1933* (Duesseldorf: Droste, 1972), pp. 289-292, and 297-399, who also points out that the expense of attending these leadership courses tended to weed out proletarian or unemployed applicants.

[31] These figures are from *Parteistatistik*, III, 70-71 and 187. Half of the 165,000 SS members were also in the party. The SA figures before 1933 are from Horn, *Führerideologie*, pp. 394-395.

The Decapitation of the SA

With an army of this magnitude, while the *Reichswehr* still consisted of only 100,000 men, Roehm's intentions in 1933-1934 were very likely to be suspect, and suspicious rivals could be found equally among the party organization, in Heinrich Himmler's SS, and in the *Reichswehr*. During the fighting years, the SA men had always been told that they were of a breed more active than and superior to that of the party members, even though as early as 1927 Hitler had ordered the political leaders of all levels not to enter the SA, and on principle had denied the SA leaders any participation in political decisions. Himmler's SS had not been able to make good its promise as an elite superior to the SA until Pfeffer resigned and the SA entered its crisis period. In the years of 1927-1929, the SA still had clear superiority over the SS, which had limited functions and experienced little growth.[32] The *Reichswehr*, finally, had every reason to fear the giant SA whose leaders had for years been eyeing the future function of the SA as the army of the Third *Reich*, a role they may have been promised by Hitler before 1933.[33] Roehm, in particular, was rumored to have plans for a takeover of or merger with the *Reichswehr* after removal of the *Reichswehr* leadership. The new *Reichswehr* leaders, Generals von Reichenau and von Blomberg, were especially apprehensive of bringing the SA leadership, which was dominated by *declassé* ex-officers and ambitious upstarts, into the *Reichswehr*, much as they might have welcomed expansion. Hitler himself had reason to see in the SA a state within the Nazi state, an immovable obstacle that barred his way to complete totalitarian control, even if it was not an immediate menace.

There had also been many complaints about unauthorized

[32] Horn, *Führerideologie*, pp. 294-298. See also Michael H. Kater, "Zum gegenseitigen Verhaeltnis von SA und SS in der Sozialgeschichte des Nationalsozialismus," *Vierteljahresschrift fuer Sozial- und Wirtschaftsgeschichte*, 62 (1975), 339-379, for an impressionistic account of the social superiority of the SS over the SA later on.

[33] See Sauer, "Mobilmachung der Gewalt," pp. 851-852.

181

stormtrooper violence and highhanded actions against enemies and innocent bystanders alike during the manhunts of 1933.[34] The auxiliary police functions of the SA were soon taken away again, but whenever the hotspurs of the SA would talk up their "revolutionary mission" or the need for a "second revolution," Hitler felt moved to call for a return to peaceful evolution. He had brought off his "legal take-over" without an SA coup, after all, and the SA was now, after the consolidation of his control, superfluous or worse. The thought of a merger of SA and *Reichswehr* into a new center of power was a menace to his hard-earned monopoly.[35] Roehm's hopes for "militarizing" the SA and "revolutionizing" the *Reichswehr* were both ominous challenges to party control. Even if he was not plotting against Hitler, he had to be eliminated before it was too late. But it was not easy to dismiss him from the head of his SA army, which had felt ill-used ever since the resignation of Pfeffer and was now more disgruntled than ever as a result of the momentous reshuffling taking place inside the whole movement.[36] As Hermann Mau has pointed out, it was symptomatic for the recognition of Roehm's claims of equality for the SA after 1933 that the Law to Safeguard the Unity of Party and State of December 1933 gave equal ministerial

[34] Roehm spoke of taking twelve lives for every SA casualty. The election violence of March 1933 alone claimed sixty-nine lives, according to newspaper reports, including fifty-one enemies of the Nazi regime. Later, some five to six hundred dead and about one hundred thousand political arrests were the toll of the terror and concentration camp phase of 1933. The SA and SS, and parts of the *Stahlhelm*, were made auxiliary policemen, the better to carry out the suppression of all opposition or even a coup. *Ibid.*, pp. 862-878.

[35] There had been *Reichswehr* feelers toward cooperation in military education and border control in the east long before the take-over, and a willingness to grant the SA militia status after 1933.

[36] See, for example, Ernst Roehm, "SA und deutsche Revolution," *Nationalsozialistische Monatshefte*, no. 31 (1933), pp. 251ff. There had been wholesale changes replacing, in particular, the bulk of the local leadership of the NSDAP with new persons in 1933-1934. See also Sauer, "Mobilmachung der Gewalt," pp. 880-885.

status to the SA chief and the chief of the party organization, the *Führer's* deputy.[37]

Given these circumstances, the purge of June 1934 was inevitable. It was preceded by a rash of rumors about an impending SA attack on the *Reichswehr* and SA fears of a *Reichswehr* coup, probably fed by the rumor mills of Goebbels, who, with Goering and Hess, was scheming against Roehm. While their leaders were vacationing in the Alps, some SA units were called out into the streets under false orders, giving credence to the later Nazi claims of an SA uprising against Hitler. Von Reichenau and von Blomberg, who had been supplying spy reports on Roehm's headquarters to Hitler, stood by and made no objection; the coup against Roehm also marked for extinction Generals von Schleicher, von Bredow, and other old enemies of Hitler like Gustav von Kahr of beer-hall putsch fame. Hitler and the SS carried out the arrests and killings in the south, while Goering did the honors in the north. Roehm and his friends, erstwhile critics like Major Schneidhuber, Gregor Strasser, who had favored von Schleicher's scheme of a coalition of labor elements from the trade unions to the NSDAP, and many others were shot, as was von Schleicher's wife, who threw herself in front of her husband. The killing went on for three days. The party, the SS, and the *Reichswehr* emerged triumphant.[38] The SA was reduced to largely ceremonial and ornamental functions. And just as the disorderly stormtrooper violence of 1933 was replaced by the quiet and deadly efficiency of the SS-guarded concentration camps, in place of Roehm's "SA state" there arose Himmler's "SS state" in all its gruesome glory.

The facts of stormtrooper history from the fighting years to the purge of 1934 have now been presented. Now we

[37] This status was promptly removed after June of 1934; Hermann Mau, "The Second Revolution—June 30, 1934," in Hajo Holborn, ed., *Republic to Reich, The Making of the Nazi Revolution* (New York: Random House/Pantheon, 1972), p. 230.

[38] See *ibid.*, pp. 235-246, and Sauer, "Mobilmachung der Gewalt," pp. 889-966.

183

must attempt to probe the social and psychological depths of this momentous drama, with the help of available statistics and the information contained in the Abel autobiographies. There are many questions about the motives of the individual stormtroopers and about the nature of such a virulent mass movement that we can answer or, at least, put in the proper context in this fashion. To begin with, the demographic trends of the period are worth a closer look, for they contain clues to the fatal coincidence of high unemployment and large masses of radicalized youth in the early thirties. Before we jump to conclusions about unemployment driving young people into the Nazi party, however, we would do well to explore, with the help of the relevant Abel stories, whether this was truly a causal relationship. How, indeed, do people become extremists of any sort, "fanatics" as many Abel respondents liked to call themselves with obvious relish?

We can explore this question both from the viewpoint of individual development and from that of organized, politicized Weimar youth. For the stormtroopers tended to be young, and their antecedents invariably lead us into a study of their adolescence or, where possible, even their childhood. We can also explore the threads of behavioral continuity between their early engagement in political violence and the activities of their adult years in the party. Violent youths turn into violent adults, just as ideologically committed youths usually become similarly inclined adults. We can analyze this mysterious process by starting with the three quintessential activities of the Hitler movement—marching, fighting, and proselytizing—and relate these activities to various social and attitudinal groups in the Nazi party. Since the movement grew to such massive proportions in the short time of two years, moreover, the features that may explain this extraordinary growth require our attention. What was it that brought all these eager bodies into the NSDAP at the crucial time? And, we need to establish, by following the most violent careers into the terror regime of the Third *Reich* what the private armies of the Weimar

184

Republic contributed to the practices of the empire of Adolf Hitler.

Political Extremism and Demography

Since the demographic trends of the later Weimar years seem to be crucial to the rise of the stormtrooper army, an inventory of the relevant developments is in order here. The postwar generation (those born after 1901), as will be recalled, amounted to nearly half the Nazi party (48.7 percent), but a good two-thirds of the SA and SS, according to our calculations.[39] We can narrow the focus of our investigation even further by placing special weight on the youngest age cohorts of the NSDAP of January 1933, namely, those aged between seventeen and twenty-five during the chief fighting and recruitment years of 1931-1932, which leaves out the relatively smaller age group of those born 1902 to 1905, the group of those often motivated by vicarious enthusiasm for the war effort. The younger group amounted to about 300,000 (35.6 percent) of the NSDAP, and consisted almost solidly of stormtroopers of the most active sort; the older ones were likely to be less active for such age-related reasons as being married and having more responsible jobs, and, perhaps, being more fearful of risking their jobs over their extremist involvement. We should look, therefore, for the relative roles of the unmarried and unemployed males of that age group in the population of the fighting years.

The age distribution in the German population of the 1930s (Table IV-2) shows a striking bulge among fifteen to thirty-year-old males, which reflects the lower birthrates of the war years (1915-1918), on the one hand, and the war casualties of the older cohorts, on the other. Although the population statistics for the years 1931 and 1932 have to be

[39] Fewer than one-fifth of the Nazis of 1933 were not in the SA or SS: 149,000 of the 849,000 NSDAP members; and only one-fifth of these nonstormtrooper Nazis were born after 1901, according to our estimates.

185

TABLE IV-2 German Males in the Fighting Years, by Age and Marital Status, 1930-1933

Age (birth date)	Males in Population Dec. 1933 (millions)	(percent)	Males in Populations 1925 (millions)	(percent)	Unmarried Males: Dec. 1933 Birth Dates	(millions)	Percent of All Males in Age Group
Up to 5	2.4	7.6	3.0	9.9			
6-10	2.7	8.5	2.0	6.7			
11-15	2.9	9.2	3.1	10.4			
16-20	2.1 (1913-1917)	6.5	3.3 (1910-1914)	10.9	1915-1919	1.96	99.4
21-25	3.1 (1908-1912)	9.7	3.6 (1908-1909)	10.1	1911-1914	2.38	90.9
26-30	3.1 (1903-1907)	9.7	2.5 (1900-1904)	8.2	1906-1910	2.35	68.3
31-35	2.9 (1898-1902)	9.0	2.0 (1895-1899)	6.7	1902-1905	.94	35.4
36-40	2.2 (1893-1897)	6.9	2.0 (1890-1894)	6.5	1898-1901	.43	18.6
41-45	1.9	6.0	1.9	6.1	1894-1897	.18	10.3
46-50	1.8	5.8	1.9	6.2			
51-	6.7	21.1	5.5	18.3	1874-1893	.38	4.9
Totals	31.8	100.0	29.0	100.0			

NOTE: The sources for Table IV-2 are *Statistisches Jahrbuch fuer das Deutsche Reich 1931*, p. 13, and *1935*, pp. 12-14. Every years' birth cohort during the highest years of 1902 through 1914 averaged about 1.2 million, while those of 1915-1918 only had 600-770,000. The older cohorts again were 10-20 percent below normal because of the casualties of the war.

interpolated from the figures of the 1925 and 1933 census, there is no mistaking the disproportionately large group that ranged from sixteen to twenty-eight years old (born 1902-1914) at the beginning of 1930, to nineteen to thirty-one at the end of 1932, a group that made up well over one-fourth of all males or one-third of all males over eighteen. The statistics on the proportion of unmarried males also show clearly that up until they were in their late twenties, this large group of young males had not yet settled down to married life.

The statistics on the ages of the employed and unemployed (Table IV-3) are not quite as satisfactory, since they fail to correspond completely, and sometimes were based only on technical definitions of the kind of aid received, thus covering only a part of the unemployed. We can, however, get a normal distribution of ages of employment in the three basic sectors from the first three columns, which deal with all gainfully employed (including independent) males. The following two columns show dependent labor only, but they also show better the importance of the large age groups between eighteen and thirty. Among the unemployed age groups, the youngest seem particularly underrepresented, because it took a certain period of gainful employment to establish eligibility for unemployment insurance, and "crisis assistance," as will be recalled, was limited to applicants over twenty-one. There was obviously no insurance for new workers among the young. For our purposes, we can assume that the entire twenty to thirty-year-old group was at least as large as their share was among the employed of 1933. Quite probably, at the onset of mass unemployment the youngest males were hit hardest.[40] By June of 1934, in any case, the share of young males of twenty-five or younger had declined spectacularly, along with the demographic bulge of the eighteen to twenty-one-year-olds, although disproportionate numbers of party members were still unemployed in January of 1935.[41]

[40] See above, Chapter I, notes 1 and 5.
[41] Of NSDAP members, 8.2 percent, including about 60,000 who

TABLE IV-3 Employed and Unemployed Males by Age (percent)

	Gainfully Employed Males, 1925, Not Including Family Helpers			Employed Males (June 1933)		Unemployed Males on Aid			
						Jan. 1932		Jan. 1933	
	Industry	Services	Agriculture	Blue Collar	White Collar	a	b	a	b
Up to 17	12.4	6.5	14.4	7.1	3.8	2.6	—	1.9	—
18-19	6.9	4.7	6.1	6.9	5.5	9.1	—	8.0	—
20-24	15.5	13.7	13.8	34.4	31.8	15.7	16.5	13.0	14.2
25-29	12.1	14.0	9.0	23.3	26.8	18.0	18.6	18.3	17.8
30-34	18.2	24.5	14.2			14.8	15.9	17.1	16.5
35-39						10.1	11.5	11.7	11.9
40-44	16.5	20.6	14.9	14.0	17.5	8.5	10.7	9.2	11.3
45-49						7.0	9.0	7.5	9.6
50-54	11.7	12.2	14.7	10.5	11.2	5.9	7.6	5.8	7.9
55-59						4.6	4.5	4.5	6.3
60-	6.1	3.8	12.9	3.8	3.4	3.7	4.7	3.0	4.5
Totals	100.0	100.0	100.0	100.0	100.0				

NOTE: Sources for Table IV-3 are *Statistisches Jahrbuch 1929*, pp. 24-25, *1933*, p. 305, and *1935*, pp. 26 and 321-322. The first three columns are for 1925, the next two for June 1933, and the last four for January 15, 1932, and 1933. By June of 1933, the unemployment curve had already declined considerably from the preceding summer. The figures in the last four columns only consider: *a*. Unemployment Insurance, and *b*. Crisis Aid that covered less than half of the known unemployed.

Against this background of demographic and economic trends, we might inquire into the extent to which the one million unemployed males aged twenty-five or less in January of 1933, or better yet the two million up to age thirty, might have been identical with the young Nazi stormtroopers, the young Red Fronters, *Reichsbanner, Stahlhelm, Jungdo,* and other unemployed young militants. It is advisable at this point to refrain from drawing any causal or attitudinal inferences between unemployment and paramilitary membership and activity, especially since we will be able to draw on sound documentary evidence on this in the analysis to follow.

Only a cautious estimate will be made of the coinciding numbers of the young unemployed and the young paramilitaries in order to gauge the "availability" of young males. If it is true, for example, that about four-fifths of the estimated 360,000 KPD members at the end of 1932 were unemployed, and of these at least one-third were male and no older than thirty, we have already about 100,000 of the two million. The *Reichsbanner, Jungbanner, Schufo,* and Iron Front had an estimated 60 to 70 percent of their 250,000 to 400,000 active militants in this age group, and of these one-half (according to the rate reported among trade union members) were unemployed: at least another 100,000, and possibly 150,000. *Stahlhelm, Jungdo,* and other bourgeois-conservative groups anxious to provide labor camps for their unemployed may have had another 50,000 to 100,000 between them, if we include the mass membership of the political youth organizations described above. And how many stormtroopers under thirty and out of work need we add? About two-thirds of the estimated 700,000 were of the

had joined before 1933, were unemployed in January of 1935 when unemployment came close to the three million mark. The highest portions of unemployed occurred in Bavaria, Pomerania, Silesia, Schleswig-Holstein, Hamburg, and Baden. *Parteistatistik,* i, 304. The unemployment statistics of 1934, when there were still more than two and half million blue and white-collar workers without jobs, show a considerable shift toward the older groups.

right age and, of these, close to one-half, another 250,000, may have been unemployed.[42] Thus, a total of perhaps one-fourth of the two million young unemployed males of 1932, half of them stormtroopers, were marching and fighting in the streets and meeting halls of the moribund republic.

Unemployment and Politicization

While there can be no doubt, then, that a very large number of the most militant elements were victims of the Great Depression, this should not yet be taken as a proof that their unemployment or other economic difficulties had politicized them and led them into the SA or other fighting organization. We cannot take for granted that "the time of soul-eating, character-murdering unemployment . . . is also the time of the greatest politicizing and revolutionizing Germany ever knew . . . [that] the poison of unemployment in the body of the German people formed its own antibody, revolutionary sentiment," as a Nazi writer put it.[43] This is much too easy a rationalization. Plausible arguments have, to be sure, been advanced that tie the motivation of the Nazi recruits to the frustration of their upward social mobility or to their social decline as results of the Great Depression. However, there are also a number of competing explanations that need to be weighed against this socio-economic motivation. The most weighty of these, as we shall see, has to do with timing: if it can be demonstrated

[42] In the Berlin SA, according to J. K. von Engelbrechten, *Eine braune Armee*, p. 172, well over half of the SA was unemployed, removed from the unemployment rolls, or without any aid; in many SA *Sturms* this was 80 to 90 percent. The corrected Abel figure is about one-third, but there may be a bias against the typical unemployed there.

[43] Engelbrechten, *Eine braune Armee*, p. 194. The author blamed unemployment on "the system," as did many Nazis and, very likely, most of the Red Fronters, *Reichsbanner*, and even *Stahlhelm* men. Richard Hamilton has argued rather persuasively that the turn to the right of the conservative and liberal parties left their working-class voters no choice but the Nazis.

190

that most members of the Hitler movement were already strongly inclined in that direction because of their political socialization at home or in a youth group, long before economic adversity struck, for example, then we must admit that it was their political socialization and not the Depression that made Nazis out of them. Also, if it can be demonstrated that a virulent ideological movement of this kind develops its own momentum and brings out the militancy in many people who come in contact with it, then the Depression also may at best only have contributed to their monomaniacal devotion by giving them free time otherwise committed to gainful employment. But unemployment per se, then, would not have been the cause of the Nazi motivation of the bulk of the stormtroopers.

The stormtroopers of the Abel Collection have a story to tell in this respect. As we indicated above, a good one-third of them, in corrected figures, were unemployed, bankrupt, or otherwise suffered severe damage by the Depression. This includes also a few cases of major changes in career and, probably, a good many young workers who had never landed their first job.[44] There were also many young people, and some not so young any more, who were going from one apprenticeship or traineeship to another without reaching a viable position in the end.[45] In addition to the casualties of the Depression, who were mostly of the postwar generation, about one-fifth of the Abel stormtroopers had become unemployed, gone bankrupt, or had to find a new career in the years before the Great Depression, when the rate of unemployment and business failure, as during the inflation of 1922-1923, was considerable. These pre-Depression troubles fell mostly on stormtroopers of the war generation, whereas the prewar generation of Nazis had a much lower rate of economic difficulties during the republican years.[46] Once a lifetime career got a good start, it seems, it

---

[44] See Theodor Geiger, *Die soziale Schichtung*, pp. 96-97.

[45] See, for example, case no. 47, who at the age of twenty-five was still making the rounds of agricultural traineeships.

[46] Well over half of the economic casualties of the Depression were

was not as easily derailed as if it were faced with economic dislocation and stagnation to begin with.

The Depression hit hardest among the blue and white-collar Nazis, and, second, among business and professional people. Its victims tended to be highly mobile among cities, in social decline, or from families distinguished by poverty or the early death of the father. There was also a significant proportion of people upwardly mobile from the urban working class, especially people with a secondary or trade-school education. In this respect there was undoubtedly an element of frustrated upward mobility, as well as the element of social decline that is often linked with fascist prejudices and a propensity for violence.

A close reading of the many Abel cases of stormtroopers unemployed or bankrupt during the Depression discloses that practically all of them held fascist beliefs or were involved in the Nazi party or similar right-wing organizations long before they were hit by the Depression.[47] Critical readers may wonder if we can really expect the Abel respondents to tell us, say, about their having become politicized and Nazified as a result of being unemployed or bankrupt. The answer is a flat yes. The respondents are so perceptive and candid on many other subjects that it would be surprising indeed if they had withheld their observations about a subject of such great topical interest at the time. The closest we come to a glimpse of the turmoil in many a breast under the impact of economic adversity are stories such as this:

> In 1926 I had to give up my bakery, as a result of the "Jewish" business practices of my creditors, and watch them auction off my inventory and the furniture. I moved to S. where I had to go on the Poor Fund for lack of a job. With this miserly municipal hand-out, I and my

of the postwar generation, whereas the war generation (born 1890 to 1901), constituted more than half of the economic casualties of 1919–1928.

[47] See, for example, cases 1, 33, 59, 67, 70, 140, 154, 172, 175, 178.

wife had to get on until 1927, with some contributions from relatives. Then I worked as a door-to-door salesman until 1929. When you think of how the measures of the red government by means of inflation, intolerable taxes, etc. had taken away my chance to make a living . . . and how instead of the "gratitude of the fatherland" we front-soldiers were governed by a bunch of sponges (*Nutzniesser*) who did not shy away from any means of taking away the last lousy *Pfennig* a person wanted to earn for his living . . . you will understand why some of the betrayed and bitter men in the street welcomed the efforts of nationalistic paramilitary organizations, and especially the Hitler movement, with enthusiasm. The combination of nationalistic goals with social reforms of the NSDAP made this movement dear to many old soldiers and idealists.

The writer was a factory worker's son (born 1897, no. 76) and an enthusiastic soldier bitter about the "treason" of the "profiteers whom the army protected for four years and for whom innumerable comrades died." He was wounded, and with the help of a small inheritance, started his bakery just in time for the inflation of 1922-1923. For years, he had to work full time in a factory to keep the shop going until the final foundering of his hopes for a middle-class existence. His combination of hard luck and self-pity may have been typical of many a victim of economic crisis, especially after 1928. But, apparently, he too had already attended *Stahlhelm* meetings for some time when he encountered the Nazi party there in 1927, and joined while selling coal door to door. Unemployed again, he used his "free time" to proselytize and propagandize among the unemployed and to protect Nazi meetings as an SA man. The villains of his story are the "red-infested public employment agencies who got Nazi comrades fired . . . and never intended to get any of us new employment," and the police who hindered and persecuted the stormtroopers.

Most of the economic casualties report that they had already been with the *Stahlhelm* or similar groups, or with the Nazi party when they lost their livelihood. In most cases, the "free time" of unemployment or bankruptcy resulted in an escalation of political involvement, but apparently never from a level of noninvolvement, and rarely from one of involvement with moderate parties. There always seems to have been at least the beginning of strong sentiments long before the economic crisis struck the individual life. Members of *Stahlhelm*, the DNVP, DVP, or Center party often described their growing alienation from their "reactionary" fellow members or relatives, usually with reference to the snobbery or lack of social concern of the latter. In these cases, an extremist identity visibly grew with nary an assist from economic adversity. In quite a few of the younger Abel cases, in fact, it was friction with the family, with fellow employees, customers, or with the boss that endangered their livelihood, and not the economic trouble that made Nazis out of them.[48] The subtle interplay between the individual on his or her way to the early Nazi party and the social environment is worth a closer look and an attempt at theoretical reflection.

A Theory of Political Deviance

One of the most illuminating writings in an otherwise rather barren literature on the personality pattern of members of political extremist groups in an article by Egon Bittner on "how radicals face down the common-sense polemic" against their bizarre behavior.[49] He took as his point of departure the fact that active members of an extremist movement, like other people, are children of parents, employees of bosses, or students of teachers, and that they are likely to have spouses, siblings, neighbors, or friends who

[48] See, for example, cases 47, 67, 72, 93, and 170. This alienation from conservative and liberal parties because they turned "reactionary" bears out Hamilton's thesis of the Nazi landslides.

[49] "Radicalism and the Organization of Radical Movements," *American Sociological Review*, 28 (December 1963), 928-940, especially p. 939.

do not approve of their political activities. The individual extremists, in other words, cannot help being a part of society and internalizing or facing some of its norms that characterize his behavior as undesirable or bizarre. He (or she) has to have very strong motivations, and is likely to develop certain ego strategies that will help him to face down his own contradictory notions and those of his everyday associates about his extremist activities. Bittner describes several such strategies, such as imagining oneself persecuted or seeking the moral support and ideological rationalizations of a group of like-minded people, which abound in the Abel vitae.

We could go a step or two further and ask qusetions about how these pre-1933 Nazis developed their extremist identities from step to step before they joined the party, and how they deepened these newly found identities in interaction with their social environment.[50] Since many of the respondents complained about the friction they encountered at work, at school, in the family, or in the neighborhood, all in supposedly nonpolitical areas of human relationships, we can take a closer look at the different scenarios that ensued, and at the active or passive role played in them by the respondents. We have to bear in mind that we are dealing with a dynamic process of the interaction between the individual and his environment, and can only speculate about the extent to which the respondent may have deliberately provoked his own persecution by imprudent words and deeds that were bound to get him "persecuted." A good deal obviously depends upon his

[50] See also Wanda von Baeyer-Katte, *Vom Zerstörerischen in der Politik* (Heidelberg: Quelle & Meyer, 1956) where the interaction between early Nazis and their social circles is likened to a deliberate game of shocking and opposing whatever the group's sensibilities happen to be. Needless to add, such an ego strategy became confused at a later point when the whole group jumped on the brown bandwagon, thus robbing the strategy of its psychological payoff. The author can indeed point to many a confused, even sulking Nazi at the time of the Nazi takeover, and at some instances of deliberately "ornery" and disruptive behavior resulting therefrom.

195

behavior. The saliency of politics in the setting and the political persuasion of his everyday associates are also important.

It seems that the process by which a young person finds out that he or she is a right-wing extremist is somewhat analogous to various forms of social deviance. There is a first moment of truth, often during a conflict in which the young person becomes involved by accident or force of circumstances. At this moment of truth the deviant label is painfully and publicly attached to him. His personality henceforth develops a kind of fixation on the discriminatory label and on the strong social and political disapproval he has encountered. One could almost say he enjoys being known as a notorious trouble-maker or disputatious radical because he has discovered his identity therein. At least he continues to engage in public activities that are sure to provoke conflict and to fix his extremist image further in the minds of those who know him. To be sure, it is next to impossible to separate the external "hassling" of the young Nazis from conflicts caused or maintained by their own exhibitionism, as long as we can judge the cases only by their own self-serving accounts. Nevertheless, it is illuminating to conceive of political extremism in terms of a deviant's style of self-presentation, and to look in the Abel cases for supporting evidence.

A good case in point is a contractor's son from Muehl-heim/Ruhr born 1907 (no. 1), whose oldest brother went into the war. A second brother broke off his apprenticeship to volunteer. The young respondent became a vicarious victory-watcher. "The enthusiasm for the fatherland seized me, too. I helped carry the soldier's rifles to the railroad station. Whenever the army reported a new German victory, I ran to the [Catholic] church in my enthusiasm and helped to ring the bells. The reports of my brothers when they came home on furlough always left a deep impression on me." His oldest brother and two cousins fell in battle. He remembered all too well the defeat and the "revolution," in particular "the shame of seeing the red revolu-

tionaries tear off officers' insignia before our eyes at school."
As soon as he was old enough to be an apprentice at the
Thyssen works, he met his moment of truth.

> Here I got to know the class struggle that the Marxists
> teach. On the very first day they tore the black-white-and-
> red ribbon from my windbreak and tried to force me to
> join a syndicalist union. I joined the Metal Workers Union
> as an apprentice, since I had no choice . . . and dropped
> out again in 1923, having entered the *Wehrvolk*
> *Deutscher Aar* [a *voelkisch* youth group]. Now I encoun-
> tered hostility from all sides at work. I got beaten up
> for my German thinking at every wild strike, but they
> could not distract me from my chosen path.

Eventually, he was fired for his views, or so he says. Actually, he missed work one day, because he was too tired from
the political exploits of the previous night to get up in the
morning. Now he became even more involved in provoca-
tive activities such as staging "patriotic" plays that attracted
Socialist and Communist raiders. At the age of eighteen, in
1925, he joined the NSDAP local that Josef Goebbels had
just founded in his area. The personal isolation of this
extremist is barely concealed by the thin veneer of righteous
pretense that almost everyone thinks as he does, or at least
ought to. Underneath is the posture of the martyr who
struggles on regardless of persecution. He longed to find
others like himself, and to merge with them in one
corpus mysticum, the movement.[51] And there is that curious,
masochistic attitude toward the political violence in which
he engaged that suggests that the urge to verbalize his guilt
feelings was nearly as strong as the urge to commit mayhem
in the first place.

> Day and night we were persecuted, dubbed day-
> dreamers, and called Nazi punks and heathens by the

[51] There are many interesting parallels with the sense of a special
identity and preciousness described by Kenneth Keniston, *Young
Radicals, Notes on Committed Youth* (New York: Harcourt, Brace
and World, 1968), pp. 25-33 and 70-74.

Center party. . . . We were outlawed as a party and had to take off the brown shirts. If we showed up in white shirts to protect the meeting hall, the police would pummel us out of the hall with their truncheons; if we were all wearing blue caps or black ties, they also considered us subversive. The Communists knocked us down, the police put us in jail, some of our comrades were shot from the back: none of this stopped us in our redoubled will to make Adolf Hitler's idea prevail among the German people. . . . The Center party fought us the hardest [the respondent is a Catholic]. The clergy refused our dead comrades a regular funeral and we were not allowed to enter the church in uniform, although we National Socialists stand on Christian principles.

The conflict at work was a very common reinforcement, even though it may be obscured in this case by the suggestion that he ought to be permitted to enter the church in his uniform. A better example is an antisemitic miller's son in 1904 (no. 19), whose fixation on the label of the *Nazischweinehund* was so strong that he put it in the mouth of the Communists long before he even joined the party. He claimed, for instance, that they mysteriously knew about his identity and followed his change of job to a town twenty-five miles away from his earlier employment. "Dirtying up my place of work, sabotage, unfounded charges, denouncing me with the boss, attacks with chairs and benches in our common room were daily occurrences . . . then I signed my name to our leaflets and my place of work became hell for me." When he was late for work, his boss shouted: "Leave politics alone. I am going to fire you if you are late again." The respondent comments: "What can you expect of the reactionaries?"

Of the nearly two-thirds of the Abel respondents who supplied information on their work environment, fewer than one in five described it as politically friendly, while over one-third described it as distinctly unfriendly and often related being fired or economically threatened for political reasons. Their job troubles, furthermore, were not limited to a hostile Socialist or Communist work environment, but also included bourgeois settings where the employer or fellow employees strongly objected to the disreputable affiliation of the youthful respondent with a right-wing (not always Nazi) action group. On the other hand, the friendly work environments also included a considerable number of Socialist or Communist settings, which may have been congenial only because the youthful respondent was either not yet a Nazi or still a left-winger. We separated out cases of security of employment in spite of political friction because of the implication that the respondent had in these cases acted with some prudence and reserve. There were also other stories to notice, such as that of a presumably sheltered middle-class youth who became aware of the miseries of lower-class life only when he first took a job, or tales of respondents proselytizing fellow workers or customers on the job.

There is a striking difference between generations with respect to the presence of political friction at work. The older respondents who never belonged to any youth group evidently grew up in a world that required neither escape from the family to a youth group nor endangering their job. The largest number of cases in which respondents were fired or economically ruined for political reasons before they turned twenty-six occurred among those who joined the Hitler Youth or the stormtroopers without previous affiliation. As many as one-half of the former members of Socialist or Communist youth groups and of the bourgeois, Youth Movement-related groups among the Abel respondents complained about a politically unfriendly work environment. About two-thirds of the members of these two categories complained about political friction ranging from hostility to firings. The friction, of course, was as likely to be the result of the respondent's militant behavior and his fixation on being politically deviant as of the "unfriendly environment." The impression that it is the political militancy of the respondent which is the cause of his economic troubles, and not the reverse, can be reinforced with further evidence. If we compare the Abel cases according to what kind of political activity the respondents engaged in as teenagers or young adults (up to twenty-five), there was a sharp division between the quasi-military types who were involved in a Freecorps, *Einwohnerwehr*, or a military training group at this age and those who engaged in partisan electioneering or street fighting. While the former overwhelmingly reported a friendly, unpoliticized work environment, nearly half of the partisan street fighters told of having been fired or economically ruined for political reasons. Three-fourths reported at least some friction on the job. Those who engaged in electioneering, demonstrations, and proselytizing at this age had only slightly lower rates of firings and of reported friction at work than the street fighters. The respondents, of course, often attribute their being fired to the hostility of the "reactionaries" or the "reds" among their employers or fellow employees. But it seems unlikely that they were simply victimized by their environment. Rather, we are dealing here with a highly politicized generation of social misfits who were bent on "doing their thing" regardless of the consequences to themselves or anyone else. The greater their political activism, the greater their urge to polarize their immediate environment.

The relevance of the youthful work environment to the developing radical lies chiefly in the fact that it constitutes one of the first settings in which his self-willed personality collides with the constraints of an adult role. The amount of friction at work as well as elsewhere obviously increases with the intense politicization of the fighting years. Other settings such as the school, the neighborhood, or the family are perhaps less fraught with role conflicts, but are nevertheless suitable for developing the deviant posture. Many respondents tell bizarre tales about neighborhood confrontations they sought out by insisting on hoisting swastika flags in a "red" neighborhood. Others tell of political clashes among their peers at school or with teachers, which led to

disciplinary measures against them. And family relationships, which usually could survive differences between
Liberals and Conservatives or Socialists by the simple
device of avoiding discussion of politics, frequently exploded in dissension over the respondent's extremism. Since
the young stormtroopers often had not yet landed their
first job or were still apprentices, the intolerance of their
parents for their extremist activism took on economic
significance, as well. Irate fathers frequently threw out their
stormtrooper sons, and the latter had to live with sympathetic Nazis or at an SA Home. The NSDAP and SA were
not "just another party." This kind of political deviance
constituted a challenge to the entire adult establishment of
the extended family that could not be ignored. Parents,
grandparents, even uncles and aunts unfailingly attempted
to dissuade the young stormtrooper from his shocking
involvement.

The SA Homes were established in response to the mush-
rooming columns of homeless young unemployed men. By
1931, the Berlin SA already had a good two dozen SA
Homes and Kitchens. For two marks fifty to three marks a
week, a fellow could sleep and eat in these hostels, which
varied widely in size and furnishings. An organization, SA
Hilfswerk, raised donations of food, furniture, and money
from sympathetic businessmen. There was also an employment service to provide occasional odd jobs. Some of the
largest, like Lindengarten, housed 250 SA men and were
commonly referred to as "the SA barracks." Like the Sturmlokale, they were frequently searched for weapons by the
police and were occasionally the targets of Communist
raiders. The suppression of the SA in 1932 also involved
the dissolution of the SA Homes and the confiscation of their
furniture and belongings. There was a great deal of resentment at this "low blow against the unemployed."[52] One of
the Abel stormtroopers related that "during my three
years of unemployment I spent most of my time with my

[52] Engelbrechten, *Eine braune Armee*, pp. 173, 217-218, 233.

SA comrades in the SA Home. From there we distributed our propaganda materials and went on marches and demonstrations" (no. 140, born 1897). A young Central German whose father died during the war (no. 72, born 1909) described the genesis of an SA Home near Magdeburg:

> Because of the unemployment [of 1930], the SA men stayed in their hangout which was surrounded day and night by the Marxists. Here we learned true comradeship . . . everyone contributed what he had to those that needed it. A kitchen was created to cook food for the unemployed. Rooms were set up where they could sleep or get warm. During the day we went out into the villages to hand out leaflets, at night to protect party meetings in the countryside, from one electoral battle to the next, conquering town after town. . . . In 1932, the SA was suppressed and all our belongings taken. We lay in the street without a place to stay.

In many cases, on the other hand, the young stormtrooper continued to enjoy the support and home of his parents, although this was not always a sign of moderation on his part. As another Central German of the same age (no. 82, born 1909), related, "after my apprenticeship . . . I was a fulltime SA man since my father was in a position to keep me. We SA men had no goal other than to make Germany national socialist without regard to jobs or private affairs." As soon as Hitler had come to power, the respondent asked to be released from his SA service and began to work for his father's newly acquired paper goods business. The respondent was not at all politically inclined to begin with, according to his own testimony, but involved in athletics and evidently attracted by the brawling prowess of the SA. He described in some detail his experiences as a commercial apprentice who, along with five or six other apprentices, made a point of marching into the office every morning with a resounding "Heil Hitler." When the older employees began to snicker, "one of us stout young men would walk

202

up to one of them and ask him to step out into the cloak-
room if he had the guts. Since none of them ever took us
up, we had the upper hand right away and could berate
them for their cowardice." The young savages who obviously knew what they wanted also strong-armed fellow employees into buying the party newspaper. With helpers like
these, the Nazi movement was bound to prosper.

Politicized Weimar Youth

At the core of the problem of explaining the stormtrooper
movement, there obviously are questions of beliefs and attitudes that we cannot ignore. The relatively young age of
most SA members before 1933 makes it all the more important to inquire how and under what influneces they
grew up. It is not unreasonable to ask what sort of children,
teenagers, or young adults the SA and SS men of the fighting years were before they joined the movement. To the
extent that the answers can be drawn by inference from the
Abel file, we can examine what other groups they may have
belonged to or how early in life they joined the brown movement. We can also try to categorize these youths according
to what they did in these early youth groups and how they
liked them. There is a wide range of possible attitudes and
behavior, and we can estimate from the Abel file how widespread some of these attitudes may have been among the
stormtroopers at large. We can also compare youthful
group activities and attitudes with those of the adult stormtroopers in order to see whether it is true that big, strapping
stormtroopers grow from little ones. Finally, we can also
examine the process of political socialization by looking at
the politics of the parents of the Abel stormtroopers.

The reader will recall the earlier discussion of the Weimar
Youth Movement and Nazi converts from left-wing and
right-wing youth groups.[53] German youth in those days was
organized in youth groups to what may seem today an un-

[53] See above, pp. 11-12 and 66-70.

believable extent. A *Reich* Committee on Youth Organizations in 1927 recorded four and a half million young Germans in youth groups. But this figure still did not include political, paramilitary, or trade union youth, such as, for example, the Hitler Youth of that day. The Weimar youth was dubbed "the political youth generation" by the German sociologist Helmut Schelsky, in contrast to both the preceding and following generations. Prewar youth had joined the romantic but not very political Youth Movement, a spontaneous hiking and guitar-playing, mostly all-male youth culture movement of protest against the sterile urban and industrial world of their middle-class elders.[54] The generation of youth of World War II and the years after that war is called the "skeptical generation" because of its disillusionment with ideology and political causes, and its preoccupation with private pursuits and accomplishments. The "political youth generation" was politicized in part by the First World War and postwar experiences. The absence of fathers and the changing role of mothers, together with the visible collapse of many prewar social norms, may explain the new attitudes of youth. There were many testimonials to the generation gap in the Abel biographies by young respondents who contrasted their own early interest in politics with the apolitical frame of mind of their bourgeois parents.

A typical response of this sort came from a vintner's son,

---

[54] See Helmut Schelsky, *Die skeptische Generation* (Duesseldorf: Diederich, 1960), and, for an overview, Werner Klose, *Lebensformen deutscher Jugend, vom Wandervogel zur Popgeneration* (Munich and Vienna: Olzog, 1970). Arthur Dix, in *Die deutschen Reichstagswahlen 1871-1930 und die Wandlungen der Volksgliederung* (Tuebingen: Mohr, 1930), describes the young generation as "frequently having a liking for playing war, for sports, discipline, and right- and left-wing radicalism, but in part also totally turned away from politics" (p. 35). See also Herbert Moller, "Youth as a Force in the Modern World," *Comparative Studies in Society and History*, 10 (October 1967-July 1968), 237-260, and Peter Loewenberg, "The Psycho-historical Origins of the Nazi Youth Cohort," *American Historical Review* 76 (December 1971), 1457-1502.

born in 1911 (no. 206) to a socially respectable family, who preferred to be in a brawling "worker's party." As he put it, "we young ones had more direct access to politics than the older generation. They were still told that politics is bad for the character, when in fact it is the bad characters that ruin politics." The "old aunties in my family," he related, were deeply shocked about his political involvements and recurrent troubles with the law. Respondents frequently mentioned that they began to read political tracts and partisan literature in their late teens, or even as early as at the age of fourteen or fifteen.

Another example is a clerk born in 1911 (no. 96), who at the age of twelve already founded a *Deutsch-voelkisch* Students' Association:

One often hears the question why it was that youth spontaneously rallied to Hitler. But the experiences of war, revolution, and inflation supply an explanation. We were not spared anything. We knew and felt the worries in the house. The shadow of necessity never left our table and made us silent. We were rudely pushed out of our childhood and not shown the right path. The struggle for life got to us early. Misery, shame, hatred, lies, and civil war imprinted themselves on our souls and made us mature early. So we searched and found Adolf Hitler. What attracted us like a magnet was precisely the fact that he only made demands of us and promised us nothing. He demanded of every person a total commitment to his movement and therefore to Germany.

Four-fifths of the Abel stormtroopers and nearly all the SA men of 1933 had been in a youth group by the time they were twenty-five years old.[55] This high figure was composed of the following:

[55] The youthful phase was defined by this age limit even though some youth groups had members older than twenty-five. All voluntary groups were counted except for trade unions and professional associations. Membership in trade union youth groups was included, as was Freecorps membership, but not military service.

Quasi-military groups	28.8%
Hitler Youth (HJ)	20.9
Voelkisch Youth	6.7
DHV Youth	2.7
Buendisch Youth	5.7
Jungdo	3.6
Bismarck Youth	7.0
Religious youth associations	1.8
Communist Youth	8.0
SPD, Socialist Youth	8.4
Others	6.4
	100.0%

The quasi-military settings included *Wehrwolf, Wiking, Oberland* (7.1 percent), *Jungstahlhelm* (2.7 percent plus 2.2 percent who joined it after belonging to another group of this category), Freecorps (5.3 percent), *Einwohnerwehr* (4.0 percent), and other military training groups (9.9 percent). The figure for Bismarck Youth, the youth affiliate of the DNVP, also includes other nationalist groups. The extent of the quasi-military and *voelkisch* elements, and of the bourgeois, Youth Movement groups, is less surprising than the left-wing groups (SPD, KJ, RJ). The Hitler Youth (HJ) was meant to be a source of SA recruits, but its small size made it unlikely that it would continue to play a large role after 1930. It had little importance among the youth groups of the SA and SS leaders, especially those with the rank of *Sturmführer* (lieutenant) up. These men were more often characterized by youthful membership in quasi-military groups, an equivalent of sorts to the old cadet school.[56] The leaders also had often been in *voelkisch* youth groups, and hardly any of them had been with KPD or SPD youth organizations.

It is difficult to exaggerate the influence of these youth groups on the development of the political attitudes and

[56] The 122 Abel SA and SS leaders had one-third of their youthful associations in quasi-military groups, nearly one-half among the *Sturmfuehrer* and *Obersturmbannfuehrer*.

beliefs of young Germans in that era. They were a way of peer group life totally separated from the home, an integral youth culture. By merging their very selves with the group or with close friends in the group, they took on a new identity, though hardly a political one in the early stages of a youth group career. The Abel stories are full of sensitive accounts of young persons groping their way toward a new identity in the youth culture and, perhaps, through several youth groups until they found the right one. Only gradually, as the young people became a little older and under the pressure of events, did political identifications and heroes emerge. If there had been no heroes and no persecutions, they would have had to be invented, for they were needed for personality growth. We may wish that the Peter Pan stage had never ended and the young person had never had to grow up. For, quite subtly, the carefree wanderings became political crusades, the occasional frictions turned into partisan street battles, and Peter Pan emerged a mindless stormtrooper slugging his way into the Third *Reich*.

A sensitive account of the search for the right youth group interwoven with coming of age politically was given by a worker's son born in 1908 (no. 250), who was prevented from getting a *Gymnasium* education by financial reasons and his father's remarriage. He was quite taken by the war effort, and used to play soldiers with his friends. He would not go into agriculture, and his father would not let him go to sea. Instead, at fourteen, he became a technician's apprentice for four years in a large company:

A short time after I started working there, I noticed a young man in strange clothes who one Saturday noon walked past us with a military knapsack. I could not resist asking him about it the following week. He was pleased to tell me that he was in a wandering group and that they went on hikes Sundays, or even Saturdays, set up tents, and cooked in the woods. I was immediately enthusiastic and asked to be allowed to come along. . . . I got to know the group, several youths between fifteen

207

and eighteen. They did not smoke or drink alcohol and rejected so-called good manners and the conventional life-style.

In an aside, the respondent distinguished three kinds of youth groups, the "purely pacifistic" (Socialist or Communist), Christian (Protestant or Catholic), and *voelkisch*-nationalistic youth movements, and continued:

The group I was in was purely pacifistic. The brother of my hiking comrade belonged to a *voelkisch*-nationalist group, the Journeymen of the DHV, with headquarters in Solingen. I did not like the pacifism of my group, but preferred the romantic and the military aspects, and hence we split off after a short time and joined the Journeymen in Duesseldorf. Our leader was an older fellow who had been a soldier in the war. He was a nationalist and during our hikes always drew our attention to the beautiful sights of the fatherland. He told us of his experiences in the war and organized our group in a somewhat military manner. Thus we received our first political education.

The respondent also learned about the *voelkisch* movement, and once after a twenty-mile hike attended a Nazi rally addressed by Ludendorff and met stormtroopers in the youth hostel.

The youth movement was split three ways, as I explained, but because of our common interests the groups of right and left often cooperated. We had our common song fests when we rehearsed and sang old German folk songs. We had our common sports evenings . . . and, while hiking, we always met other groups in the hostels or elsewhere and got to know everyone. I used to go with my hiking comrade several times to the "nest evenings" of a pacifist group and had great discussions there. For hours we talked about one affair which we ourselves considered downright dishonorable. This group wanted to send their members to France and Belgium in their love

208

of mankind in order to help rebuild what our fathers and the hostile troops had had to destroy there.

These youth groups, invincible though they seemed in their hold on a young person's mind, had an obvious weakness that contained the seeds of their destruction: the attraction of the opposite sex.

Our group, the Journeymen, was not working out anymore, because the leader wanted to get married and no longer had enough time for us. So we were looking for another youth group and I met this comrade in vocational school who belonged to the German Boy Scouts.[57] He told me that the French occupation of Duesseldorf had outlawed the Boy Scouts. . . .

I liked the whole approach of Scouting better than the purely *buendisch* (Youth Movement) affairs earlier. Here we had literature and guidance on the meaning of Scouting and how to organize the hikes and encampments. In the earlier groups there had been such a search for something new and no one had a clear picture before his eyes. Here there was a goal and the work was laid out in a program, so to speak. There followed wonderful "nest evenings" and hikes and we also tried to recruit by all means one or another classmate or other acquaintances. In this fashion we got one fellow, who is still my friend, but who is now a high-up stormtrooper leader. . . .

On one occasion, the respondent again met one of the pacifists who had meanwhile joined the *Nerother Bund*, a right-wing group of university and secondary-school students. They agreed to bicycle together to a *Stahlhelm* meeting outside the occupied area, which was also attended by *Jungdo* and the stormtroopers, all in uniforms and with

[57] For a description of the *voelkisch*, conservative-revolutionary leanings of the German Boy Scouts, see Hotzel, *Deutscher Aufstand*, pp. 239 ff. This book also relates the takeover of the initially unpolitical Youth Movement by Freecorps officers, pp. 228 ff., and describes *Jungstahlhelm*, pp. 222 ff., and the unpolitical motives that drove many students into the Freecorps.

flags. On the way, they also met a group of the *voelkisch Wikingbund* who had been expelled by the French and told stories about skirmishes with Communists. The *Stahlhelm* rally left "an enormous impression," all these "nationalist-thinking men" with their uniforms, insignia, and various flags. The former pacifist was sorely tempted to join one of these organizations, but could not make up his mind, and in the meantime the respondent recruited him for his Boy Scouts. The group prospered and grew, and subtly became more involved in politics.

> We *experienced* the death of Schlageter. We knew somehow that he was shot as a freedom fighter and not just as an adventurer. We understood his deed. We *experienced* how Willi Schwarz threw a hand grenade into a French patrol and was subsequently tortured in French jails to the edge of insanity. We *experienced* how even the Youth Movement leaders were arrested; how our houses were searched for military items like regulation knapsacks, and there were occasional small clashes with the occupation troops. And we *experienced* the passive resistance . . . in a hidden water-mill near Duisburg where the activists of the passive resistance had found a hiding place. . . . A big iron swastika was outside the door. Every Saturday young people from Duisburg, Essen, Duesseldorf, etc. gathered here to tell each other of the new deeds of the Ruhr fighters. An old officer from the World War read from his war diary and told us a little war adventure. Monday morning we would be back at work with renewed strength, the heart full of resistance against the oppressors and full of faith in Germany's future.

SA and Hitler Youth (HJ)

The respondent then told of the frequent need to change the name of his Boy Scouts in order to elude their prohibition, and of physical skirmishes with Socialist or Communist youth and, later, with the *Reichsbanner*. The group became more and more committed to *voelkisch* principles. The respondent, now eighteen, finished his apprenticeship and went with a hiking comrade on a three months' trip through Bavarian and Austria. After a series of sporadic jobs interspersed with further roaming, he finally began to lose interest in youth group activities because he had acquired a girl friend.

> The group life and hiking declined more and more. Various members got too old, some had already joined the NSDAP, others like me had girl friends, and some were too busy with their jobs. . . . I had been approached now and then to join the NSDAP, the *Stahlhelm*, or some other organization. I had always declined because I felt too young to be a party member and would not permit myself a definite political opinion. I did not like the *Stahlhelm* anyway because there was no spirit of comrade-ship . . . and there were class distinctions there.

But soon he began to go to Nazi rallies and became "strongly enthusiastic." He joined the NSDAP in March 1930. At first, he was not inclined to become a stormtrooper, because their evening schedule would have interfered with his love life. But, witnessing a white-shirted SA demonstration at the time the brown shirts were outlawed, he marched along and, having received his share of hateful "red" insults and attacks, he joined the SA.

The vast panorama of these youth-group backgrounds can be subdivided by age groups and location. The few storm-troopers who had no youthful association were invariably older. They grew up at a time when the organized youth culture was not yet universal to German youth. The young-est were those stormtroopers for whom the SA or HJ was their first group, which was probably a consequence of the late availability of the spreading Hitler movement. These respondents also tended to come from smaller towns and rural areas where youth groups and political activism may have been novelties. The next youngest were those who

211

were with *Jungdo*, or with *buendisch* or *voelkisch* youth. There were also socio-economic differences that set off the relatively urban and bourgeois Youth Movement from its proletarian equivalents. Communist, Socialist, and trade union youth shared some of the *buendisch* Youth Movement outlook and practices such as hiking and a love of nature and folklore. Yet working-class youth of necessity had a different perspective on youth group activity, since they generally had to go to work from the age of fourteen, while middle-class youth would still be in school. Leisure-time activities for working-class youth, as a result, were less characterized by a need to demonstrate personal independence from home. These young men were less foot-loose and, in particular, less prone to the building of castles in the sky. It is hard to imagine a working-class organization with a name like the *Jungdeutscher Orden* (*Jungdo*), with its connotations of medieval knights and crusades. A young apprentice or worker was more likely to want to belong to a *Arbeitersportverein* or to the Friends of Nature. The Socialist Workers' Youth (SAJ) was a more integral youth culture group, and quite noticeably less politicized and militarized than Communist youth (KJ). Just as we may consider most Youth Movement groups to have been still relatively unpolitical, the typical SAJ member did not yet consider himself a full-fledged Socialist fighter in a manner comparable to the young Red Fronter or SA stormtrooper. In the political life cycle, so to speak, Youth-Movement-type group memberships were still a part of the moratorium of youth culture halfway between the political innocence of childhood and adult involvement. Communist and Nazi youth, however, strove directly for an adult political role.

The Hitler Youth (HJ) of the Weimar Republic is worth a closer look in this context. The early antecedents of the HJ, the *Jugendbund* of 1922 and the Greater German Youth of Saxony, were of modest size and each was only one of several active *voelkisch* youth organizations.[58] The *Jugend-*

[58] The HJ antecedents did not exceed 2,500, and its 1,200 members

bund was divided into a *Jungmannschaft* of fourteen to six-teen-year-olds, a *Jungsturm Adolf Hitler* of sixteen to eight-een-year-olds, and a girls' section; the members wore wind-breaks, white shirts, and blue caps with black-white-red cockade and swastika, as well as the familiar armband. There were Youth Movement touches, to be sure, but the emphatically political orientation clearly emerged even then from "organizational and ideological affinity between the *Jugendbund* and the SA."[59] The Saxonian Greater German Youth of Kurt Gruber was more independent, because it flourished while Hitler was in jail and the party was out-lawed. But it clearly understood its role as a youth organiza-tion of the Hitler movement and, after some transient align-ments with substitutes such as Ludendorff's *Tannenberg-bund* and Roehm's *Frontbann*, succeeded in becoming the HJ of 1926. By this time, Hitler had come around to the realization of the crucial importance of youth in planning the conquest of Germany, and was ready to give it a more prominent role in the reconstruction of the party.[60]

The new HJ was organized, like its predecessors, into fourteen to sixteen and sixteen to eighteen-year-olds, with the addition of a children's section for the ten to fourteen-year-olds. Members wore the SA uniform without the arm-band and were subordinated to the SA Commander, Cap-tain Pfeffer. This made the HJ, for all effects and purposes, the youth group of the SA, although the latter was now also kept more tightly under the reins of the party than in

---

in 1923 played a negligible role in a movement of 55,000 Nazis. Other *voelkisch* groups were the Eagles and Falcons of 1920 (3,300 mem-bers in 1932), the *Artamanen* of 1924 (1,800 in 1930), the *Geusen* of 1919 (1,150 in 1930), the *Freischar Schill* (1,500 in 1932), and smaller groups.

[59] Peter D. Stachura, *Nazi Youth in the Weimar Republic* (Santa Barbara: ABC-Clio, 1975), p. 8. The *Jugendbund* was outlawed along with the SA and NSDAP after the beer-hall putsch, although it had not participated in the events.

[60] *Mein Kampf*, p. 348. The "youth question" received a prominent place on the agenda of the Weimar convention of the party in July of 1926.

the hectic days of 1922-1923, when it was a nearly autonomous, paramilitary formation under Captain Roehm. As SA youth, or rather NSDAP youth,[61] it was not expected to participate in street violence, at least not until the early 1930s, but only in propaganda activities and in its group life, which the adult organization promised to protect against "the terror." HJ members turning eighteen were expected to graduate to the NSDAP, although this rule was waived later in the case of HJ leaders, who were not required to resign their positions. The party had to authorize all HJ appearances in public and was entitled to be represented at HJ meetings.

Under these circumstances and with all kinds of organizational difficulties, the HJ grew only very slowly in the early years. In 1929, by Peter Stachura's estimate, it had no more than 13,000 members in 450 branches, which is not large in comparison with the 4.3 million youths organized in the *Reich Committee on Youth Organizations* of 1927.[62] By the end of 1930, this figure had hardly increased, but then the HJ began to grow rapidly: by January 1932, it had 37,304 members and, a year later, 55,365,[63] though this still did not amount to very much in comparison with the 291,000 SA troopers of January, 1932, and an estimated 700,000 on the eve of Hitler's appointment as chancellor.[64] At this point, we need to recall the drop in the birthrate, which may have kept the younger HJ age groups much smaller and less affected by the Depression than the SA age group.

Who were the members of the HJ and how did they differ from most of the other youth organizations of the Weimar

[61] The most recent German history of the HJ describes its life as "in the shadow of the party." Hans-Christian Brandenburg, *Die Geschichte der HJ, Wege und Irrwege einer Generation* (Cologne: Wissenschaft und Politik, 1968). Stachura believes that the HJ nevertheless retained considerable autonomy, *Nazi Youth*, pp. 27-30.

[62] This organization was not even all-inclusive, and at first rejected, for example, the HJ. Stachura, *Nazi Youth*, pp. 37 and 41.

[63] *Ibid.*, pp. 180 and 185.

[64] See Werner, "SA und NSDAP," pp. 544-552.

Republic? The rank and file of the HJ evidently differed dramatically from the almost exclusively bourgeois Youth Movement by being composed of 69 percent workers and industrial apprentices, 10 percent shopkeepers' assistants; 12 percent students; and 9 percent unemployed or other.[65] This heavily proletarian makeup differs strikingly from the HJ leadership, which by all accounts was heavily middle-class—in fact much more so than the known composition of the NSDAP itself.[66] The composition of the HJ rank and file is, in fact, very similar to that of the SPD in 1930, which was 64.1 percent working-class,[67] while the HJ leadership was as overwhelmingly bourgeois as the Youth Movement. A tabulation of the ages of 186 of the 200 HJ leaders in the Stachura book further adds to this impression:

Prewar generation (born 1894 or earlier)		4.5%
War generation (born 1895-1901)		11.0
Postwar generation	1902-1905	22.5
	1906-1908	24.5
	1909-1911	22.0
	1912-1914	8.5
	NA	7.0

The HJ leaders were overwhelmingly of the postwar generation and at least 90 percent, in fact, were eighteen years or older by 1929. O   percent of them, therefore, were in the Freecorps,   war-generation calling, and 19.5 percent came fro   r youth groups, especially from the

[65] Cited by Stacl   Nazi Youth, pp. 58-59. There is no evidence for his assertion, h   ver, that the HJ were the "sons of the proletarianised bourgeoi   Stachura found a percentage of only 6.5 to be working-class among   admittedly partial and sketchy sample of HJ leaders of the 1926 to 1933 period.

[66] With 31.5 percent workers and 45.4 percent independents, white-collar workers   vil servants, the NSDAP was midway between the two. N   teistatistik (1935), I, 185.

[67] SPD Jahrbuc   . See also David Schoenbaum, Hitler's Social Revolution: tatus in Nazi Germany 1933-1939 (Garden City, N.Y.: Doubleday, 1966), chapter 1.

Youth Movement and from *voelkisch* groups, most of which were eventually absorbed by the HJ.[68] These HJ leaders, furthermore, joined the NSDAP at the following periods:

to 1925	18.5%
1926-1928	27.0
1929-1930	28.0
1931-1933	14.5
Later	2.5
NA	9.5

They tended to join the party far more heavily during the period prior to the September 1930 landslide election than did the total NSDAP membership of 1933, of whom only 15.3 percent had joined before that date. Finally, they appear to have "graduated" to the SA in surprisingly small numbers for an organization that was supposed to be the "SA youth": Only 26 percent joined the SA or SS, and again two-thirds of them before the 1930 elections—in fact, three-fifths by 1928, when all three, the HJ, the SA, and the NSDAP were still rather small. This, incidentally, did not prevent about 16.5 percent of them from entering an SS or Security Service (SD) career in the Third *Reich*. A considerable number of HJ leaders were expelled or dropped out before and after 1933, though it is not known whether this was because of their Youth Movement or social revolutionary attitudes or for other reasons.[69] Still, the different social origins and the reluctance to join the SA in the proportions typical of the rank and file of the HJ suggests either that

[68] Beginning in 1929, there was cooperation and, by 1931, there were local mergers and joint membership with several *voelkisch* youth groups. See Dietrich Orlow, *History of the Nazi Party, 1919-1933*, pp. 197-198.

[69] Beginning in 1928, the party and later the new HJ leader, Baldur von Schirach, moved emphatically toward the right, which led to many internal conflicts in the HJ, the SA, and the NSDAP left wing. For the HJ and university students in the NS Students' Federation, it meant cooperation with bourgeois and conservative groups and a switch from social-revolutionary pretensions to militant nationalism and *voelkisch* antisemitism.

216

they were an alien (Youth Movement) element or that, given the division of labor between the SA street fighters and the party functionaries, they definitely preferred the latter, nonviolent career to doing the dirty work.[70]

[70] Stachura's account of the sixteen HJ casualties of the political clashes also stresses their heavily proletarian character. There were evidently no HJ leaders among them. See also Orlow's report of a massive purge of the HJ leadership in the wake of the Stennes revolt. *History of the Nazi Party*, p. 227.

The Vortex of the Movement

THE SWATH cut by the Nazi movement through German society in the early 1930s can be likened to the path of a hurricane over tropical waters. Given the right atmospheric conditions and water temperature, the falling air mass comes into violent, counter-clockwise motion around a center of very low pressure, generating extremely destructive winds and torrential rains. The atmospheric conditions of Weimar culture and politics were, indeed, highly favorable to this eruption of revivalist nationalism complete with images of the devil. And there were ever-widening circles of disoriented and discontented individuals—veterans, young people, the unemployed—ready to be swept up into the self-accelerating motion of the great storm. Only people with a strong sense of other loyalties, Socialist or Catholic for example, could have hoped to resist the suction of the brown hurricane. We have already described the prevailing atmosphere and the various kinds of people "available" for the gathering storm. Now we need to link propensities to actions and show the dynamic nature of the movement.

Violent Youth, Violent Adults

The high incidence of prior youth group memberships among the Abel stormtroopers suggests that it may well be in the youthful setting that we find the seeds of the adult stormtrooper career. However, we still need to clarify whether the patterns were primarily behavioral or attitudinal. What did the stormtroopers do and think in their youth? Almost two-thirds of their youth group memberships already involved political violence, and most of these were partisan street and meeting-hall battles rather than the organized Freecorps-type of violence that many of the quasi-military groups may have engaged in during the years between the years 1919 and 1923. The nonviolent third by no means limited itself to unpolitical pursuits like hiking or singing folksongs. Three-fourths of them tended to be in demonstrations, election campaigns, or proselytizing for their youth groups. The same respondents who were violent youths in partisan street violence were also in the forefront of adult stormtrooper violence during the fighting years of the movement. By way of contrast, those who had been involved in organized, Freecorps-style violence during their salad days were more prominent in demonstrations and election campaigns during the fighting years. The contagion of political violence, in other words, did not simply come from Freecorps-type involvement during those years of upheaval. The violent respondents of those years were ten years older by the early thirties, and apparently no longer as prone to violence, even though their nationalistic, anti-Communist attitudes still drove them into the Nazi movement. The violent youth of the early thirties belonged to a younger group, mostly born after 1905.

In the process of trying to untangle the behavioral and the ideological continuities between the Abel respondents as youth group members and as fully grown stormtroopers and party members, we developed a typology of youthful extremist attitudes that may help to clarify the processes at hand. The youthful activists were divided into

1. *politically militarized youths* who were characterized by: a. a great urge to march and fight; and b. an astonishing unconcern about the ideological goals and programs of the movement. These youths were by far the youngest and the

219

most likely to be involved with the SA or SS and with their street violence;

2. *fully politicized youths* who were defined as: a. highly ideological (*voelkisch*) and politically knowledgeable; and b. more interested in organizing than in violence;

3. *hostile militants* who typically straddled the war and postwar generations. They were characterized by: a. a sociopathic degree of hostility to certain groups and to authority in society; and b. heavy engagement in violence;

4. *authoritarian youth*, motivated by the leadership cult and an obsession with restoring law and order;

5. attitude groups that could be described as prepolitical, parochial, or romantic.

We can recognize readily some of the groups we have described and the generational dimensions. The third and fourth groups were likely to be older and heavily represented among the Freecorps, veterans' youth, and among conservative nationalists, especially those with a military background. The fully politicized youths, on the other hand, were more likely to be found among *voelkisch* youth organizations, including the early NSDAP youth (*Jugendbund*), and only in individual cases among the other groups, such as antisemitic defectors from the extreme left or among the bourgeois or conservative groups. These politicized youngsters often went through several diverse groups before homing in on the Nazi party. The politically militarized group, by way of contrast, was very simple in its motivation, craving above all military-like action and good fellowship, and probably feeling equally at home among stormtroopers or Communist and *Reichsbanner* street fighters.

Let us compare the composition of the Abel stormtroopers with the rest of the Nazi members in regard to these typical youthful postures. The type we described as politically militarized is obviously the dominant one among the SA and SS men, and especially among the latter, who generally represented a selection of "the best" from among the SA men available (Table V-1). The politically militarized youths also stand out prominently among the lower and

220

TABLE V-1   Youthful Postures of Abel Stormtroopers
and Party Members (percent)

Youthful Postures	SA/SS	NSDAP Only
Politically militarized	39.9	6.2
Fully politicized	10.3	9.8
Hostile militants	12.8	7.2
Authoritarians	4.3	8.2
Prepolitical, etc.	10.2	22.2
Others, including people of no youthful association	22.5	46.4
Totals	100.0	100.0

middle echelons of SA and SS leaders. This is evidently the
type of person, juvenile or fully grown, who embodied the
behavioral continuity of violence in the lives of the stormtroopers far better than the handful of Freecorps fighters
still active in the top stormtrooper leadership in the 1930s.

The ideological element was secondary among the stormtroopers, and in this respect the fully politicized youths
played about the same role in the SA/SS as in the party.
This does not mean that party members were as rarely
ideologically motivated as the stormtroopers, but rather
that their political development grew from a fully politicized youth in as few cases as among the SA and SS. A
tabulation of the varied strands of ideology typical of the
Nazis, without regard to the intensity of beliefs, in fact,
shows only minor differences between the stormtroopers
and the rest of the party (Table V-2). To the extent that
they expressed their beliefs, the stormtroopers' ideology tended to be made up of superpatriotism, the Hitler
cult, and revanchism, while the rest of the party put more
stress on antisemitism and *voelkisch* beliefs. The SA and SS
leadership again resembled the rank and file to a fault. On
a more superficial, tactical level, however, anti-Communism
and anti-Socialism—the bogus enemy, in other words—
must be added to the stormtroopers' ideology, while the
other party members were more likely to tie their anti-Com-

221

TABLE V-2 Ideological Themes of Abel SA/SS and NSDAP
(percent)

Ideological Main Theme	SA/SS	NSDAP Only
Solidarism (*Volksgemeinschaft*)	30.4	31.7
Superpatriotism	22.3	21.6
Hitler cult	21.3	19.6
Antisemitism	10.7	14.9
Revanchism, authoritarianism	6.6	3.7
Nordic, agrarian romanticism	4.7	6.8
No ideology worth noting	4.0	1.7
Totals	100.0	100.0

munism to antisemitism and to project their hatred also on the "reactionaries," that is the conservatives, liberals, or the Center party. The stormtroopers' anti-Communism obviously did not go very deep, and was an attitude related to their daily combat, a phobia rather than an ideology.

Stormtrooper Antisemitism

Antisemitism, on the other hand, was at the core of the beliefs typical of the NSDAP, and it is interesting to see how the SA/SS differed from the rest of the party in this respect. We ranked all the Abel respondents according to the kind and virulence of their prejudice (Table V-3). The stormtroopers differed quite markedly from the rest of the party,

TABLE V-3 Antisemitic Prejudice of Abel SA/SS and NSDAP
(percent)

Degree of Prejudice	SA/SS	NSDAP Only
No evidence of prejudice	37.7	30.2
Mild verbal clichés	15.9	10.5
Sudden *Judenkoller*	24.9	33.7
Anecdote-tellers	7.3	14.5
Conspiracy/paranoia	14.2	11.0
Totals	100.0	100.0

222

especially from its choleric and anecdote-telling elements.[1] Our scale of antisemitic attitudes requires further comment. Some theories attempt to assign ethnic prejudice a function relating it to the cohesion of a movement or the aims of a regime. But none of these hatreds, as Hannah Arendt has pointed out convincingly, fulfilled any rational purpose or followed any vital necessity except for the warped logic of hate-filled minds.[2] The empirical material of the Abel Collection gives few clues to the function of prejudice for the movement or the regime that followed. Instead it allows us to document the presence of extraordinary amounts of prejudice and hatred in the respondents, a feature that still has to be fully acknowledged in much of the literature.[3] It further permits us to ascertain different degrees of prejudice, and to relate them to the background, socialization, and other attitudes and behavior of the respondents.

Our scale begins with the respondents whose vitae contain no evidence of their prejudice one way or the other. There is no telling how many of them deliberately omitted this theme because in their social circles there was a sense of shame attached to talking about such phobias. In a manner of speaking, all the other cases can be considered those without a sense of shame about their prejudice. But a truly prejudiced person, according to Gordon Allport, tends to assume that everybody shares his or her prejudice. Many

[1] The SA and SS leaders again resembled their rank and file, except that even more of them gave no evidence of prejudice.

[2] *The Origins of Totalitarianism*, new ed. (New York: Harcourt, Brace and World, 1966), pp. 423-429, 452.

[3] Books that tackle the pivotal role of the hatreds and phobias in Nazi policy, such as Karl A. Schleunes, *The Twisted Road to Auschwitz* (Urbana: University of Illinois Press, 1970), are still in the minority. See also Werner Mosse, ed., *Entscheidungsjahr 1932, Zur Judenfrage in der Endphase der Weimarer Republik* (Tuebingen: Mohr, 1966). But there are now a number of regional and intellectual histories that show the derivation of the Nazi movement from prewar (and the immediate postwar) antisemitic movements. See, for example, Eberhart Schoen, *Die Entstehung des Nationalsozialismus in Hessen* (Meisenheim: Hain, 1972), pp. 8-21 and 104-116.

223

Nazis are known to have regarded the United States of the early thirties as a country full of antisemitic prejudice. We can safely assume that most of those who give no evidence of prejudice were, indeed, not "truly prejudiced" in this sense, and had other motives for joining the NSDAP. This may have been true especially of the younger, more naive respondents. It is hard to imagine a reasonably perceptive, mature person who would join the NSDAP without being fully aware of its chief issue.

The next entry on the scale takes account of mild verbal projections and cliché-like mouthings of prejudice, such as one would expect at Nazi social gatherings. We can assume that persons of weak prejudice would use the language of prejudice in a perfunctory way to establish rapport with their fellows.[4] These first two categories abounded among the stormtroopers, while the cholerics and anecdote-tellers did not. From the weak motivation of the verbal cliché, there is a huge step to the severity of a *Judenkoller* or the anecdote-telling habit we discussed above.[5] As will be recalled, the choleric outbreak of prejudice appears to restore the mental balance of the respondent, if at a price, and may later be rationalized with an anecdote. The anecdote is not a true story of an event that "caused" the prejudice, but a vehicle for self-presentation and a label of social deviance the respondent has accepted. Many of the Abel vitae begin with the respondent saying something like: "If you want to understand me as a person, you will have to know the following anecdote about me."

While the anecdote-teller is a confirmed, self-rationalizing antisemite, he is still a person relatively at a static balance between his displacement and his rational self. He can leave his scapegoat alone except for symbolic vilifications. At the last point in our scale, however, there is no longer even

---

[4] See especially the interpretation of the use of prejudicial language in popular agitation to establish rapport between the demagogue and his audience by Leo Lowenthal and Norbert Guterman, *Prophets of Deceit* (New York: Harper, 1949).

[5] See above, Chapter III, "Occupation of the Rhineland."

a sense of balance between the person and his sickness, but the dynamic disequilibrium of paranoia. Cornered by his surging fears of "the conspiracy" and of personal persecutions, the paranoid is a dangerous man. He has become a "political antisemite" who feels compelled to take political action against the object of his displacement. He will lash out at his imagined tormentors, plot counter-conspiracies against their alleged conspiracy, and go around warning people about the fancied menace. These paranoids, too, are represented more heavily among the SA/SS rank and file, and also among the leaders of both the SA/SS and the party, than among ordinary party members. The movement was literally led by the paranoids.

There are many stories about the distribution of handbills and attaching of antisemitic posters and stickers on walls, park benches, and places of public convenience. There are also a number of accounts in the Abel file of obscure prewar antisemitic associations and of the antisemitic underground literature of that period. None of the Abel respondents seems to have read Walther Darré, Alfred Rosenberg, or the *voelkisch* literature that is often blamed for their mania. But quite a few were familiar with one Theodor Fritsch (1844-1933), whose *Handbook on the Jewish Question* went through an awesome forty editions between 1888 and 1936, and with other publications of his Hammer Verlag, which also published a monthly. This prewar antisemitic element and its ramifications in the Weimar setting come closest to supplying a kind of ideological core, especially if we throw in scattered *voelkisch* ideas that crop up here and there in the autobiographies of the Abel collection. However, even this *voelkisch*/antisemitic core is too limited in its acceptance and salience among the bulk of the Abel respondents to serve as a basis for studying the movement as an ideological movement. The typical antisemite was no philosopher, but more similar to a woman born about 1895 (no. 44), who "due to inherited, sound feelings" used to volunteer in school to sing *Deutschland, Deutschland ueber alles* despite the teasing

225

of her classmates. "It was not a matter of vanity with me, but from the desire of my heart." Canvassing for the People's Party (DVP) after the war, she wanted to "struggle for the German soul" and "peel off the alien layers from the German soul," until she became disillusioned with the DVP and got married. After the failure of her marriage, she was vehemently attracted to the Nazi movement because of its stress on *the race question!!!!*" *"With this an ideological leader could not make any money. For this he needed idealism, faith in ultimate verities for which we have been ardently longing for all these years, knowingly or not. Yes, our people needed idealism, the awareness of the meaning of the words: to be a member of a certain people!!!!"* (italics and punctuation of the respondent). It would appear that we cannot truly understand the minds of the rank-and-file Nazi activists, much less the minds of the stormtroopers, by intellectualizing their motivations.

The paranoid elements among the party and SA/SS tended to be business and professional people, white-collar workers, and a few workers driven by their antisemitism to switch from left-wing activism to the swastika. Many paranoids were also in social decline or were upwardly mobile from the urban underclass, second-generation urbanites. This latter group showed the most prejudice, and was in the forefront of all Nazi activities. While the cholerics often railed at society from an underdog's perspective, moreover, the story-tellers and paranoids were more likely to be the sons or daughters of military-civil servants or well-situated professional people.

It is an intriguing question to find out how the intensity of prejudice in our sample was related to the partisan activities the respondents engaged in. Was intense prejudice an advantage or a hindrance to an activist's career? We have already seen that the paranoids played a major role among the lower and middle-level leadership of both the stormtroopers and the rest of the party while, conversely, the anecdote-tellers and the cholerics did not. The partisan activities tell a similar story. The paranoids were the most heavily involved in street fighting and meeting-hall brawls, often "day and night." The next heaviest fighters were the verbal cliché and the no-evidence groups. The cholerics and anecdote-tellers were noticeably less involved, especially in "day-and-night" fighting at the peak time, 1931-1932. Instead they stood out for proselytizing and electioneering. The story-tellers were still a good step ahead of the cholerics in fighting, and behind them in proselytizing. Here, it would appear, they reveal themselves as having gone beyond the *Judenkoller* toward the fighting stance of the paranoid political antisemites.

What did they get out of the struggle? Neither the anecdote-tellers nor the cholerics were getting much of a sense of personal integration out of the struggle itself. Neither group came close to the disproportionate numbers of no-evidence and paranoid respondents for whom this sense of integration was their chief satisfaction in the party. The cholerics and the story-tellers instead tended to feel uplifted by the thought of striving for utopia and, among the cholerics only, by the Hitler cult. The verbal cliché group tended to be gratified mostly by the classless comradeship in the movement.

The upshot of this and the preceding comparisons is, then, that there is a rather important difference in the degree of political mobilization of the various prejudice groups. It is chiefly those with no evidence of prejudice and the paranoids, and the verbal cliché group to a limited extent, who are driven by a deep inner need for the political struggle. The strong prejudice of the choleric and the anecdote-tellers may, indeed, be an inhibiting factor on political activity other than proselytizing. As *Judenkoller* and facetiousness turn into paranoia, prejudice evidently drives people into violent and aggressive political actions, which explains the consistently leading role of the paranoids in party officeholding and in stormtrooper violence. The no-evidence group participated without inhibition in storm-trooper activities, but evidently held few offices in the NSDAP precisely because of its lack of prejudice. The party

227

was dominated by the political antisemites, and even the verbal cliché group seems to have readily followed their maniacal leadership.

The Background of Prejudice

The genesis of strong prejudice is a fascinating topic that would deserve detailed exploration with clinical methods. The Abel vitae, unfortunately, allow only broad categories of childhood settings to be compared and, for obvious reasons, they tell more about the adolescence than about the childhood of the respondents. Respondents who grew up in poverty showed the least prejudice. Those with a disciplinarian upbringing and the many orphans, on the other hand, had the highest number of paranoids and fewer respondents who exhibited no prejudice than any other group. Here the theories of the "authoritarian mind" or a disturbed father-son relationship obviously seem to apply.[6] We also divided their childhoods into better-off and worse-off settings. Of the economically well-off childhoods, the freewheeling were high in prejudice, especially in *Judenkoller*, while the sheltered were among the least prejudiced of all the groups. Considering the importance attached to freewheeling childhoods in some cultures, including our own, this is a startling discovery. The disease of *Judenkoller*, moreover, is about the last consequence we would expect of a freewheeling childhood—unless, of course, we view this freewheeling permissiveness, from a conservative point of view, as self-destructive.[7]

The influences of the parents, and especially the fathers, follow predictable lines. The least prejudiced by far were the children from an unpolitical home environment,

[6] The literature speaks of "an ambivalence toward the parents" rather than of authoritarian childhood influences. Allport, *Dynamics of Prejudice*, p. 374.

[7] This only means that freewheeling childhoods *among Nazis* and not necessarily among the general public, tend to be correlated with a higher level of prejudice.

228

followed by those from a nationalistic or patriotic environment. The most prejudiced, as we would expect, were the
children of *voelkisch* or antisemitic parents. These also supply the largest share of aggressive paranoids and of the
mildly verbal, as well as more than their share of tellers
of prejudicial anecdotes. Most of the choleric, however,
came from nationalistic or militaristic homes, where they
may well have learned to identify closely with the glories of
the empire that disintegrated in 1918.

Their reported school environments follow similar lines.
Those who reported an influential *voelkisch*, antisemitic, or
Nazi teacher, or conflict with Jewish fellow students were
the most prejudiced and included the largest numbers of
paranoids and story-tellers. Students in a nationalist school
environment were also more likely to engage in mild verbal
projections or to have the *Judenkoller*. The respondents' reports on their school environments, of course, represent less
of a causal nexus than those about their parents, for children cannot choose their parents or defend their minds
against early parental influences. Students who report an
influential antisemitic teacher out of the many teachers they
had in eight or more years of school very likely selected this
particular teacher's influence because they already tended
in this direction.

The process by which a person becomes a Nazi militant
needs to be explored still further. How fast did an average
young German turn into a stormtrooper or a paranoid antisemite? Under what influences and by what stages? There
are glimpses of the process to be gathered from the Abel
stories. The paranoids, for example, were often classified as
"hostile militants" in their youth association, which leaves
us to speculate about the psychodynamics of their personalities, as does the frequency among them of a disciplinarian
or orphaned childhood. Were these cases of battered children, or children without fathers, turning into brown
bruisers? Was their "hostile militancy" in young adulthood
the missing link between their childhood traumas and adult
paranoia and activism? If we compare how many years a

229

person took from his (or her) first involvement in quasi-military or political activity to becoming a full-fledged Nazi, the *Judenkoller* takes on added significance, for it seemed to speed up the process of escalation as no other influence did.

Were these prejudiced militants loners in German society, people lacking social integration? The family settings of the different types of antisemites also can tell something about the personality of the respondent. The fully mobilized paranoid, it turns out, was less likely than members of other groups to have any family members other than rather distant ones in the party.[8] By way of contrast, the spouses of cholerics were often in the party, and the mildly verbal group tended to have practically their whole family in the NSDAP. The general impression is that the paranoids were loners whose pseudo-political obsessions were their whole lives. Interestingly, respondents who give no evidence of prejudice and who were quite involved in fighting and far less in party offices also tend to be loners. A person who joins an antisemitic movement just for the sake of street fighting is psychologically rather marginal, too. By contrast, the choleric married to a party member and the mildly verbal conformist with his whole Nazi family seem socially well integrated.

What did it really mean, "coming out" as a brazen anti-semite or superpatriotic extremist, or "acting out" the role in street violence or hectic propaganda campaigns? There was a curious bifurcation, at least among the Abel Nazis, between those who exhibited their strong views in some fashion and those who engaged in street violence or meeting-hall brawls with the extreme left. The former included those with the strongest prejudices against Jews and aliens, ideological obsessions, and great missionary zeal. They were

---

[8] Oddly enough and, in spite of their fears of persecution, the paranoids report not nearly as much political friction in any of these settings as, for example, the anecdote tellers. Their political mobilization evidently made them meeker and less likely to cause friction with their environment, since they had an outlet for their self-representation in their political roles.

mostly older, and included the women of the Abel Collection, but this did not keep them from engaging in proselytizing and propaganda to the limit of their ability. They also held more than their share of party offices at the local level. The violent types, on the other hand, were relatively low in prejudice and also in ideological awareness in general. They were predominantly young and made up the bulk of the SA and SS. The physical struggle in itself, rather than the dreams of utopia typical of the other group, was to them the great payoff. This may have been due in part to the large numbers of them who were depressed by their unemployment or because they had lowly, humdrum jobs from which they derived neither excitement nor even satisfaction. When a stormtrooper put on his uniform and went to do his "service" he literally stripped off his humdrum worker's life, or meek bourgeois habit, and became a heroic superman to himself and his comrades. Marching and fighting in closed formation, in particular, he felt powerful and masculine beyond compare. Longing for the heroics of World War I and for the *machismo* of the all-male cult of the veterans' or Youth Movement group, to him the "fighting years were the best time of our lives" (no. 67).

Marching, Fighting, Proselytizing

The three quintessential activities of the NSDAP in the fighting years were marching, fighting, and proselytizing; all three served the propaganda purpose. Large numbers of Germans mobilized by war, counterrevolution, and the youth culture had been marching prodigiously ever since the end of the war. Hitler himself derisively called them "the eternal marchers" in *Meim Kampf*, and yet he obviously needed them for his SA. Fighting with the Communists and the *Reichsbanner* was important both for attracting the following of parties to the right of the SPD and as a test of dedication of the younger Nazis.[9] At the same time, fight-

[9] Very considerable pressure was put upon members of the Nazi

231

ing the bogus enemy was also a symbolic act, representing the struggle for power of the NSDAP as an ideological crusade. Proselytizing, finally, was the activity most likely to make the movement grow into a huge wave of the faithful, a missionary juggernaut much like revivalist movements or the great religious movements of old. To make the NSDAP grow from 129,000 in September of 1930 to 849,000 in January of 1933 required that every follower recruit at least five more in a little more than two years. To be sure, the well-organized propaganda machine made sure that there would be many converts coming to the party of their own accord.[10] But there were quite a few Abel respondents who plausibly related their personal recruiting efforts, and each of them, of course, was himself recruited. This was another activity by which a member could prove his dedication to the movement. If he (or she) really believed in Hitler, as the phrase went, he could go out and prove his missionary zeal every day.

We tabulated the Abel stormtroopers and their leaders as against the rest of the party according to the character and intensity of their participation in Nazi activities in the fighting years (Table V-4). There are, of course, certain overlapping activities. Nearly all respondents were engaged in marching and election propaganda. But mere marching (M) was not enough. A good SA or SS man had to be involved in fighting the battles as well, as over three-fourths of the stormtroopers and over four-fifths of their leaders were. The rest of the party had few marcher-fighters (MFs), but it had a substantial share of another combina-

---

Student Federation (NS.D.St.B) to force them into the SA, according to Michael H. Kater, *Studentenschaft und Rechtsradikalismus in Deutschland 1918-1933* (Hamburg: Hoffmann & Campe, 1975), pp. 186-189. Nevertheless and contrary to the Nazi myth, no more than 40 percent of the Nazi students were willing to back up their beliefs by putting their bodies on the line.

[10] It should be noted that the SA and SS were generally not supposed to hand out propaganda leaflets, at least not in the big cities, where other party formations were assigned that task.

TABLE V-4   NSDAP Activity of Abel SA/SS and NSDAP (percent)

Activity in NSDAP	SA/SS	SA/SS Leaders	NSDAP Only
Mere member/sympathizer	7.0	4.3	43.7
Marching & electioneering (M)	4.7	2.7	8.8
Marching & fighting (MF)	44.3	45.7	1.9
Marching & proselytizing (MP)	10.6	9.7	40.0
Marching, fighting & proselytizing (MFP)	33.4	37.6	5.6
Totals	100.0	100.0	100.0
Number	341	186	215

tion of great value to the movement, the marcher-prose-lytizers (MPs). Since fewer than half of all the Abel respondents report any proselytizing on their part, the number of new recruits each proselytizer had to bring in during the years 1931-1932 was in the neighborhood of twelve. Hence being a proselytizer was very important, even if a person was too old to do any fighting, or was female. The three quintessential activities, finally, were sometimes combined in those who marched, fought, and proselytized (MFPs). They too loomed large among the stormtroopers and their leaders.

There are significant differences among these groups. The mere members/sympathizers and the MPs were the oldest (mostly over thirty-five) of the five groups, and included many rural-urban migrants of peasant stock as well as children of military-civil servants and artisans. They tended to live in Berlin and other metropoles. They had been enthusiastic soldiers in the war and the *Fronterlebnis* meant a lot to them, although they were not much involved in any postwar counterrevolutionary activity except for the *Einwohnerwehr*. The mere members had often been with the DNVP, while the MPs had been in *voelkisch* parties or the early (pre-1924) NSDAP before joining the reconstructed movement again. Some were with the *Stahlhelm*. Their most prominent reasons for joining the post-1924

233

NSDAP were the dynamic impression of the Hitler movement or, especially with the MPs, their own ideological and
antisemitic fervor.

Those who only participated in demonstrations and rallies
(Ms) were generally rather young and gave every indication that, given time, they would have become MFs or
MFPs, too. They included many converts from conservative
or bourgeois opposition groups, *voelkisch* outfits, and even
republican or communist groups. What attracted them to
the NSDAP were the spirit of camaraderie among the stormtroopers, their resentment of "police and governmental
repression," and the dynamic impression of the Hitler movement. With this, we come to the more violent bulk of the
stormtroopers, the MFs and MFPs, which we will describe
and then compare in various ways with the MPs, who were
more typical of the rest of the party than of the SA and SS.

The young marcher-fighters (MFs) were obviously more
advanced in revolutionary consciousness, although they
were the youngest of all the groups. MFs were often from
the French-occupied areas, and included many highly
mobile people, mostly from middle-sized towns and metropoles other than Berlin. Large numbers among them were
blue (nearly one-half) or white-collar (one-fifth) workers,
or farmers (one-tenth). Their fathers had been workers,
artisans, or military-civil servants. Half of their families had
made no attempt to rise and an unusual number were in
social decline. Of the few upwardly mobile, only those rising from the city proletariat stand out. They tended to join
the NSDAP only when it had become a substantial minority
in their area. In the war, they were enthusiastic soldiers with
some animosity toward civilians and draft-dodgers. Like the
Ms, they had a disproportionate share (one-fourth) of war
invalids and POWs, who may well have felt particular ire
at the disparagement of military honor after the war. The
Abel data permit us to trace the evolution of the various
relevant activities of a group such as the MFs, MPs, or
MFPs over the entire Weimar period. Unlike the MPs,

whose involvement in violence decreased with advancing age, the MFs' violence obviously grew.

Over one-half of them, indeed, were already either marching or engaged in organized violence in the first five years of the republic. They were with the Freecorps and the *Bürgerwehr*, and in *Wehrwolf*-type organizations. In 1923, many were involved in antioccupation activity or were members of militant veterans' or *voelkisch* groups. Later they tended to be distrustful of parties or just shopping around, or actually in republican parties. Half of them were under twenty-five, and a fourth under twenty-one when they joined the NSDAP. The reasons for their joining were the stormtroopers' spirit of comradeship, "free time" because of unemployment, and clashes with the occupation or with the Communists. The dates of their joining cluster around two points, the period of 1925 to 1927 and that following the 1930 elections, which brought a lot of old right-wing war horses into the NSDAP. During the height of the battle in 1931-1932, indeed, the MFs were by far the most violent group in the NSDAP.[11] Their perception of the Weimar Republic tells much about their mental make-up. One-third insisted that Marxists were "running the republic," with overtones of longing for deliverance.

The outstanding characteristic of the marcher-fighters, next to their awesome bent for violence, was their almost complete failure to engage in the other essential activity of an extremist movement, proselytizing. As Table V-5 shows clearly, they did far less proselytizing than either the MPS or the MFPs. Were they the mindless sluggers of the movement? Let us take a closer look at their ideology and attitudes over the different periods of the republic.

The MFs differ markedly from the MPs and MFPs in their dominant ideological motifs. The latter two tended to

[11] With 39.4 percent engaged in violence in 1919-1924, 35.3 percent in the quiet years of 1925-1928, 58.5 percent in 1929-1930, and 76.4 percent in 1931-1932, the MFs were on the average twice as violent as the MFPs.

TABLE V-5 Demonstrations, Violence, and Proselytizing,
1919-1932 (percent)

		1919-1924	1925-1928	1929-1930	1931-1932
	Demonstrations	16.0	16.8	15.6	13.9
MFs	Violence	39.4	35.3	58.5	76.4
	Proselytizing	6.4	3.4	4.8	8.5
	Totals	61.8	55.5	78.9	98.8
	Demonstrations	12.1	9.0	19.2	20.6
MPs	Violence	15.9	4.1	9.0	9.7
	Proselytizing	17.8	25.4	44.9	62.9
	Totals	45.8	38.5	73.1	93.1
	Demonstrations	26.7	21.9	23.7	26.2
MFPs	Violence	18.8	23.9	30.6	32.1
	Proselytizing	16.8	26.3	37.6	41.2
	Totals	62.3	72.1	91.9	99.5

emphasize antisemitism, the Nordic-German cult, and the *Volksgemeinschaft*. The MFs, by way of contrast, stressed the Hitler cult, revanchism, and superpatriotism. They were evidently, in spite of their youth,[12] a kind of missing link to the violent nationalistic and counterrevolutionary strains of the immediate postwar era and 1923.

Their hate lists, as compared to those of the other two groups, tend to be either all-embracing or simply anti-Communist and anti-Socialist. They also felt a lively hatred for the police and the government. The MFPs likewise stressed their anti-Marxism, while the MPs instead tended to pillory the "reactionaries" and the Jews. On the antisemitism scale, indeed, the MFs (and also the Ms) were the least prejudiced, with over one-third giving no evidence of bias and another one-fifth engaging only in mild verbal projections. A good third of the MPs, by comparison, were suffering

[12] Half of them joined the post-1924 NSDAP at the age of twenty-five or younger, and 70.9 percent joined it before they had passed the age of thirty. This contrasts with 36.7 percent of the MPs, 59.4 percent of the Ms, and 65.7 percent of the MFPs who joined before they were past thirty.

236

from *Judenkoller* and, like the MFPs, about one-eighth indulged in personal antisemitic anecdotes. The MFPs, furthermore, stood out with an unusual number (23 percent) of paranoid persons who spoke of conspiracies and hinted at threats and counterthreats.

There is further evidnece that the MFs were merely the footsoldiers of the movement who, for reasons of their own, did the dirty work. Almost three-fourths of the MFs held no office in the Nazi party, in striking contrast to the MPs and MFPs, of whom two-thirds and three-fourths, respectively, were in party offices. The MFPs, in particular, held more than their share of higher offices and special functions. On the other hand, the MFs had the highest proportion of respondents who immediately joined the SA stormtroopers (two-thirds) and of those who graduated to the SS (one-seventh). Nearly three-fourths of the MPs were in neither the SA nor the SS. The MFPs came close to the high involvement of the MFs, but tended to join the stormtroopers a year or more after they had entered the NSDAP. The MFs consequently held a lot of offices in the SA or SS, more than the MFPs, but they tended to be the lower offices of *Truppfuehrer* or *Rottenfuehrer*. The MFPs held just as many of the higher offices, such as *Sturmfuehrer* or *Sturmbannfuehrer*, and in addition a number of special organizing functions.

Although the MFPs held as many or more SA and SS offices, the MFs did far more of the fighting in streets and meeting halls. Only in the most intense category, campaigning and fighting "day and night" in 1932, did the MFPs have the edge over the MFs. We get the impression that even in political violence there was some stratification that assigned the common or garden variety of violence to the MFs, while the MFPs were involved in a more rarefied way. Their concern with ideology and proselytizing made them far from mindless, but rather men "with malice aforethought." They also tended to join the party first and warm up to the stormtrooper role only later. This makes their "day and night" fighting a climax of their extremist career, rather than just an increase in quantity of the same mindless slugging that seems to have attracted men to the MFs to begin with.

What did these various groups get out of their activities during the fighting years? The MFs derived their greatest satisfaction in the movement from the struggle itself and from the Hitler cult. The MFPs, instead, stressed the classless comradeship and, less strongly, the struggle, and the satisfaction of striving for utopia. Among the MPs, this utopian consciousness was quite dominant, although they also appreciated the classless comradeship of the movement. In this connection, it is worth juxtaposing all these satisfactions of Nazi membership to the grosser one of expecting a job or promotion as a reward. The latter expectation, interestingly enough, was highest among the mere Nazi members (about 10 percent) and lowest among the Ms, MPs, and MFPs (2-5 percent). The MFs included 8 percent with this expectation who evidently believed that they were entitled to something like a pension for their pains. To them, apparently, utopia was not enough.

Perhaps an experienced psychoanalyst could arrive at a better grasp of the respondents' personalities. The challenge of the available information proved to be too much for our approach. But there were a few meaningful questions we could ask of each case: 1. What were the formative experiences in the lives of the MFs, as compared to the other groups? They seemed to be the experience of youthful comradeship and educational or literary influences, two experiences the MFPs tended to share. Many MFs were also deeply impressed by an experience of social humiliation or unemployment, and so were many MPs. Otherwise, the MPs had been formed by the war and its aftermath. Many MFPs also projected alleged episodes with Jews or aliens as their formative experiences, which may well be a reflection of their ideological preoccupation.[13] 2. If we ask ourselves what

[13] The MFPs are the only one of these groups that had disproportionate numbers of unemployed or bankrupt members during the fighting and even before 1929, far more than the MFs or MPs who seem to have taken it harder.

was most abnormal about each of the cases, the MFs stand out with disproportionate numbers of very insecure, self-pitying respondents. Like the MFPs, the MFs also had many who seem to have had a great desire to merge their individuality with the movement. The MFPs also had more than their share of persons with an extreme case of leadership cult. The MPs, on the other hand, included disproportionate numbers of respondents who suffered high cultural shock in 1918 or exhibited extremes of irrationality or paranoia. Many MFs possessed a low ideological kind of understanding of politics. The MFPs and MPs, in this order, were considerably more perceptive in their grasp of Weimar politics. 3. In their personal lives, too, the groups differed markedly. The MPs, for example, tended to have their families and especially their spouses in the NSDAP. The MFPs often had the whole family in the party, a sign of the penetration of family life and marriages by the Nazi virus. The MFs, by contrast, seemed to be loners, for their family involvement lagged far behind the other groups. This is also the impression we get from their patterns of political friction. The MFs report in disproportionate numbers having been fired or boycotted (economic suicide), or having gone out of their way to seek out friction, which suggests a lack of social integration.

Here are some more or less typical MF cases. One was an illegitimate child, born in 1903 and raised by grandparents (no. 490), who had to work as a teenage dockworker to support them. He was pressured to join the union and, when he refused, life became difficult for him on the job. So he quit and volunteered instead in 1919 for the border protection units of the *Reichswehr*, which sent him to various places for action. When he returned to civilian life in 1924, he again encountered Communists and Socialists dominant in most employment situations, which greatly offended his patriotic soul.

The decisive change in my political view of the world occurred in 1932 after several NSDAP rallies when I met

239

my current *Obersturmfuehrer* (with the same name as respondent) at work, who had long served in the SS. This man got me so enthusiastic about the goals of the *Fuehrer* that I joined without hesitation. After an overwhelming rally in May 1932 I joined both the party and the SS in order to contribute to the realization of the ideals and goals of the *Fuehrer*.

The respondent had evidently found the father substitute he was looking for. "There ensued a time of plenty of battles and sacrifices. We dropped everything and rushed into the fray, taking the gaff and insults of the reds. They never had the guts to attack us few comrades physically. But I shall always remember the wonderful times when we broke up many an opposition rally or demonstration and chased them away."

Another young respondent, born 1907 (no. 488), witnessed at close hand the suppression of the Ruhr uprising of 1920 by the Freecorps von Epp and the French occupation of 1923, which was painful to him and his family. He emerged with a deep-seated hatred for the French and a strong aversion to the reds and the republican parties. Expelled to Kassel by the occupation, the respondent immediately joined the *voelkisch Jungsturm*, which offered him *voelkisch* indoctrination and military training. Years later, while studying agriculture, he became an agricultural trainee under another *Jungsturm* leader and rejoined. His new youth group, however, fell under the spell of an old Freecorps fighter who indoctrinated the boys and their leader with National Socialism. The entire group joined the stormtroopers in August of 1930.

And then we former *Jungsturm* men worked untiringly under and for the swastika banner. In rain or shine, with or without a speaker, we went into the villages every Sunday to make propaganda. From here many an SA *Trupp* and base and many an NSDAP local were started. I really hated to leave Prechtau when I changed jobs and went to Dortmund. Here I joined the SS and liked the service in it even better. It was harder, full of responsibility, and more dangerous, especially in the red industrial center where I did all kinds of things for the SS.

The commitment of the marcher-fighters was usually rather nonideological, but what they themselves would call "idealistic" and passionate. As one of them put it (no. 480, born 1910):[14]

A non-Nazi who has not experienced the enormous elementary power of the idea of our *Fuehrer* will never understand any of this. But let me tell these people as the deepest truth: whenever I worked for the movement and applied myself for our *Fuehrer*, I always felt that there was nothing higher or nobler I could do for Adolf Hitler and thereby for Germany, our people and fatherland. . . .

When I say so little in this vita about *my external life*, my job etc., this is only because *my real life*, the real content of my life is my work for and commitment to Hitler and toward a national socialist Germany. . . . Hitler is the purest embodiment of the German character, the purest embodiment of a national socialist Germany (italics added).

The last of the larger groups, the marcher-fighter-proselytizers (MFP), was the epitome of the Nazi storm against the established authorities. By origin heavily from highly mobile strata or rural-urban migrants, these men were living mainly in medium-sized towns of 2,000 to 100,000 residents. By occupation, blue and white-collar workers (one-half), business and professional people, and military-civil servants stood out among them. Military-civil service and artisans predominated among the occupations of their fathers. There were many respondents who were upwardly mobile (two-fifths), especially up from the city proletariat by means of a better education. Yet no other group was as hard hit by unemployment or bankruptcy before 1928 (22.5

[14] For further cases of MFs, see Merkl, *Political Violence*, pp. 397-401, and of MFPs, *ibid.*, pp. 403-407.

241

percent) and even more during the Depression (38.3 percent).[15] There is a parallel here to the social dynamics of revolution, as many historians and social scientists from Crane Brinton to James C. Davies and Ted Gurr have explained them.

This was also the sprouting dragon-seed of the last years of the war. Due to their youth, 55.6 percent of the MFPs, 67.6 percent of the Ms, and 58.9 percent of the MFs saw no military service. Disproportionate numbers of the MFPs viewed the war with disaffection after initial enthusiasm, but also with hostility toward the civilians and shirkers who would not "stick it out." They tended to blame the defeat on international Bolshevism. Many were youthful "victory-watchers" (born 1902-1905). Their fathers were often militaristic, *voelkisch*, or unpolitical, and their school environment was disproportionately reported as *voelkisch* or nationalistic. One out of eight had to go to work before he was fourteen years old, which adds deprivation and hard luck to the seeds of militarism and antisemitism.

The MFPs were highly involved in such groups as *Wehrwolf*, the bourgeois and left-wing poposition to the republic, *Stahlhelm*, *voelkisch* action groups, and the Freecorps. They were in the *voelkisch* parties, including the early NSDAP (23.4 percent), as well as in the DNVP, and in moderate parties. In 1923, too, they were more involved than the Ms and MFs, particularly in militant veterans' groups, other legitimate parties, and participating in or sympathizing with the beer-hall putsch in Munich. It is difficult to escape the conclusion that, unlike most other groups, the MFPs were political activists throughout the years of the unhappy republic.

When they finally joined the NSDAP, they stood out among those that founded or cofounded local organizations (two-fifths); they were at least a part of the first nucleus in their locality in proportions rivaled only by the older zealots,

---

[15] The averages for the entire sample are 16.2 percent before and 25.6 percent after 1929.

242

the MPs. Nearly half of them were at the time under twenty-five, and two-thirds were under thirty years of age. They were attracted chiefly by the stormtroopers' comradeship, and driven to join by their own ideological fervor.

Since the MFPs embodied all the essential qualities of effective members of an extremist movement, there is a special quality about many of the vitae, be they long or short. A good example is a young carpenter, born in 1908, the son of a bricklayer (no. 409), who told how during his apprenticeship he met and joined some young people who liked to go on "marching exercises into the environs every weekend singing soldiers' songs." The respondent was seventeen and greatly enthusiastic about the spirit of comradeship in this group. He "really liked the wonderful romantic life in nature," especially camping overnight. During these camping trips two older comrades who were already with the SS indoctrinated the boys with national socialism. "As soon as we had more or less mastered the basic ideas, they took us to NSDAP meetings. We got to know the faults of the other parties and the great idea of our *Fuehrer* and thus became political soldiers of the movement." In 1926 and part of 1927 the respondent served as a stormtrooper without having joined the party. Finally he was officially enrolled and began proselytizing.

> And so we were forever trying to recruit new members for our idea, which was particularly difficult because of the French occupation of the Palatinate. But we were not to be discouraged. We fought on with redoubled effort which soon bore fruits in the growth of the SA, despite some setbacks. . . .
>
> We were not spared brawls with people of different conviction and there was often a court trial afterwards. As our *Sturm* grew enough to be divided, we looked for a new hangout in the reddest part of town, in fact quite close to the Communist headquarters. . . . Since the Communists were so close there were often massive clashes, and we were exposed to many a danger.

243

Another MFP, a self-styled former Marxist and member of the "red" Metal Workers Union (no. 440, born 1898) related:

> Since I was full of the idea I began to spread it. Although it was slow going, I kept thinking back on my own political development which had pointed me in a different direction. It was relatively easy to convince young people and bring them into the party. But with their [older] relations it was often necessary to point out the faults of the other parties again and again and to make clear with all my energy the will and desire of national socialism. Our untiring proselytizing for the new view of the world thus created a movement which by its steady growth was bound to come to power some day.

In the Vortex of the Movement

In the broader context of German history and of the history of other countries, few aspects of the Nazi surge are as striking as its landslide character. Within a space of less than three years, from early 1930 to the end of 1932, the main surge of the Nazi vote and membership took place. The vote suddenly rose by a factor of seventeen from the 810,000 of 1928 to the 13.5 million of July 1932.[16] The membership of the NSDAP jumped by a factor of eight from 116,000 in December 1929 to an estimated 900,000 in December of 1932. The SA, finally, must have grown by a factor of about twelve to fourteen in the period in question, and then grew again in a huge surge that was powered by nationalist enthusiasm and opportunism after January of 1933. All this suggests that we look for the special qualities that may account for this veritable vortex of Nazi mania,

---

[16] The NSDAP declined by 2 million in the November elections, and there was an exodus of members. The renewed surge of the March elections of 1933 took place under conditions of terror and harassment as well as mass hysteria related to the *Reichstag* fire.

the self-accelerating nature of the movement, or the attitudes that might sustain such extraordinary growth.

One way of doing this is by tabulating the reasons that, according to their own statements, drove the Abel Nazis into the party (Table V-6). The stormtroopers and their leaders,

TABLE V-6 Reasons for Joining of Abel SA/SS and NSDAP (percent)

Reasons for Joining NSDAP	SA/SS	SA/SS Leaders	NSDAP Only
Friction with French occupation	5.6	6.8	.3
Unemployment, agricultural revolt	5.8	5.5	3.8
Repression by police, government	7.5	8.1	7.3
Rough opposition by KPD, etc. (including threat of red revolution)	7.0	5.1	6.7
Comradeship among stormtroopers, NSDAP	11.8	13.1	5.1
Dynamic impression of Hitler movement	18.9	16.9	31.2
Ideological fervor, antisemitism	43.4	44.5	45.5
Totals	100.0	100.0	100.0

as we can see, differed only in minor ways from the rest of the party, which was less likely to be motivated by the occupation, by unemployment, or by comradeship among the stormtroopers. The party members were more likely to be attracted by the dynamic impression of the Hitler movement, a factor we can estimate to have loomed largest also among the landslide voters of 1930 and 1932. Stormtroopers, leaders, and party had in common that they were moved by factors peculiar to the vortex of the rapidly expanding movement—the opposition of police and political opponents, the camaraderie of the movement, and, most of all, its "dynamic impression" and their own fervor—far more than they were moved by the French occupation or even unemployment.

To emphasize this point further, we can compare the reasons the Abel respondents gave for: 1. their first quasi-military involvement, 2. their first political activity, and 3.

joining the post-1924 Nazi party or one of its affiliates.[17] Quasi-military in this context means marching or fighting with Freecorps, *Stahlhelm, Jungdo,* and so on, while political activity signifies interest in parties and elections. Since we are dealing only with people who eventually joined the reconstructed party, the accelerating effect of the movement in the fighting years should be evident from the increasing concentration on movement-related rather than war-related or other environmental motives. The history of the Weimar Republic and the individual histories of the majority of the Abel respondents make this sequence a plausible one for their individual political development. Our Table V-7 shows indeed, how the war-related motives were soon replaced by motives central to the mushroom growth and virulence of the movement. The differences between stormtroopers and nonstormtroopers appear minor at the first glance. But with respect to the motives for the first quasi-military activity they are significant: the stormtroopers were more motivated by war and occupation, the rest of the party more by the desire to oppose the Marxist revolutionaries. The stormtroopers' motives to join the post-1924 movement still were more related to war and occupation, but by this time the nonstormtroopers differed mostly in that they were more impressed by the dynamism of the movement than the SA/SS members and leaders, who embodied much of this dynamism.

We also recorded the age at which the Abel respondents first engaged in these quasi-military or political activities in order to find out if there was a certain personality type in such movements that became "militarized" or "politicized" early in life and then might constitute the most violent core of the movement. We found that no fewer than two-fifths of the Abel respondents who were thus "militarized" or politi-

---

[17] Depending on the nature of their activities, of course, their first quasi-military activity may have been with the pre-1924 NSDAP or other *voelkisch* paramilitary groups, and their first electoral or other political activity likewise, though not at the same time.

TABLE V-7 The Shift to Movement-Related Motives for Joining, 1919-1933 (percent)

Motives for Joining	First Quasi-military Activity			First Political Involvement		Post-1924 NSDAP		
	SA/SS	SA/SS Leaders	NSDAP Only	SA/SS	NSDAP Only	SA/SS	SA/SS Leaders	NSDAP Only
Impact of war, defeat, occupation	43.1	40.6	34.4	14.0	23.2	5.6	6.8	.8
Shock of opposition to revolution, Marxists, friction with political enemies	39.8	44.8	46.5	37.6	29.9	7.0	5.1	4.4
Unemployment, economic troubles	—	—	—	11.9	7.2	5.8	5.5	4.0
Opposition to Weimar leaders, police repression	8.9	8.3	9.6	11.9	22.4	7.5	8.1	8.4
Ideological fervor, antisemitism	8.2	6.3	9.6 }	24.6 }	17.3 }	43.4	44.5	44.1
Dynamic impression of Hitler movement	—	—	—	—	—	30.7	30.0	38.3
Totals	100.0	100.0	100.0	100.0	100.0	100.0	100.0	100.0
Number	158	96	73	143	125	414*	236*	251*

* Multiple responses

cized" between the ages of twelve and seventeen turned up among the marcher-fighters (MFs) of the brown movement. One-third of those thus mobilized between eighteen and twenty and one-fourth mobilized between twenty-one and twenty-five turned out among the MFs. If they were mobilized any later in life, their chances of becoming MFs were small. To become a marcher-fighter-proselytizer (MFP), on the other hand, was a process requiring a noticeable upward shift in the ages of militarization and politicization, with a peak between eighteen and twenty-five and a dropping off only after the group of twenty-six to thirty-five year-olds. The upshot of this inquiry was that to be a mindless slugger of such a movement one had to start early, whereas the missionary fighter type was the product of a more mature genesis. The marcher-proselytizers (MPs), who were older, were scattered all over the age range from twenty-one to sixty in their period of militarization or politicization.

The fit between the Weimar chronology and the individual life cycles of the Abel respondents had a large effect on what they did when they joined the movement. This emphasizes once more the importance of a population bulge of rebellious youth in the later years of the republic in determining the violent nature and direction of the Nazi movement. Without this youthful revolt, Hitler would have remained a minor figure of Weimar politics and there would have been no Third *Reich* and, probably, no Second World War—and no holocaust.

Most Weimar stormtroopers (over two-thirds) joined the SA almost immediately after they joined the movement. They were evidently so highly motivated toward putting their bodies into the line of fire that, in their minds, the stormtroopers' role was the important one, not that of the party membership. Nevertheless, there were some (one-fifth) who first joined the party, and only after a year or more of political concerns decided to become active stormtroopers as well. The difference between these two groups,

248

from all the evidence available, was considerable.[18] The delay in most cases signified a process of gradual extremist escalation among upwardly mobile or middle-class respondents—the instant SA man tended to be working-class—spurred on by unemployment or radicalization for whatever reason. The delayed stormtroopers were generally more ideologically inclined, and presented ideological rationalizations of their violent behavior, whereas the immediate SA men felt none was required. At the other end of this scale of stormtrooper attitudes, there was the SS man, who was generally handpicked from among the most spontaneous of the stormtroopers in a ratio set at one to ten in the early thirties. The role of the SS was still that of a bodyguard and special squad under the Supreme SA leader (OSAF). We shall come back to its later role in the Third *Reich*.

This account would hardly be complete without some attention to how the stormtroopers were recruited, considering the broadly-gauged propaganda and proselytizing efforts of the NSDAP. If the Abel Collection is any guide, proselytizing person-to-person brought in less than a third of the total number of stormtroopers, and even less of the rest of the party (Table V-8). Of these persons recruited by proselytizers, only one in twelve of the SA/SS (but almost one in two of the other party members) was recruited by a relative, and even fewer by strangers. By far the greatest bulk, especially of the stormtroopers, were taken to a party meeting or rally by a friend or colleague who was already a member or sympathizer. This must have been the typical form of proselytizing. It may well be typical for the politics of industrial societies that politics is most often discussed at work and recruitment for new parties takes this route.[19] For the young stormtroopers who were unemployed

[18] For a detailed comparison between these immediate SA men and the delayed variety, see Merkl, *Political Violence*, pp. 585-593.

[19] This may be particularly important when a person encounters a party of political belief that differs from common political ground among the person's family.

249

TABLE V-8 Personal Introduction of Able SA/SS and NSDAP
(percent)

Personal Introduction to NSDAP	SA/SS	SA/SS Leaders	NSDAP Only
Proselytizing by a relative, friend, colleague, or stranger	32.5	29.6	28.8
Went to NSDAP rallies, saw marching, violence	27.2	38.3	35.6
Attracted by ideology, written propaganda	30.3	32.1	34.6
Totals	100.0	100.0	100.0
Number	290	162	188

or not yet working, friends or youth group chums may well have fulfilled the same function. In fact, about one out of six of those recruited by proselytizers reports that his youth group joined *in toto*.

A good third of all three groups joined the brown movement as a result of another kind of propaganda, that of Nazi demonstrations and rallies. The "closed formations" and street battles of the SA, the monster rallies with Nazi speakers, and the meeting-hall battles of the stormtroopers obviously bore the expected fruit. Uniforms, disciplined marching, flags, and quasi-military behavior may have been as attractive in this context as was witnessing the violent encounters with Communists and the *Reichsbanner*. Somewhat less than a third, at least among the SA/SS, were attracted by what they heard or read about Nazi ideology, presumably because they more or less shared it beforehand. This is the category that most people imagine to have been the chief or even the only way such a movement might recruit people. In fact, it is only one of several, and moreover, probably requires the presence of the other nationalistic groups of which these prospective Nazis had often been members or were well aware. It is a common misconception to think of the Nazi recruits as politically naive or ill-informed about Weimar politics. Most of them (with

250

the possible exception of the youngest stormtroopers) had a long record of participation in many other groups before they discovered the Nazi party.

Let us look at a few examples of the different kinds of personal introduction to the NSDAP. A typical rally-goer was a young clerk, born in 1910 (no. 4), whose political interest was stirred by the occupation of the Rhineland. He considered joining the *Stahlhelm* or *Jungdo* in his town, but found neither of them to his liking. The *Stahlhelm* was "not revolutionary enough," and *Jungdo* "lacking in the comradeship I considered necessary for a successful revolutionary struggle." Barely eighteen, he went from one party's rally to the next.

> One evening before the *Landtag* elections of 1929 I attended first a DNVP, then a Centrist, and finally an NSDAP rally. The speakers of the first two meetings came up with the usual fine words and comments about their programs, but I heard no tangible proposal on how we as a people could get out of our misery and return to honor. The speaker of the new movement, however, was quite different. I was swept along not only by his passionate speech, but also by his sincere commitment to the German people as a whole, whose greatest misfortune was being divided into so many parties and classes. Finally a practical proposal for the renewal of the people! Destroy the parties! Do away with classes! True *Volksgemeinschaft*! These were goals to which I could commit myself without reservation. The same night it became clear to me where I belonged: to the new movement. It alone gave hope of saving the German fatherland. Thus I entered the Hitler Youth and found what I had sought: real comradeship. . . . Soon I was appointed local leader (*Ortsgruppenführer*) of the NS *Schülerbund* (high-school students' federation) and experienced and led the fight in the front lines.

A mixed case of rally-going and introduction by a fellow worker was that of a gardener's son and apprentice, born in

1908 (no. 5), whose father was a superpatriot and bitter anti-Marxist. The son joined the DNVP youth and canvassed actively for the DNVP in the face of all kinds of friction at work. He also had a growing suspicion that his DNVP buddies, the "sons of the better families," were leaving all the dirty work to him. His apprenticeship completed, the respondent began to work in his parents' gardening business where an older employee, a pre-1924 Nazi, began to talk to him about the NSDAP. His DNVP friends always referred to the Nazis as "brainless fantasy-spinners." He still voted for the DNVP in 1929, even though its phrase-making seemed emptier and its "youth leaders" more aged every year. In the fall of 1929, he finally quit in disgust and swore never to join another party. But the excitement of the September elections of 1930 did not permit the respondent to remain aloof for long.

> Like most people I often went to election rallies, and also to a Nazi rally. The speaker of the evening, a well-known National Socialist of the Ruhr area, tore off the masks of all the parties from left to right with a ruthlessness that had no equal. This was too much for the police officer present, a Socialist of course, and he dissolved the meeting without a good reason. I was so incensed about this repression of opinion that I quickly decided to join at the end of the meeting.

An example of a person introduced by a close relative was an industrial clerk, born in 1901 (no. 15), who on occasion switched to blue-collar jobs because the pay was better. He had been raised by his devout, patriotic mother after losing his father at the age of three. Disillusioned with the war and the miserable food supply, he became interested in Socialist and Communist literature and joined a Communist trade union. The "excesses" during the workers' 1920 uprising in the Ruhr soured him on the Communists, but he still remained a pacifist and socialist for a number of years. In 1926 he first happened to hear about the NSDAP and to read a copy of the Nazis' *Voelkischer Beobachter*.

252

The contents were of great interest to me. They put into words what I felt inside. But the description of the SPD I found objectionable. I got so enraged, I put down the paper because it kept referring to the black-red-golden flag as black-red-and-*yellow*, which I regarded as very insulting and nasty. . . . When I saw the first SA men in uniform, I was just as unsympathetic as the rest of the populace. Much of this was due to the brown uniform, which reminded me of the Belgian occupation troops, and the cap, which looked like the Austrian army, an outfit not exactly known as great soldiers. People used to call these first Hitler men scornfully Comrade Laceboot (*Schnür-schuh*).

However, the respondent's attitude slowly changed because his younger brother (he had four older siblings) began to bring home Nazi propaganda material.

My younger brother, who had been with the *Marine-jugend*, became associated with this little [Nazi] circle and joined it after a short while. Every now and then he would bring me the *Voelkischer Beobachter* (VB) and invite me also to discussion evenings although I did not want to go. We often had vehement arguments about the contents of the VB. He also brought home various other pieces of Nazi literature which I read with great interest. Most of all, I was fascinated by the Jewish question, to which I devoted my attention. I acquired all kinds of tracts and countertracts to clarify the question in my mind, looked up passages in the Old Testament, transla-tions from the Talmud, and the *Protocols of the Elders of Zion* by Alfred Rosenberg [sic]. I compared past and present and finally broke with Marxism, Communism, and democracy.

His *Judenkoller* reached its climax after a turbulent left-wing rally at which the featured anti-Nazi speaker was a former SPD deputy allegedly convicted eleven times for morals offenses and accorded the status of *non compos mentis* by a court. Since the SPD still tolerated this man as a leader, the respondent turned away from it and attended his first NSDAP discussion evening.

A party comrade . . . spoke about Marxism and national socialism in such a vivid way that I realized that this was precisely the way I felt inside. When he declared that nationalism and socialism were not opposites but in reality one and the same, I was ripe for national socialism and joined the party. . . . I began to save money to buy the uniform I had once derided, and described to the weekly *Der Nationalsozialist*. I had the best comradely relations with the other party members. We eagerly discussed the Nazi ideology and became more and more firmly committed.

While the role of the respondent's younger brother was pivotal, this case has many other elements as well—the influence of Nazi propaganda literature, attending a Nazi meeting, and the background split between patriotic and socialist loyalties. Like other Socialists and Communists in the Abel collection, the respondent was alienated from the left by an outbreak of *Judenkoller*. There is also an air of the revival meeting in his description of the discussion evenings (*Sprechabende*) at which the members sought to strengthen each other's faith.

How are these different modes of introduction related to the three generations of early Nazis? By far the youngest group, with about half in the postwar generation, are those introduced by a friend or colleague. The group that was attracted by the propaganda and publicity had the largest number of members of the war generation (1894-1901) and, like those introduced by a relative, nearly half in the prewar generation (born before 1894).

Being recruited by rallies or demonstrations, on the other hand, was particularly frequent among inhabitants of rural areas, a fact that obviously reflects the impact of Nazi campaigning there. Those introduced by friends or fellow workers, by comparison, tended to live in small and larger towns (2,000-100,000). By occupation, both the rally-goers and those introduced by friends and colleagues were most often workers or pensioners. Those persuaded by the ideological propaganda were often military-civil servants, farmers, business or professional people, or white-collar workers. There were evidently class-related differences between going to an extremist political rally and being attracted by the ideology of the party: the former was more proletarian and the latter more typically bourgeois. Those introduced by relatives included disproportionate numbers of women, whose social contacts and freedom to attend rallies were probably limited.

In their patterns of social mobility, the typical rally-goer also turns out to have been in social decline or socially static —which may well have been the best condition to favor these occasions. Those who had been introduced by friends or colleagues were upwardly mobile from urban backgrounds or also in decline. Respondents attracted by the written propaganda tended to be upwardly mobile from either a farm or a city background.

We can also look at the process of personal introduction as part of the broader patterns of political participation. Attending rallies, reading propaganda leaflets, or joining a militant movement are all varieties of participational behavior. There were some striking relationships, for example, between patterns of youthful participation and the modes of personal introduction to the party. The respondents who were introduced by friends or colleagues were by far the most active before the age of twenty-six, having participated in partisan street fighting, electioneering, proselytizing, and in the Freecorps type of violence. They included many who were either politically militarized or hostile militants in their youth. Those who joined because of rallies and those introduced by relatives were much more apt to be the spectator type, with only moderate participation in demonstrations or individual provocation. Those susceptible to Nazi propaganda, again, showed a different if not unexpected paramilitary pattern. They tended to have

255

been involved in Freecorps or vigilante activities, or in voluntary military training groups.

The close link between work and activist politics, which came out in the many cases in which respondents were introduced to the party by fellow workers or in the pattern of proselytizing on the job, is a good reason to look closely at the youthful work settings. The rally-goers and those introduced by friends or colleagues reported the most friction on the job, often with disastrous consequences. They often lost their livelihoods during the Depression. Those who were susceptible to propaganda, by comparison, tended to experience a friendly work environment. Since they were older, their economic troubles usually took place before 1929 or not at all.

Even the ideological attitudes of the various introduction groups differ substantially. Respondents introduced to the party by friends or colleagues, for example, tended to have antisemitism or superpatriotism as their main ideological motives. The rally-goers, by way of contrast, were mostly revanchists, Nordic-German romantics, and, incidentally, anti-Marxists. Those introduced by relatives were frequently Hitler worshipers, which goes with their evidently restricted social contacts outside the family.[20] Those attracted by the propaganda, finally, tend to be solidarists, revanchists, or superpatriots. They tend to be particularly hostile to "reactionaries"—which also fits into their military-civil servant background.

What do these unexpected differences signify? Evidently the activists introduced by friends or fellow-workers were attracted to the party largely by their own virulent superpatriotism and antisemitism. On the antisemitism scale, in-

[20] Most of those introduced by a relative had their entire family in the party, while those introduced by a friend or colleague tended to pursue their politics by themselves or, like the respondents attracted by propaganda, had their spouses in it, too. Thus the mode of introduction also relates to the degree of general social integration of a respondent. For statistical breakdowns, see Merkl, *Political Violence*, pp. 569-578.

256

deed, they turn out to have the largest percentage of paranoids who speak of conspiracies and threats. The rally-goers
were a good deal more conventional, with their vintage
revanchism, anti-Marxism, and *voelkisch* romanticism.
These three elements frequently showed up in Nazi
speeches and evidently constituted what the NSDAP meant
to the audiences. From this description, it is hardly surprising to find that those who were introduced to the party by
friends or fellow-workers were more often in the SA or SS
and engaged in political violence than anyone else. Those
attracted by the ideological propaganda, by way of contrast, had the largest share of party offices, including many
at the level of *Ortsgruppenleiter.* Being socially middle-
class or at least white-collar and ideologically committed,
they were far ahead in this respect of the more proletarian
but passive rally-goers.

Third Reich Careers

Having surveyed the history of the Weimar stormtroopers,
the reader may well wonder what became of them after the
Abel vitae break off in 1933-1934. While the stormtrooper
movement was obviously pivotal in helping Hitler to attain
and consolidate his power, it also was purged and finally
decapitated and demoted to a position of insignificance
after 1934. Did many of the old fighters manage to overcome this crisis and make a career in the Third *Reich* they
had fought for? What kind of careers did they attain? Many
of the Abel respondents sounded so sincere and harmless
that it seemed difficult at first to associate them with the
monstrous misdeeds of the Third *Reich.* Since an attempt
to locate and reinterview surviving Abel respondents after
nearly forty years was unlikely to be worth the effort and
expense, we decided instead to look up as many as were
identifiable in the NSDAP membership files in the Berlin
Document Center.[21] It was our hope that the information

---

[21] Acknowledgment for this work is due to Horst W. Schmollinger

on the Third *Reich* careers of the Abel respondents might shed some light on the question of what kinds of early Nazis tended to make what kind of career in the totalitarian state.

As was to be expected, the information in the membership catalog had a good many limitations due to poor record-keeping and an obvious lack of interest by the party in certain kinds of information. There was no record, for example, of any private wealth acquired by an old fighter as a result of his past record and, perhaps, from the expropriation of the property of Jews and political opponents. The party evidently was not interested in recording information about a member's property or even his career in private industry. To complicate matters, we had to identify each case by a handwritten name and date of birth, with the result that about one out of ten of the Abel respondents could not be positively identified in the membership file. One-third of the respondents' files gave no clear evidence of whether they had or had not benefited from their pre-1933 involvement. One out of seven showed no unusual advancement,[22] and another one out of ten had died or been expelled for generally nonpolitical reasons by 1945. All told, less than a third of the Abel respondents and even fewer of the stormtroopers (one-sixth) could clearly be shown to have made an unusual Third *Reich* career out of their early membership.[23]

As careers go, the party careers were hardly spectacular, for the old fighters were always up against stiff competition from waves of better-educated opportunists who el-

of the Institute of Political Science at the Free University of Berlin. For further details, see Merkl, *Political Violence*, pp. 634-638.

[22] By definition, "unusual advancement" required judgments regarding normal advancement in a line of work.

[23] In this context, it is important to note that about one hundred cases of the original Abel Collection were requisitioned by the FBI in 1950 and never returned. No reason was given, but it seems likely that these were prominent cases involved in denazification proceedings.

bowed their way into the party offices. Our tabulation shows, furthermore, that these party careerists tended not to have been in the SA or SS (Table V-9). The one-fourth

TABLE V-9   Third *Reich* Careers of Abel SA/SS and NSDAP
(percent)

Third Reich *Careers*	SA/SS	SA/SS Leaders	NSDAP Only
Party career	28.6	24.7	55.1
Administrative career	24.8	25.8	39.1
Enforcers	46.6	49.5	5.8
Totals	100.0	100.0	100.0

each of the stormtroopers and their leaders who did make party careers tended to hold offices in the various NSDAP auxiliaries, including the post-1934 SA and its affiliates. A high office in the latter or in the Nazi Motor Corps (NSKK) hardly held the promise and status of its equivalent in the pre-1933 SA. The administrative careers, by comparison, were often far more remarkable, as people of very limited education and low-status employment took advantage of the purges of "politically unreliable" or "racially objectionable" civil servants in 1933. A former bricklayer, born in 1897 (no. 258), a technical employee in 1933, for example, was a *Regierungsbauinspektor* in 1934. A former teacher, born in 1894 (no. 404), vaulted into the state school administration as a *Kreisschulrat* in 1934 and then, by a circuitous route of party offices such as *Kreisleiter*, became the appointive lord mayor of a large city. A lowly bank employee, born in 1893 (no. 272), became a civil servant (*Regierungsinspektor*) in the Ministry of Economics, and during the war, in 1942-1943, got himself transferred to the Office Rosenberg in Rome. A mere party member holding no office in 1933 might make *Ortsgruppenleiter* by 1942 (see no. 56, born 1897), when some of his more able-bodied rivals were already in the war. By comparison, those who had acquired such offices prior to 1933 received these offices much sooner

259

after their entry into the party. This is even true of women, such as a long-time stalwart of the People's party (DVP) born 1894 (no. 44), who joined the NSDAP in mid-1930, became *Ortsgruppenleiterin* in a metropolitan area within the same year, and held this office until 1937. Such early office-holders often increased their further chances of advancement by a judiciously timed entry into the SS. One *Ortsgruppenleiter* of 1928-1930, born in 1908 (no. 389), for instance, joined the SS in March 1933, rose to the rank of sergeant by 1935, and thus moved on to director of the *Kreisleitung* and the appointive position of a city council-man of a large town.

Of the three careers, the enforcers of the totalitarian state naturally command our special attention in spite of their small numbers (forty-two). We counted as enforcement careers functions in the Gestapo, SS (pre-1939), SD, and RSHA, concentration camp guards, and occupation police,[24] which were all recorded in the membership file in Berlin. Some careers with the domestic police that were not clearly identifiable as related to the Nazi terror were listed with the administrative careers instead. Let us compare the blood-hounds of the Third *Reich* with the other careerists and with those not ascertained or with the motley group of those who died, made no noticeable gains, or were expelled. The youngest by far, with well over one-half in the postwar generation, were the enforcers of the terror. Their average age was about twenty-nine in 1933, in or about the victory-watcher cohort, and hardly any of them were over forty. The administrative and party careerists, by comparison, had only one-third in the postwar generation and an average age of about thirty-five in 1933. Both careerist groups tended to be military-civil servants or white-collar workers, as would seem to be appropriate for careers in various kinds of

[24] The abbreviation *Gestapo* denotes *Geheime Staatspolizei*; SD, *Sicherheitsdienst*; and RSHA, *Reichssicherheitshauptamt*. "Occupation police" refers to the police function in the occupied areas in the east, which was deeply involved with the rounding up of Jews and political enemies.

bureaucratic organizations. The enforcers of the terror, however, were mostly blue-collar workers or farmers—a fact that, perhaps, made them more ready for the dirty work. Both kinds of careerists, as we would expect, were upwardly mobile, especially from the urban proletariat. The terrorists, on the other hand, tended to be in social decline, or had never attempted to rise. There appears to be a strong causal link between their kind of sociopathic destructiveness and social decline or stagnation in the midst of an upwardly mobile society.

There are several other such marks of Cain on the enforcers. More than any other group, they tended heavily to have lost their fathers before reaching the age of eighteen (32.3 percent). Many also lost their jobs or livelihoods during the Great Depression (38.6 percent), which might explain their readiness for any career available. They exhibited the greatest propensity (72.1 percent) not to indicate any religious affiliation, although this was not much more than the party careerists. Neither one of these groups, it seems, was in the vanguard of the defense of Christianity against Communism. In their educational level, finally, the enforcers were mostly of very modest attainments. While nearly half of the administrative careerists and a third of the party careerists had completed a secondary education (*mittlere Reife*), this was true of only one-fifth of the enforcers. It becomes painfully clear what kind of person tended to go into the enforcement activities of the totalitarian state. Callow youths with minimal education, who grew up without a father and without religious commitment; workers or farmers, with families in social decline or foundering in the Depression, they had no higher ambition than to subject some of their less fortunate contemporaries to the regime of terror. With the rise of the dregs of society to the top, the Nazi revolution had taken on its most characteristic meaning.

The youth group background of the different groups of Nazi careerists gives us some clues to their later development. The people who made a career of party office tended heavily to come from the *Bismarckjugend* (DNVP), the *voelkisch* DHV, *Jungdo*, or liberal (DVP, DDP) youth groups, including those of the Youth Movement. Many of them belonged to *voelkisch* youth groups long before they became Nazis. The ideological, mainly *voelkisch* emphasis was pronounced from the very beginning. The administrative careerists came from a wider range of youth organizations, including paramilitary groups, the DNVP and DHV youth, and religious or unpolitical associations. The enforcers of the terror, finally, came largely from paramilitary (including the Freecorps) and left-wing youth, such as the Red Front or SAJ, or they had joined the SA or Hitler Youth (HJ) directly.

What were the attitudes of these respondents toward their youth groups? The enforcers predictably liked political violence and marching best, and "unnational views" or a lack of a social conscience the least. The left-wing converts among them account for their concern for social conscience. The administrative careerists also liked violence best, but they also liked hiking, cultural appreciation, and a spirit of comradeship. They expressed a dislike for class-struggle slogans and for a lack of political direction and violent action. There appears to have been a distinctively military attitude about this group. The party careerists, finally, preferred hiking and cultural appreciation in the true *voelkisch* style, as well as marching with a sense of ideological direction. Their dislikes centered on a lack of social conscience and on the ideology of particular youth leaders.

The prospensity for violence of the enforcers expressed itself early in their lives. A good one-third of them were involved in partisan street fights or meeting-hall brawls, and another fifth in the Freecorps type of violence before they were twenty-six.[25] The party careerist typically engaged more often in proselytizing and electioneering when they

[25] The party men had one-fourth in partisan and one-sixth in Free-corps-type violence, the administrators one-fifth and one-eighth, respectively.

262

were young, while the administrative careerists were mostly in military training groups as their most extreme youthful activity. In their political youth postures, therefore, over two-fifths of the enforcers could be classified as politically militarized, while the party careerists were most often fully politicized youths or political romantics, probably of the *voelkisch* type. All three groups had more than their share of hostile militants, especially the enforcers (one out of six). Political militarization thus seems to have been the process often leading to a career as enforcer, while early politicization or political daydreaming was more likely to lead to a party career. The office-holding style of the party man also differentiated itself early from the violent, militarized style of politics. As many as half of the party careerists had already held an office in their youth organization, but only a third of the administrative careerists and enforcers had done so.

The Bloodhounds of Adolf Hitler

Let us take a closer look at some of the vitae of enforcers who were especially groomed by the Third *Reich* for careers in terrorist enforcement. One of the purposes of concentration camp brutality, from the very beginnings under SS *Obersturmbannfuehrer* (Lieutenant Colonel) Theodor Eicke at Dachau, was to toughen the SS guards. Eicke regarded Dachau as "his school" and, indeed, one of his early pupils there was ex-Freecorpsman Rudolf Hoess, the later commandant at Auschwitz. His notions of the education of an SS man in impersonal, systematized brutality were shared by Himmler and Heydrich, who frequently expressed their conviction that this experience was a most desirable one.[26] There are a number of concentration camp guards and the like in the Abel Collection who are worth a closer look.

One example is the son of a peasant, born in 1891 (no.

[26] See esp. Helmut Krausnick et al., *Anatomy of the SS-State* (New York: Walker, 1968), pp. 429-446.

263

444), who served in the prewar army and felt great patriotic enthusiasm in 1914. Gravely wounded in 1915, he emerged partly invalid. He had no comment on the German defeat, but viewed the "revolution" as a Marxist plot to expunge *voelkisch* traditions. He was with the DNVP until that party, too, became too "liberal-capitalistic" for him. Much of his venom is reserved for the "Marxist and Jesuitic press" and its calumnies regarding the NSDAP, which he eventually discovered as just right for him "as a peasant at the southwest border of Germany . . . related to the people and the soil by my blood."

In 1928, he began to fall under the spell of the Nazis and their appeal to "our arch-German, undistorted peasant sense." He joined in 1930, after two years of bankruptcy and fellow-traveling with the movement. A year later he helped to found an SS *Sturm*, and from then on his energies were completely absorbed in fighting and propagandizing. He gives a long list of alleged harassments and false accusations by the police, beginning with a charge of resisting a police officer "because I had stopped the police from working over a comrade." It was always the police or the Communists who were at fault. In 1932 he and others were wanted by the police and, after thirteen weeks, "betrayed, caught, and jailed." A court sentenced him to five months for breach of the peace "because I and some SS men went to help other comrades who were threatened by the Marxists." On another charge of rioting, the prosecutor wanted to put him in prison for twelve years of hard labor, but the court decided on three years of jail, "because I had straightened out a police officer who had searched my house, while I was in hiding, for insulting my wife and being disorderly." He was saved by the amnesty of December 1932.

After the 1933 elections, he wrote: "Today there are only a few people, either of alien blood or dedicated to nothing but money who still oppose us and our idea. It will be our task in the future, in loyal and unquestioning obedience, and with pure National Socialist will, to stand by the side

264

of the *Fuehrer, ready to strike* so that these people cannot do as they please" (italics added). In 1934, the respondent was a *Haupttruppfuehrer* of the SS. As the membership file discloses, ten years later he was an *Obersturmfuehrer* (first lieutenant)—no spectacular advancement. But his skills of violence had brought him to the SS Death's Head unit in Dachau.

Another case is that of a worker and worker's son (no. 369, born 1893), who also served with dedication in the war. He gave no details about his life before 1926, when a Nazi rally persuaded him to join. Subsequently,

> as an SA man I participated in many battles. It was particularly hard to hold a meeting in Fuerstenwalde. Only at about the tenth try did we thirty to fifty Nazis manage to survive the onslaught of hundreds of Marxists and Communists. The Marxists did not seem to understand that we were fighting not only for a better Germany, but also for a freer lot for the worker.

The respondent casually mentioned a time when he and a couple of SS comrades broke up an SPD rally. His record lists him as a *Rottenfuehrer* (corporal) in 1939 and, from 1943, as a member of the SS Guard Battalion of Sachsenhausen.[27]

While these men were older than most of the enforcers, there were plenty of younger ones to compare. There was, for example, the son of a village blacksmith, born in 1904 (no. 306), who completed the *Abitur* but could not go to a university because inflation wiped out the family's savings. The Ruhr invasion of 1923 politicized him and he belonged to the *Wehrwolf* from 1923 until 1925. He fondly remembered his days with this group, which took him to flag consecrations and German Days all over the region. "The comradeship was great. Politically, we were nationalistic

[27] See also no. 478, another enforcer of the Death's Head *Sturmbann* Sachsenhausen, who in 1940 was a SD *Hauptsturmfuehrer* and in 1944 held the same rank with the SS in the *Volksdeutsche Mittelstelle* of Cracow.

and monarchistic. But the *Wehrwolf* movement, after a brilliant rise in 1923-1924, began to decline in the whole Reich and in my area. At fault was the lack of political direction."

In 1925, a *Wehrwolf* leader and former Freecorps officer from a neighboring town took his group and the respondent into the NSDAP. Two cousins of his had already traveled the same route. The respondent, a bank clerk, had just been dismissed as a consequence of an audit by "a Jewish auditor" in the central office in Berlin, which awakened his mind to "the Jewish problem." He began to read Nazi literature and to set his faith in "the unconditional, goal-conscious policies of Hitler." He told very little of his early fighting years except that it was "very hard" to increase the membership until the 1930 elections. In that year, the respondent moved to Berlin, where he had found a new bank job, and immediately joined the SA. The electoral campaigns of 1932 were accompanied by many meeting-hall battles and SA service nearly every night. The respondent described one major battle, taking care to stress that "the Communists provoked us in the first place." He also related how, during the suppression of the SA, his unit became the Brandenburg Sports Club and merrily went on with their drills. He concluded with a word about how "the movement began its storm after the seeming setback of the elections of November 1932 in January . . . and pushed open the gates to power on that historical January 30, 1933." He went on to make a career with the SS, which took him to the position of a *Hauptsturmfuehrer* (captain) in Auschwitz in 1940 and to a high rank with the SS Economic Administration, looting Hungary in 1944.

Of similar age was the son of a locomotive engineer, born in 1904 (no. 422), who well represents the mindless hostility typical of many young Nazis in the collection. He was in the underground against the occupation, "like so many patriotic Germans." He met and admired members of the *Bund Oberland* and also heard about the Hitler movement which, to his mind, embodied "German manhood (*Manneszucht*) and comradeship, unlike the republican outfits." The failure of the beer-hall putsch put an end to his efforts to join the Nazis. But as soon as party and SA were once more available, in 1925, the respondent joined both. He gave no details about his activities with the SA or, after 1930, with the SS except to say that he always fought "in the foremost line." In 1933 he was a *Sturmfuehrer* (lieutenant). After 1941 he became a leader of the SS Guard Battalion South East.

Another young respondent, born in 1903 (no. 469), was a victory-watcher who commented on his mother's strictness while her husband was away in the war. He learned farming from his father, and later had to go to help him periodically because of the old man's war injuries. He also learned to drive heavy equipment, an ability that stood him in good stead until 1930 when he lost his job on an estate in Mecklenburg. As he reports, in 1929 he "had to belong to the *Reichsbanner*" for six months to keep his job. In 1932, he joined the SS, but he does not say a word about his activities there. Being unemployed left him free for stormtrooper service, and he received no other job until, in April 1933, the Nazis gave him a factory job. They also put him through an SS leadership training program of six weeks, after which he was made an SS *Oberscharfuehrer* (sergeant first class). In 1936 he joined the SS Guard Commando in the SS Camp Koenigstaedt.

A number of the original vitae (such as nos. 214, 226, 557, and 559) mention how SA and SS members were made auxiliary policemen the moment the Nazis took over. Their function involved rounding up political opponents of the pre-1933 struggles, mostly Communists and Socialists, into the new political jails and concentration camps. A clerk, born in 1893 (no. 426), who had an extremely violent record before 1933, told revealing details about their activities in this connection. He had already collected all kinds of inside information on the local KPD by pretending he was going to defect.[28] When the SS there became part of the auxiliary police, the respondent and his stormtrooper gang carried out unauthorized searches and seizures with such abandon that the local police was cowed into cooperation. The arrested KPD leaders were at first compelled to carry out such assignments as removing old election posters in public places. The respondent wrote:

This gave me an opportunity, by means of small favors and gifts, to win some of those who were of weak character. I got one released from protective custody who then did good work for us. Even before that we had already tracked down SAP people distributing the paper Spartakus. . . . These people were all arrested and have since been sentenced.[29]

In June 1933 my informer led me to newly organized Communist cells which were totally captured and interned. We also found a group distributing the red *Berliner Zeitung* and they were also taken to [the concentration camp] Oranienburg.

The respondent's talents in this detective work—in his words, "my successes during the revolution"—were rewarded with a criminal police job. The violent stormtrooper bully became a police officer. His membership file lists him as an SS *Obersturmbannfuehrer* (lieutenant colonel) in 1944 without further indication of where and how he served the SS state.

Another testimonial of 1933 is from a teacher and war invalid, born in 1897 (no. 199), who delights in gory hints about "the bloody year of 1932." His account is all too typical of the self-serving reasoning underlying the violence of the takeover:

[28] See also no. 162, who hints at some undercover work among the Communists for the SS.

[29] The SAP (*Sozialistische Arbeiterpartei*) was a radical SPD offshoot of which Willy Brandt was briefly a member before fleeing to Scandinavia.

It is my firm conviction that we old fighters would have paid with our lives, had the Communists won power instead of us. . . . Now that it was our revolution that had come we could easily have paid the political enemy back [sic] in the same coin. But nothing of the kind happened in our suburb. We did not touch a single Communist, which surprised them more than anybody. . . . They associated streets aflame and rolling heads with a revolution. . . . But many of them interpreted this treatment as weakness and their propaganda began to show up again here. We had to hit them harder. One morning in November 1933, when everybody was going to work, the police had blocked off the roads and sixty former Social Democrats and Communists, including all their former leaders, had to go to the Police Presidium. Some returned after a few days; others had to go for several weeks to the concentration camp.

It is refreshing to hear at least some early Nazis acknowledging the SA terror, which in 1933 alone led to the detention of at least 60,000-75,000 political enemies.[30] The respondent allegedly helped to take care of some of the families of inmates, and claimed that they were all back in a month or two. There also were some SS men who acknowledged having been employed, often after prolonged unemployment, as auxiliary policemen in the concentration camps of Dachau or Oranienburg (for example, no. 474, born 1900). Such early concentration camp duty does not appear in the membership files. The membership file also fails to disclose the SS membership and rank of another case (no. 162, born 1886), who told how he participated in the executions of June 30, 1934.

The careers within the SS, if we consider only rank, often evolved faster than in the party organization because of the rapid growth of the SS after 1933. It was never again as fast

[30] See Bracher, *The German Dictatorship*, p. 358, and the description of the early mass arrests, terror, and concentration camps in Hans Buchheim et al., *Anatomy of the SS-State*, pp. 400-420.

269

a road from SS man to *Sturmfuehrer* (lieutenant) as it had been during the fighting years, when a man could, under favorable circumstances, build up his own *Sturm* within a period of one to two years. An old fighter joining the SS in 1938 might make it by 1941 (no. 450, born 1906). To get from the lowest rank to that of *Sturmbannfuehrer* (major) might take as long as a decade (see no. 421, born 1898; no. 475, born 1900; and no. 427, born 1893). A pre-1933 *Sturmfuehrer* could be a *Gruppenfuehrer* (general) by 1938 (no. 443, born 1902), or by 1939 (no. 385, born 1906), or by 1942, a time of rapidly widening opportunities in the top ranks of the Armed SS (no. 462, born 1896). To rise to such heights from the lowest rank after 1933 was evidently helped greatly by membership in the Security Service (SD), the secret police watching SS and party members (no. 440, born 1898).[31]

The SS and *Gestapo* (Secret State Police) were among the organizations specifically proscribed in the war crime and denazification proceedings after the war. They and later services such as the SD, the SS Special Commandos, the new Office of the Chief of the German Police (Himler), and the RSHA (Reich Security Office) were the hub of the Nazi police state, of the coercive system at the heart of the Third *Reich*.[32] There was some objection at the time of the denazification trials that a person should not be considered guilty for merely having belonged to the SS, but only for specific acts of wrongdoing. Considering the solidarity and mobility among the SS members, the deaths of victims, and the confusion of the times, such acts were rarely proven or even known beyond a small circle. Among the enforcers of the Abel Collection, the membership file in the Berlin Document Center often listed very incriminating assignments that we shall examine more closely below. But

[31] This respondent, a lathe worker, was an SS *Truppfuehrer* in 1933 and became an SS general in the SD main office as early as 1939.

[32] See esp. Bracher, *The German Dictatorship*, pp. 350-362, and Buchheim et al., *Anatomy of the SS-State*, pp. 172ff.

there were also SS men with no such entries or with entries suggesting a different order of wrongdoing, if any.

A case of this latter sort was a young traveling salesman, born in 1900 (no. 526), who complained about having had a mean stepmother since the age of ten and about losing his father, a bookkeeper, in the war seven years later. He was drafted at the same time as many unwilling Socialist recruits, but never saw any action. After the war, the respondent served some time with the *Buergerwehr* and as a *Zeitfreiwilliger*. Through a "noble Communist" friend he was also exposed to the writings of Rosa Luxemburg, Karl Liebknecht, and Ernst Toller. At every election until 1929, the respondent related, "in his confusion" he voted for a different party. In 1929, while he was unemployed, he went to a big Nazi rally and was immediately captivated by a Goebbels' speech.

> It was as if I had heard the gospel. Politically completely neutral, I immediately awakened to the significance of the idea and found what I had always been looking for: justice and progress. Justice in the socialist demands of the program toward the workers whose bitterness I had gotten to understand. . . . Progress in awakening the natural forces of personality and race. . . .
>
> It was fighting time! I had a goal and, being unemployed, I could devote myself completely to party work.

He became an SA man and propaganda assistant, and served nearly every night at one rally or the other. He comments on this service: "We SA men of that period were, of course, no saints, but we never resorted to one thing: we never broke the discipline to tolerate in our midst elements who were in it only for the adventure. For we were no mercenaries (*Landsknechte*) but political soldiers fighting for a new view of the world which was to unite our whole people and lead them into a better future."

In October of 1930, the respondent graduated to the SS, which he described as "on the average the best-selected

271

material of men available in Germany in a special organization for certain tasks and with rigorous discipline." When
he completed his vita for Abel, he was an SS *Sturmfuehrer*.
By 1941, according to the Berlin files, he had become an
Obersturmbannfuehrer (lieutenant colonel) in the staff of
the SS Main Office. The last entry identifies him as a film
director and producer with the Ufa, Tobis, and Terra com-
panies and a functionary of the *Reichsfilmkammer*. Thus
the menace of his black SS uniform with the officer's insignia
was probably confined to the starlets of the motion picture
sets.

But there are many others whose SS or other enforcement career ends with more ominous entries. There was,
for example, a druggist from Silesia, born in 1905 (no. 522),
who found all parties, right and left, distasteful until the
Nazi landslide of 1930 swept him up. He began to read
the *Voelkischer Beobachter, Mein Kampf*, and other Nazi
propaganda, and soon joined the NSDAP. He claimed having witnessed "the fury and meanness of the Marxist rabble and its helpers" during an alleged assault by the "Moscow disciples" on an SA man. He also accused the police of
having deprived the injured man of available medical assistance. Then he told of an attack of "the *Reichsbanner*
hordes" on his SA home, which received such "a hearty
reception" that it was not repeated. According to the
respondent, it was always the others, the "hordes," that
attacked.

He began to proselytize among friends and fellow-
workers and recruited the majority of the eighteen employees of his company before his superiors, allegedly a
Freemason and a left-winger, followed up on "Jewish
accusations" and fired him. He went to live with his parents
and, after his father's death, joined the SS. His record in
the party files indicates that he joined the Gestapo late in
1933 and eventually became a *Kriminalsekretaer* with this
organization in occupied Poland. In 1944, he also served
with the Reich Security Office (RSHA) as an *Untersturm-
fuehrer* of the SS.

Another case was a gardener, born in 1905 (no. 466), the son of a furniture manufacturer and at seventeen a member of the Red Hundreds. After a clash between his Red Hundreds and the *Voelkisch* Hundreds, the respondent was irresistibly attracted by the latter and their swastika banner. He began to study *voelkisch* propaganda, including Fritsch's *Handbook of the Jewish Question*, and joined the *voelkisch* squads. His account of his years as a stormtrooper was a series of descriptions of inspiring moments presented in the special inspirational style typical of some Nazi propagandists. He also spoke of a "common front against the Jews and the lower races" and the "final victory of the Germanic tribes." His account of violent encounters depicted the *Reichsbanner*, the Communist, and the police as the aggressors, even "animal-like murderers," but with fewer undertones of hidden brutality than the previous case. His wife was also an "old fighter" of the movement. In 1934, he was already an SS *Sturmhauptfuehrer* (captain). Ten years later he was a *Sturmbannfuehrer* (major) of the Armed SS in a special section on police affairs with one of the regional Higher SS and Police Chiefs. His inspirational preaching evidently masked a terrorist mind.

A third case of the same generation was a plumber, born in 1904 (no. 59), who at the age of nine lost his father. His Catholic mother raised him to religious devotion, and he joined a Catholic young men's association. Under the influence of a meeting of the *voelkisch-sozialer Block* and his own antisemitic disposition, however, he soon found himself isolated among his Catholic fellows, and left the group. His experiences in the militant Metal Workers Union during a wildcat strike also were a great disappointment, in spite of enthusiastic beginnings. He quit the union and claims always to have done well in negotiating with employers by himself. In 1923, the respondent and a friend fell under the spell of a young Nazi who had been expelled from the occupied area and who supplied them with information about the movement in Bavaria. Another Nazi swore them to secrecy and asked them to be ready for the call of Novem-

273

ber 9 that never came. The next day, the newspapers told about the abortive beer-hall putsch.

The respondent was far more ideologically committed and politically active from an earlier date than most enforcers. After 1923, he helped to form a Nazi front, *Treubund*, and got into violent encounters with the local "rabble." After a short stint with the *Reichswehr*, he went back to work among Socialists and Centrists, and attempted to propagandize the cause at work. Since the *Treubund* had been outlawed, too, he and his friends founded a *Stahlhelm* chapter in 1927, but after about a year the respondent moved away. In 1931, he lost his job just as the Nazis were coming to his town. A rally that ended in a wild melée with Communists, Socialists, and the police battling an SS team finally induced the respondent to join the party and the SS.

> Now the fight started in [this city]. We found some more men and women to form a local. When we were planning another meeting at the end of October, we were prepared to give the Reds something to think about in case they wanted to disrupt our meeting. . . . I was living with my brother who wanted to throw me out so he would not have to put up with the danger of being accosted by the Reds. . . . My relatives were particularly mad at me, since they all belonged to the Center party, except for my brothers. My uncle once refused to eat for three days because I had sullied the family name by marching at the head of an SA demonstration. At the unemployment office it was like running the gauntlet, being the only SS man who needed unemployment benefits. Rocks were frequently flung at me from behind and from dark corners.

By the beginning of 1932, the respondent was already heading his *Sturm*. He told of the comradeship and togetherness in the movement. But he also told of "the terror of police and government against us":

> In January 1933, a comrade from the edge of town asked me to see him home because he was threatened by about

274

twenty Communists. I went with him until he was safe. Now the toughs cornered me as I reentered the town. I defended myself and knocked one down with a heavy wrench. The police appeared and took me down to the station, where the wrench was called a weapon. I was sentenced to four days in jail. But I need not have worried for . . . our *Fuehrer* Adolf Hitler became *Reich* Chancellor a few days later. . . . Our erstwhile enemies went into hiding for fear of our revenge.

This respondent joined the police in 1934, and soon began to work for Himmler's Reich Commissariat for Strengthening German Folkdom (RKFDV), which was entrusted with shuffling about the various ethnic minorities in the east. He became an RKF Commissar in Poland and an SS *Obersturmfuehrer* of the Armed SS in 1943. His advancement appears to have been slower than that of other enforcers.

The Mark of Cain

These three cases show certain common features, such as early involvement in extremist violence. Evidently, the most violent pre-1933 stormtroopers simply went on to enforcement roles in which they could further indulge in brutality. They all tended to see their violent encounters in masochistic terms, that is, with the antagonists always the aggressors. Frequently, their fathers had died prematurely, were absent, or were at odds with their sons. And there was usually a long record of previous involvement in extremist politics that prepared the respondent, stage by stage, as it were, for the hostility and militant attitude he showed as a violent stormtrooper and later as an enforcer of the Third *Reich*.

When we compare the political development of the three career groups systematically, the differences become even clearer. Already in childhood, the enforcers had a very high number of orphans or children growing up away from the parents, while the other careerists came mostly from eco-

275

nomically secure homes. All three reported a large share of disciplinarian fathers (up to one-fifth), but the enforcers stand out with extreme expressions of hostility toward the police and government, and with their Hitler cult. The identification with the authority figure is evidently needed to legitimize violent enforcement activities that may, in large part, stem from the individual motivations of fatherless or battered children. Poverty marked the childhoods of about one-third of all three groups equally, which would exclude it as a factor making for violence. The fathers of the enforcers and the party careerists tended to be military men (another hint of excessive discipline) or identified with moderate parties. In school, both groups tended to pick out *voelkisch* or antisemitic teachers or peers. During the youthful years of work experience of the enforcers, an astounding three-fourths reported friction on the job or having been fired for political reasons.[33]

The differences marking the enforcers off from the other two groups continued as they went through their first experiences of militarization or politicization. The administrative careerists tended to join the Freecorps, *Wehrwolf*, or *Stahlhelm* after they passed the age of twenty-five, many of them probably in logical continuation of military-civil or wartime service.[34] The party careerists either tended to become militarized just as late, or before they were even eighteen. But they did so in an ideological and political manner. They mostly joined *Jungdo*, left-wing groups, or pre-1925 *voelkisch* groups such as the *Schutz-und-Trutz-*

[33] Among the other two careerist groups, only two-fifths have the same complaint.

[34] Party and administrative careerists more often went through militarization than did the enforcers and the rest of the sample. It is remarkable that half of the enforcers, in fact, became militarized at all, considering that 57.4 percent of them were born in 1902 or later, and hence could have been no older than twenty-one in 1923. This may also help to explain their early militarization, as may organizations such as *Wehrwolf* or *Stahlhelm* that were available after 1923. But it does not detract from the youthful militarization that seems to be a hallmark of the bloodhound group.

276

bund or the early NSDAP. One out of five in this group belonged to the pre-1925 party. The enforcers shared some of the features of both careerist groups by tending to join the Freecorps or the *Wehrwolf*, but they did so heavily before the age of twenty-one. In fact, three-fourths of them became militarized before that age, as compared to only two-fifths of the administrative and nearly half of the party careerists who went through this experience. Their motives for militarization round out the picture. The administrative careerists were militarized mainly by the impact of the defeat and their shock at the new leadership of Weimar. The party careerists, by way of contrast, were militarized mostly by their own antisemitic predisposition or by their opposition to the revolutionaries. The accent was clearly on ideological motivation. The enforcers tended to be mobilized by the shock of the occupation or by their opposition to the revolutionaries, presumably a gut reaction rather than the result of intellectual deliberation. In their first politicization, finally, the enforcers were mostly motivated by opposition to Marxists and revolutionaries, or by unemployment or other economic difficulties of their working-class or farming way of life. Even in those early involvements, nearly half the enforcers were already engaged in violence and demonstrations, while the party men were more likely to have been holding office or waging election campaigns.

In the post-1924 NSDAP, the enforcers tended to be either marcher-fighters (MF) or marcher-fighter-proselytizers (MFP) (Table V-10). The party careerists, by comparison, tended to be MFPs or marcher-proselytizers (MP),

TABLE V-10 Third *Reich* Careers and Pre-1933 NSDAP Activity
(percent)

	Ms	MFs	MPs	MFPs	Totals
Party careerists	8.6	16.1	24.7	23.6	71.0
Administrators	4.4	22.1	22.1	19.1	67.7
Enforcers	3.4	52.5	10.2	28.8	94.9

or simply marchers (M). The accent was on fighting among the enforcers and on proselytizing among the party men. The administrators had no unusual concentrations in any one category. The large percentage of MFs, the "mindless sluggers," among the enforcers is particularly notable. They also joined at a much younger age—45.7 percent under twenty-one, and three-fourths no older than thirty. The comparable figures for the other careers were one-third under twenty-one and nearly half under thirty. Their chief motive for joining the NSDAP was the dynamic impression of the Hitler movement. The enforcers, in contrast, were attracted mostly by the spirit of comradeship among the stormtroopers, or motivated by their economic troubles.

There is a certain obliqueness and opacity about the way the enforcers came to join, almost by accident rather than motivated by deliberate, political goals, as were the other careerists. And yet their lives speak of a continuous thread of violent behavior that links the early stages with their careers in the Weimar SA or SS and, finally, with grisly enforcement careers in the Third *Reich*. The party men, on the other hand, knew from the beginning what they wanted, their ideological obsession. They were the earliest to join the party; one-fifth of them were in the pre-1925 party, and another fifth joined immediately upon the party's reconstruction. They also tended to be the first to join in their locality, and often were founders of their Nazi local. The enforcers heavily joined in the years of reconstruction, 1925-1927, and again right after the landslide elections of 1930. They tended to join the party only after it had become a substantial minority in their area. We would not be wrong to see in them the young Freecorps and stormtrooper types who crowded into the party at these times, attracted by the opportunities for violent action, and little else. The administrative careerists joined mostly after September of 1930; they have the highest number of *Septemberlinge*, far in excess of the entire sample. They also tended to join not immediately after the 1930 election, as did the enforcers, but —with the caution befitting bureaucrats—only after mid-

1931, when the further growth of the movement and its final triumph seemed likely. Here, in other words, we have the opportunists for whom the word *Septemberlinge* was really coined.

In their manner of introduction, the party careerists and enforcers conform to the model typical of the most active stormtroopers. They were introduced by friends or fellow workers who presumably took them to a Nazi meeting knowing that they would like it, given their previous attitudes or behavior. The administrative careerists, on the other hand, were mostly attracted by an awareness of the Nazi ideology, as were many of those who joined after mid-1931 and at middle age. Once they were in it, moreover, the attitude of both party and administrative careerists toward the NSDAP was strongly colored by the expectation of a job or other material reward, and much less by a sense of personal integration derived from the pursuit of utopia. The enforcers, by way of contract, tended to derive their satisfactions from the struggle itself, and also from the Hitler cult that lent legitimacy to the mayhem. This combination is evidently a strong indication of the enforcement career to come.

A glimpse of the personalities of these groups of men emerges from their patterns of prejudice and of family membership in the party.[35] They rarely had their whole families in the party. The good fellowship of the fighting years alone was evidently not enough to make a career. Instead, both the party men and the enforcers showed a tendency to be loners, which was quite at variance with our earlier finding about the violent stormtroopers. Evidently the enforcers were somewhat odd even among the bulk of the stormtroopers. The administrators tended to have spouses in the party. In many cases they also indicated their "formative experiences" either as the *Fronterlebnis* of World War I or as alleged episodes with aliens or Jews. In fact,

[35] Of the thirty-six Nazi women in our sample, only four appeared in any of our career groups, including three in a party career and none among the enforcers.

their level of antisemitic prejudice was even higher than that of the party men, especially with regard to anecdote-telling and expressions of antisemitic paranoia. The enforcers, like the other groupings of violent men we have examined, were not particularly prejudiced, although they had a larger number of respondents with a sudden outbreak of *Judenkoller* than any other group. It is hard to interpret this finding except by interpreting the choler as a sign of deteriorating mental balance. That the party careerists should be the most prejudiced is hardly surprising, though the extent of virulent prejudice among the administrative careerists is. It must signify a high degree of penetration of the civil service with Nazi ideas that such men could make a career in it.

In all this, it goes without saying that the enforcers were not particularly intelligent. Their level of political understanding tended to be either of the low, ideological, or the dimwit-romantic type. The administrators, by comparison, were far more often knowledgeable about Weimar politics, and even the party men and women were at a medium level. The enigma of the motivations of the enforcers remains, in spite of our search and the speculations about a man like Rudolf Hoess, the "face in the crowd," who ran the Auschwitz camp. Were they really just dim-witted brutes who did not mind doing the dirty jobs of the totalitarian SS state? We have already looked at one or two who rose to higher authority in Himmler's empire of terror.[36] Obviously, they did not tell us all there may be to know about their persons and conduct even before 1933.

The three groups look in many ways like groupings we have encountered earlier. The party careerists resembled the *voelkisch* ideologues and office-holders of the pre-1925 party. The administrative careerists were a mixture of the prewar military-civil servant strain, the front generation, and the more passive antisemites who jumped on the bandwagon only after 1930. The enforcers, however, have to

[36] For further SS and SD cases, see Merkl, *Political Violence*, pp. 661-666. One-third of the enforcers were already in the pre-1933 SS.

be placed more specifically among the styles of violence we discussed earlier. In addition to their large share of "instant" stormtroopers, for example, the enforcers accounted for half of the pre-1933 SS members of the Abel Collection. Nearly one-third of the enforcers held middle-echelon ranks, and almost half of them lower ranks in the SA or SS. There were very few "day-and-night fighters" among them, far fewer than among the party men and administrative careerists.

To come to a conclusion, we have to fall back on their personal background for an explanation of their grisly role in the Third *Reich*: their social frustrations, lower-class and poverty-stricken backgrounds, lack of paternal or religious guidance, fatherless or disciplinarian childhoods, low education, and poor school environment seem to have turned these youths toward very early militarization, violent youth activities, and eventually Nazi extremism. They seem to have joined the NSDAP for lack of something better to do, and because it promised them more violence under the cover of a legitimizing ideology, and it was supported by a charismatic leader and a comradely organization. Hence the intense leadership cult and the stress on the comradeship of the stormtroopers, and on merging their individual selves with the movement.

As the movement took over power in the country, the romanticism of the violent brotherhood of outlaws waned, but the new regime was anxious to continue to exploit their bent for violence. And it appears to have been precisely their overwhelmingly masochistic attitude toward violence that made it possible for them to work as concentration camp guards and other minions of the SS state.[37] The

[37] With all respondents engaged in violence, we recorded whether their accounts of their involvement stressed the blows they dealt (sadism) or those they received (masochism), and found that most of the respondents who felt no compulsion to rationalize their violence were inured to the violence of war and counterrevolution or were highly ideological bullies. The administrative careerists conformed to this model. The enforcers, instead, tended to rationalize their violence in terms of how they had been attacked and assaulted (masochism).

281

masochistic attitude, which had manifested itself in the curious habit of relating all violence as if it was initiated by the antagonists and imposed on the respondent, is an extrapunitive, sociopathic attitude that is extremely well suited to the enforcement role. These men and many others like them probably blamed even their victims in the concentration camps for the violence they visited upon them. The extraordinary wave of political violence that swept over Germany after the end of World War I and manifested itself in private armies and pitched battles thus ended in the terrorist regime of the Third *Reich*. A nation whose civilized abhorrence of violent strife had been under attack too long no longer shrank from Adolf Hitler, the man who had publicly endorsed the brutal SA murderers of Potempa and who had announced, with due respect to the "legality" of his takeover, that "heads would roll" after his victory.[38] The most violent of his men then took on the task of licensed murder and mayhem.

[38] The murder at Potempa (Upper Silesia) involved the invasion of an unemployed Polish Communist worker's home by five uniformed SA men who beat him to death in his own bed and before the eyes of his mother. They also injured his brother seriously. Sentenced to death under a new decree against political violence, they drew a supportive telegram from Hitler, and Nazi editorials that clearly showed every German who was willing to listen what to expect of a Nazi regime. See also the article by Richard Bessel, "The Potempa Murder," *Central European History*, 10 (September 1977), 241-254. The SA men involved were border Germans or German ethnic exiles from Polish Upper Silesia.

The Violent Face of Fascism

THE TIME has come to reflect upon the path we have traveled in this book. We began by reviewing the setting of Weimar paramilitary organizations and their political violence long before the SA and NSDAP began to play a prominent role. The revolutionary waves of the far left and their suppression; the plotting of the right wing and the whole atmosphere of secret armies in the shadow, and often under the wing, of the *Reichswehr*; and the pathetic efforts of the *Reichsbanner* to gird itself for the defense of the unhappy republic against left and right—this was the background without which it is impossible to understand the rise of the stormtroopers. The NSDAP, to be sure, had older antecedents in the form of prewar ideological movements and traditions, the war generation and its Freecorps and vigilante violence, and the hundreds of political murders of the first half of the republic. In this context we also examined the social dynamics of the early Nazi movement that reach back into imperial society: rural-urban migration, upward mobility, social decline, and the frustrations of the old middle classes, of the professional military, the farmers, and of newly rising strata presented a varied picture that gainsaid any simplistic explanation such as the "lower middle-class thesis."

But the real historical drama lies in the sudden develop-

283

ment of the NSDAP from a fringe movement of the far right into the mass movement of the early 1930s. The example of the so-called conquest of Berlin clearly showed the important role of combat with the Communists, deliberately sought in order to frighten and radicalize working-class Tories and the bourgeois right. It thereby showed the role of the stormtroopers as part of a grandiose propaganda undertaking. Even though they were in many ways like the *Stahlhelm*, the Red Front, and the *Reichsbanner*, and shared many of their problems and concerns (including the fatal desire to elect their own *Reichstag* candidates in 1930), the stormtroopers were a key to the transition of a fringe movement to a mass movement, and hence to the success of Adolf Hitler in taking over the country. Their marches, battles, and campaigns were the battering ram against the democratic republic that swayed vast masses in the countryside, the small towns, and, of course, the big cities. This is not to deny the other side of the "double strategy" of the NSDAP, the infiltration and takeover of the many intermediary organizations from within.[1] But without the pressure of the street, the well-engineered appearances of mass enthusiasm, and the pressures at the bases of these intermediary organizations, they would not have fallen into the hands of the usurper.

We were hardly the first to apply social science and social psychology—disciplines that have long sought to penetrate the mysteries of revolutionary movements—to the rich record assembled by the historians of the Nazi takeover. The demographic trends, that is, mass unemployment at the precise movement when large numbers of young men born before the drastic decline of the birthrate in 1915 were look-

[1] See, for example, Jeremy Noakes, *The Nazi Party in Lower Saxony* (Oxford: Oxford University Press, 1971), or Heinrich August Winkler, *Mittelstand, Demokratie und Nationalsozialismus. Die politische Entwicklung von Handwerk und Kleinhandel in der Weimarer Republik* (Cologne: Kiepenheuer & Witsch, 1972), and in Wolfgang Schieder, ed., *Faschismus als soziale Bewegung, Deutschland und Italien im Vergleich* (Hamburg: Hoffmann & Campe, 1976), pp. 97-118.

284

ing for their first job explains the hundreds of thousands of extra bodies available for paramilitary organizations of every sort. But their presence was obviously not enough. We needed to find strong motivation and initiative other than prewar or war-related factors. We found them in the politicized youth of the Weimar era and in the dynamics of the movement itself, which we then examined systematically in terms of: 1. the process by which a young person becomes an activist of a fringe movement; 2. the relation between an early bent for political violence and later involvement; and 3. the three quintessential activities of the Nazi movement on the way to mass membership and electoral success, namely, marching, fighting, and proselytizing.

The Abel stories enabled us to look into the motivations of these groups of "old fighters." The Nazi movement in this phase was essentially a self-sustaining whirlwind of propaganda that all three of these activities served.[2] This whirlwind of propaganda stirred up individuals like so many grains of dust, used them, and dropped them again. Less than half of the members who had joined before September 1930 were still in the party at the time the official party statistics appeared in 1935. The turnover among leadership cadres and men was at a level comparable to that of the KPD.[3]

This whirlwind succeeded in making Adolf Hitler eligible for appointment as Chancellor in January 1933 without actually conquering power for him, but it had little influence on the developments to follow. The SA was already in a deep crisis at the time of the 1930 elections, and remained

[2] See especially the interpretation of Hans Mommsen, "National Socialism—Continuity and Change" in Walter Laqueur, ed., *Fascism, A Reader's Guide* (Berkeley and Los Angeles: University of California Press, 1976), p. 181.

[3] *Parteistatistik*, I, 26. The fluctuations among the voters must have been very considerable, too; witness the drop of the Nazi vote in November 1932. See also Wolfgang Schaefer, *NSDAP, Entwicklung und Struktur der Staatspartei dee Dritten Reiches* (Hanover: NVA Goedel, 1957).

so in spite of its mushroom growth. After the takeover, it became gorged with masses of new followers who had not earned their spurs during the fighting years, and it was embittered by the deliberate policy of the party to keep the SA away from the councils of power. The party organization had itself entered a state of crisis in 1932, if not earlier, and fared little better after 1933, except that many party men received local government or bureaucratic positions.[4] Hitler, still true to his strategy of "legal revolution," preferred an alliance with the old conservative forces of the *Wehrmacht*, the bureaucracy, and German industry to giving a position of authority in his new state to the "old fighters." Roehm and his old fighters dreamt of the continuing whirlwind, a permanent revolution of vague specifics, and did not want to permit SA ranks to be diluted with minor public officials. Thus there was a painful gap between the party leadership, national and regional, which succeeded in taking its place among and above the traditional elites of the German establishment,[5] and the rank and file of the old fighters, whose role soon became that of a mere ceremonial ornament at propaganda functions, the ever-ready columns of "spontaneous mass enthusiasm" of the regime. Heinrich Himmler and his SS eventually inherited the role as the real instrument of power, an efficient new elite willing to serve every whim of the dictator.

It was at this point that we took a last look at the Abel Nazis, or rather at those among them who managed to make a Third *Reich* career out of their early membership and

[4] The disappointment of many old fighters in the NSDAP and SA was undoubtedly a major motive for many of the old fighters to write their stories for Abel's essay contest, especially since it was the party that solicited and collected these vitae. An old fighter thus could tell the party how he had fought and suffered for the cause.

[5] As Nazi leaders took governmental positions, large numbers of high civil servants and military men, and even some industrialists, became eager party members. See Hans Mommsen, "Zur Verschraenkung traditioneller und faschistischer Fuehrungsgruppen in Deutschland beim Uebergang von der Bewegungs-zur Systemphase," in Schieder, *Faschismus als soziale Bewegung*, pp. 157-176.

fighting records. Not many were so lucky as to make a modest party or administrative career. But some storm-troopers managed to become enforcers of Himmler's SS state. This, of course, is the point of continuity between the violent movement and the system, and the Abel autobiographies give us a second opportunity to examine and compare what manner of "old fighters" became the bloodhounds of the Third *Reich*.

History and Political Motivation

It would be one-sided not to acknowledge the extraordinarily rich contribution that a number of historians have made to our knowledge of the Weimar republic and the Nazi takeover. But there has been a seemingly unbridgeable gap between the approaches of social science and history, which has often given the impression that the social scientists were not keeping up with their history, which the historians often disdained the theories and methods with which social scientists had attempted to explain the nature and rise of the Nazi movement. Until social scientists became historians, or historians became social scientists, we could never really understand what transpired in Germany during those fateful years.

A number of current trends in the writing of history (and among some social scientists) have tended toward the creation of a consensus on methods to be used on appropriate subjects which is quite capable of bringing about the desired union of history and social science. There is, for example, the long-standing trend toward writing the history of little people rather than great historical personalities and their deeds. In fact, the new history has become a history of conditions rather than of deeds. Historians and social scientists alike have long been writing histories of working-class movements, but now they also write about unorganized labor, about servants, or about the poor. They write about women in settings such as Victorian England, childhood and the family in colonial America or seventeenth century Europe, peasants, miners, and other callings in particular historical settings, or slaves on pre-Civil War plantations. They study the impact of unemployment on families during the Great Depression[6] and political violence or strikes in nineteenth-century Europe.[7] They use sophisticated social science models and quantitative methods wherever a historical situation provides the necessary information. Economics, sociology, social psychology, anthropology, and political science can supply the methods required for appropriate historical problems. The more recent in history, the more likely can the basic material be found or generated to permit a combined social science approach to historical subjects.

This is the background against which the study of the Abel stormtroopers and party members should be viewed. It relies heavily on the historical research that historians of the period have assembled. It is obviously not a study of great historical personalities and their deeds. The individual SA man, in fact, is less worthy of attention and less likely to contribute to our knowledge than the study of a Hitler or Goering. As a collectivity, however, an organized movement, the SA was indeed capable of historic deeds and misdeeds. In fact, Hitler would have been a political nobody without all these little SA men whose opinions, actions, and motivations in the plural mattered indeed as a historical force. It was this motivation, as it seemed to arise from the conditions and events of their lives and as it manifested itself in their beliefs and actions (and in their self-told personal histories) that is central to the use of masses of autobiographies for the study of a revolutionary movement.

The motivation of individuals, great and small, has always supplied historians with meat for controversy. Contrary to the stereotype of conservatism or scholarly caution, his-

[6] See, for example, Glen Elder, *Children of the Great Depression* (Chicago: University of Chicago Press, 1974).

[7] See Charles, Louise, and Richard Tilly, *The Rebellious Century, 1830-1930* (Cambridge: Harvard University Press, 1975).

torians have often tended to make sweeping statements about the motivation of whole classes and movements of people. Some of these statements are only implicit, while other are simply taken over from contemporary antagonists or ruling classes who were quick to jump to conclusions about "what the negroes really want" or what motivated "all women of natural feelings" in a given historical setting. With political movements, it was even more likely that the stereotypes of motivation would be supplied either by their antagonists ("the Nazis are the lackeys of the bourgeoisie") or the movement in question ("we Nazis only want to save Germany from Communism"). Social scientists have learned, however, especially from public opinion studies, that such generalized statements are to be distrusted. They are at best crude simplifications that apply only at a superficial level to some of the persons concerned.

In a fraternal organization like the SA, instead, group life and the vaunted camaraderie of the fighting community account for a large part of the attraction of the movement. Antecedent group memberships in youth groups or anti-revolutionary organizations may have been relevant at a behavorial and at an attitudinal level.[8] An early bent for political violence could draw a person into a fighting movement regardless of ideology. Intensely private motives could be mixed with political motives in subtle ways. Motives of political ideology or of social background could be very im-

---

[8] See the remarks of Werner, "SA und NSDAP," pp. xxxi-xxxiii on the importance of "the group," even the gang, the networks of personal friendship among young graduates of schools or youth groups, and other factors in SA recruitment. Quite similarly, according to Adrian Lyttelton, *The Seizure of Power* (New York: Scribner 1973), p. 244: "the origins of many [Italian fascist] squads are to be found in the loose informal relationship between a group of adolescents somewhat resembling that of a youth gang . . . small group solidarity served to protect the Fascist from the feelings of impotence and ennui common among those in the grip of large, impersonal bureaucratic organizations . . . the violence which was the essence of *squadrismo* allowed an outlet for aggression."

289

portant in this context, but they would need to be demonstrated in all their complexity and interrelatedness. It would not do to smuggle in huge and simplified motivational assumptions on the strength of nothing more than lists of occupations that are presumed to predetermine Nazi motivation.

The relative lack of information about group phenomena before the age of public opinion research, of course, invites sweeping generalizations from a slender and uncertain data base such as aggregate voting statistics or a listing of occupations of very young men who, moreover, were likely to have been in their respective occupations only a short time, if at all. For lack of something better and empirically stronger, such evidence is not to be disdained. It can be used with profit especially in macrocomparisons among fascist movements of different countries, to bring out differences among them.[9] But for the more detailed knowledge desirable in a study of motivation in one movement, such slender and uncertain information is no match for the insights to be gained from first-person accounts of members and observers at close hand. This is particularly true for the most basic question of the wellsprings of political motivation of revolutionary movements: whether the individual member is motivated by a purely political will or whether his political intent derives from socioeconomic, psychological, or any other essentially nonpolitical origin.

To tackle this difficult, basic question, we must first become aware and dispose of some of the historical and political prejudices that insisted that there could be only one "revolution," that of the organized working class, and that any opposition to that one and only legitimate revolution

[9] See, for example, Juan J. Linz's excellent "Some Notes toward a Comparative Study of Fascism in Sociological Historical Perspective" in Laqueur, *Fascism, A Reader's Guide*, pp. 59-73, and this writer's concluding chapter, "Comparing Fascist Movements" in the forthcoming symposium by Stein U. Larsen and Bernt Hagtvet et al., eds., *Who Were the Fascists?* (Oslo: Norwegian University Presses forthcoming).

must be counterrevolutionary or "reactionary." According to this dichotomous view of the politics of the interwar years, fascist movements could never be "revolutionary," no matter how much they might have espoused radical changes in state and society. A more objective view of political movements, however, should be able to establish a more encompassing typology in which revolutionary consciousness is distinguished by degrees of intensity and not according to a partisan point of view. Whether a particular movement— or rather the mass of its members—was motivated by social origins, economic or social frustrations, or by political notions such as racism or imperialism, for example requires demonstration in each case. A careful study will very likely arrive at a highly differentiated result that gives each source of motivation its due and establishes its relative importance in comparison to all the others. This is just as true of the history of Socialist, anarchist, or Communist movements, which is hardly objective history if it accepts without further examination partisan, ideological assertions that a. there is a proletariat, and only one, to which political consciousness and collective action are clearly attributable at all times; b. that all proletarians are predeterimed in their politics by their socioeconomic origins, rather than individually capable of an autonomous, political choice for or against the movement, or simply for or against political participation; and c. that there are no important differences in the kind and intensity of political motivation between, say, a member of a goon squad or terrorist gang, a passive working-class follower, or an intellectual sympathizer, or that such differences are not worth exploring. One does not have to accept the obsolete concept of totalitarianism or be an anti-Communist to rebel against primitive, partisan simplifications in recent history. Nor does one have to deny the importance of social class altogether in order to demand that the nexus between political motivation and social class in a particular case be explained and demonstrated in some detail.

Fascist Movements Compared

In the last two decades, historians and social scientists have assembled more and more comparative evidence on fascist movements in many countries in their quest for a broader understanding of the phenomenon.[10] We are still far from having all the relevant information in many countries, especially in Eastern Europe, but also in Germany and Italy. Despite the incompleteness of information, such comparisons are unsurpassed as a method for penetrating the nature of fascism. Instead of the premature rush toward a quasi-Platonic definition of the "essence of fascism," for example, the comparative method can help us to determine and test the boundaries of any one definition. Thus, mariginal cases can be eliminated, or set aside in parentheses, and allegedly essential characteristics of fascism have to prove themselves

[10] Among the more notable comparisons are the late William Ebenstein's *Today's Isms* (Englewood Cliffs, N.J.: Prentice-Hall, 1954) now in its seventh edition (1973); Seymour M. Lipset, "Fascism-Left, Right, and Center," in Lipset, *Political Man* (Garden City, N.Y.: Doubleday, 1960); Ernst Nolte, *Three Faces of Fascism* (New York: Holt, Rinehart, 1966) and *Die faschistischen Bewegungen* (Munich: DTV, 1966); Hans Rogger and Eugen Weber, *The European Right* (Berkeley and Los Angeles: University of California Press, 1965); Weber, *The Varieties of Fascism* (Princeton: Van Nostrand, 1964); Walter Laqueur and George L. Mosse, eds., *International Fascism, 1920-1945* (New York: Harper Torchbooks, 1964); John Weiss, *The Fascist Tradition: Radical Rightwing Extremism in Modern Europe* (New York: Harper & Row, 1967); S. J. Woolf, ed., *European Fascism* and *The Nature of Fascism* (both New York: Vintage Books, 1969); F. L. Carsten, *The Rise of Fascism* (Berkeley and Los Angeles: University of California Press, 1967); *Fasismus a Europa—Fascism and Europe, an International Symposium, Prague, 18th-29th August, 1969* (Prague: Institute of History, 1969); Charles F. Delzell, ed., *Mediterranean Fascism 1919-1945* (New York: Macmillan, 1970); Peter F. Sugar, ed., *Native Fascism in the Successor States, 1918-1945* (Santa Barbara: ABC-Clio Press, 1971); Henry A. Turner, ed., *Reappraisals of Fascism* (New York: Franklin Watts, 1975); and the forthcoming Larsen and Hagtvet et al., eds., *Who Were the Fascists?* The literature on particular fascist movements frequently includes comparative excursions.

292

by being present in most of the movements. By the same token, comparison clearly shows what might have been typically German about the Nazis, or an outgrowth of the particular situation in Spain at the time of the rise of the Falange.[11]

A comparison of nearly forty fascist movements in some twenty-one European countries between the wars, for example, suggests the close relationship of nearly all of them to the three great watersheds of the first half of the twentieth century: the First World War, the Russian Revolution, and the Great Depression. To be sure, the antecedents of fascist movements frequently go back to certain literary figures, student circles, and nationalistic organization of the decades before World War I—Maurice Barrès, Enrico Corradini, the *voelkisch* literature, and prewar organizations like the *Action Française* or the Pan-German League.[12] But it took the great mass upheaval of World War I—its territorial changes and irredentist legacies, its unemployed veterans and students, the disappointed officers and officials of fallen empires—and its shattering effect on the prewar bourgeois society and moral values to create the conditions for massive fascist recruitment, at least in the countries involved in the war. It would be quite impossible to understand the genesis of fascist movements in Germany, Austria, Italy, Belgium, and all of Eastern Europe without reference to the war.

The Russian Revolution and the vast Socialist mobilization of the years 1917 to 1921 in many of the countries concerned, including the establishment of Workers and Soldiers Councils' (*Soviet*) dictatorships in Russia, Budapest, and Munich, or the seizure of the factories in Italy, provided another major setting for massive anti-Socialist or anti-Communist recruitment. Among the mass organizations assembled in reaction to the perceived threat of revolutionary

[11] For an excellent example of such comparative analysis, see the contributions of Juan Linz to Laqueur, *Fascism, A Reader's Guide* and Larsen and Hagtvet, *Who Were the Fascists?*

[12] See especially Zeev Sternhell, "Fascist Ideology," in Laqueur, *Fascism, A Reader's Guide*, pp. 327-335.

293

Socialism were especially the Italian *squadristi*, but also the German *Einwohnerwehr* and *Stahlhelm* or the Austrian *Heimwehr*, which were not really fascist, although some of their members later went on to join the NSDAP. For Mussolini's Fascist party (PNF), the mobilization effects of the war and of the great red scare were enough to turn his motley band of revolutionary syndicalists, futurists, and dissident nationalists in a very short time into a powerful mass movement that could push itself into the existing vacuum of power and take over the state. Hitler's attempt to follow in his footsteps in 1923 fell short of success despite the external and domestic crises of that year.

During the second half of the 1920s, the situation was evidently not threatening enough to create further fascist ground swells, and the war was already too remote to be of much help to the French *Faisceau* of George Valois, Taittinger's *Jeunesses Patriotes*, or Redier's *Legionnaires*, not to mention Codreanu's Iron Guard in Rumania, the Croat *Ustasha*, the Slovak *Hlinka*, or the Czech, Polish, or Finnish fascists. It took the third major event, the politics of the Great Depression to boost the chances of the German NSDAP, the Norwegian, Swedish, Danish, Icelandic, British, Irish, Dutch, Belgian (Walloon and Flemish), and Swiss movements, as well as the French *Francistes* (Bucard), *Solidarité Française* (Renaud), the Hungarian Arrow Cross and Scythe Cross, and once more the Rumanian and Polish movements. Spain and Portugal also sprouted fascist movements in the 1930s, but they were less directly related to these historical crises.

The comparison of these movements (Table VI-1) also shows at a glance, and despite some rather dubious membership figures, that only a few of over thirty separate organizations ever reached mass-movement dimensions, at least before getting into power or before the country was conquered by Nazi Germany or Fascist Italy: the Dutch NSB, Jaques Doriot's PPF and, earlier, the *Faisceau* and the *Jeunesses Patriotes*, the German and Austrian NSDAP, the Italian PNF, the Iron Guard, and the Arrow Cross move-

294

ments. The Spanish JONS/Falange and the Portuguese National Syndicalists, the several Belgian organizations, the Finnish Lapua/IKL, and perhaps the Polish movement of the late 1930s may also qualify as incipient mass movements, considering the size of the population of these countries. Of the larger movements, only the Italians and Germans won power unaided, while another half dozen shared it with foreign occupations or powerful domestic forces. The size of the membership after such a takeover is more revealing of the character of the political system at the time than of the social forces that raised the fascist movements in the first place.

Comparison can also help to take the mystifications out of the question of socio-economic motivation as contrasted to other political or social-psychological motives. The occupational composition of the party membership that has been central to the great German debate over definitions of fascism can be elucidated with comparative materials about the composition of Dutch, Belgian, French, Norwegian, Italian, Austrian, and Spanish fascist movements.[13] Far from a confirmation of the lower-middle-class thesis, such a comparison of the occupational composition turns up a bewildering variety, ranging from strongly proletarian elements (French PPF, Italy, Switzerland, Spain) to farmers and fishermen in countries afflicted by agricultural crisis (Norway, Iceland, Ireland, Finland, Slovakia, and northern Germany). Strong old middle-class elements were present in Belgium and the Netherlands, and white-collar elements were present in most of the industrialized countries. In countries with several fascist movement, such as France and Czechoslovakia, they differed in the occupational elements they attracted. It may be more illuminating to note the role of university students in the Scandinavian, French (*Faisceau*), Spanish, Italian, Rumanian, German, and Fin-

[13] See my concluding essay, "Comparing Fascist Movements" in Larsen and Hagtvet, *Who Were the Fascists?*, Table 5. Table 1 of the same article compares the reported sizes of each movement before takeover.

295

TABLE VI-1 Starting Point, Degree of Violence, and Paramilitary Organization of European Fascist Movements

Country	Movement	Name of Group Leader	Start	Paramilitary Organization	Youth Group	Degree of Violence	Kind of Political Violence
Norway	Nasjonal Samling	Quisling	1933	—	idem	Low	Some rural and labor violence
Iceland	Icelandic Nationalists		1933	Marching squad	yes	Low	Street harassment
Denmark	DNSAP	Clausen	1930	SA	yes	Low	
Netherlds.	NSB	Mussert	1931		yes	None	
Belgium	Rex	Degrelle	1936	Guards	yes	Medium	Rally violence
	Flemish Nationalists						
Ireland	Blueshirts	O'Duffy	1932	ACA/Blueshirts	yes	Medium	Attacks on IRA, police, bailiffs
Gr. Brit.	British Union of Fascists	Mosley	1931	Biff boys		High	Street violence, demonstrations
France	Faisceau	Valois	1925	Uniformed guards	idem	Medium	Street violence, demonstrations
	Jeunesses Patriotes	Taittinger	1924	Uniformed guards		Medium	Street violence, demonstrations
	Legion	Redier	1933				
	Solidarité Française	Renaud	1933			Low	Feb. 1934 demonstrations
	Francistes	Bucard	1933	Cagoulards		High	Attempted coups, murder
	PPF	Doriot	1936	Militia Union	Pop. JF	Medium	Street violence, demonstrations
	RNP	Déat	1941	MSR			
Spain	JONS/Falange	José Ant.	1931	Blueshirts	SEU	High	Random terrorism, street violence

insisted on marching in formation in brown shirts, with Nazi salute, and in other ways showed the crudest contempt. The same fascist attitude was displayed toward the bureaucrats, the teachers, the capitalists, or all the worthy old men of a previous generation.

Violence also symbolized the impatience with international treaties that had given Anatolia to the Greeks, Fiume to the Yugoslavs, or part of Silesia to the Poles. It was a soldier's way of making short shrift with the presumably illegitimate interlopers from the far left. It was also a young man's way of forcing his will onto unwilling antagonists, just as the typical fascist pose was always a cult of exaggerated masculinity, a heroic display of *machismo* not unlike the posturing of youth gangs in a decaying neighborhood.

A look at our last table (VI-2) also shows that the SA and SS had its equivalents in most fascist movements in Europe. In the PNF (and some other movements), the *squadristi* were not so much a separate organization as simply the young activists of the movement. The British Union of Fascists had its Biff Boys, the Falange its milita, the Swiss National Front its Harst. The Rexists and the Slovak Hlinka had their guards, the Iron Guard its green-shirted Legionnaires, and the Icelandic Nationalists their Marching quad. In many cases, partisan youth organizations also rved the purposes of marching, fighting, and proselytizing r the great fascist leaders, who themselves liked to posture youthful, strapping stormtrooper heroes with riding boots uniform. The uneven information on the propaganda ies and demonstrations of these movements is replete accounts of Quisling's parades, DeGrelle's and Mos- monster rallies, and similar activities of most of the groups from Rumania to Iceland.

re to the point, there was a great deal of fascist ce, ranging from the rural violence of Norway, Ire- and Schleswig-Holstein (directed at bailiffs and , and the random terrorism of the Falange and Arrow to the attempted coups and putsches of Austria, Fin-

Country	Movement	Name of Group Leader	Start	Paramilitary Organization	Youth Group	Degree of Violence	Kind of Political Violence
Portugal	National Syndicalists	Preto	1932	Blueshirt militia		Low	Street demonstrations
Switzerld.	National Front		1930	Harst/Auszug	NJ	Low	Street & rally violence
Germany	NSDAP	Hitler	1919	SA & SS	HJ	High	Organized violence, terror
Italy	PNF	Mussolini	1919	Squadristi	GF	High	Assassination, putsch, terror
Austria	DNSAP/NSDAP		1919	SA & SS	HJ	High	Street violence, coups
	Heimwehr	Starhembg.	1918	SA & SS		High	Terror, bombings, uprising
Hungary	Arrow Cross	Szalasi	1935	SA & SS		High	Terror, uprisings
	National Socialists	Gömbös	1919	Special squads		High	
	Scythe Cross	Böszörmeny	1932				
Romania	Iron Guard	Codreanu	1923	Greenshirts/legionaries		High	Assassinations, terror
Yugoslavia	Ustasha	Pavelic	1929	Greenshirts/legionaries		High	Assassinations, terror
	Orjuna		1921	Paramilitary units			
CSR	DNSAP (DAP)	Henlein	1920	Volkssportverband			
	Slovak People's Party	Hlinka	1920	Armed auxiliary	yes	Low	
	Czech Nationalists	Gajda	1925				
Poland	Great Poland/ONR	Dmowski	1926	Falanga		High	Assassination, coup plans
Finland	Lapua/IKL	Kosola	1929		Blue-black youth	High	Terror, coup plans

nish movements, or that of veterans and officers among the Irish Blue Shirts, the Italian Black Shirts, the German Brown Shirts, as well as in France, Spain, Austria, Hungary, and Yugoslavia (*Orjuna*).

The age factor[14] loomed large in all of these movements because they tended to rest on specific generational experiences, such as the alienation of the war generation; the cultural despair of prewar intellectuals in such countries as France, Italy, Spain, and Germany; the antibourgeois anger of the unemployed of the Depression; or the disgust of young socialists with the timidity of the German SPD or of the Italian Socialists when the moments of truth arrived in 1914 and again in 1918-1919. This youthful character appears to be one of the few attributes distinctive to all of these movements. In an age marked by a series of historic cataclysms, youth was obviously an important characteristic of fascism everywhere.

Even the question of whether there is a core of ideological beliefs that characterized all fascist movements can benefit from such comparative treatment. The most widely shared issues among these movements were varieties of ethnic hatred, including antisemitism and xenophobia. Some of these hatreds were undoubtedly aggravated by the territorial changes and the collapsing empires of Central and Eastern Europe. A second set of widely shared concerns consisted of antiparliamentarism, anticapitalism, and identification with Mussolini's empire or Hitler's Third *Reich* (after 1933). Antiparliamentarism was both a reaction of traditional elites against the newfangled institutions of liberal democracy and the two-fisted reaction of veterans and violent youth to politics as usual. Anticapitalism similarly reflected traditional prejudices as well as the disdain of soldiers and youths for money. Syndicalism and corporatism here entered a curious alliance against the modern market economy. Finally, there was a melange of anti-Bolshevism and imperialism among the Central and Eastern European

[14] See *ibid.*, Table 3 on the age structures of several fascist movements.

movements that often mirrored the agonies of the disintegrating empires, along with the fear of the Bolshevik presence both outside and inside one's country—for example, as the Soviet threat to take Finland back either by armed force or by means of a fifth column, the Finnish "reds" inside. German National Socialism may seem extreme in its views, and monstrous in its deeds once Hitler to power, but its ideology was not at all unusual in the text of all the other fascist movements. Since it succe in putting the resources of a major power behin nefarious plans, of course, its tenets achieved an aw degree of reality that other movements were spare

Reflections on Fascist Violence

When the fascist storm first broke over Europe of the Italian *squadristi*, it earned its reputatio uncertain ideological or socio-economic pedigr extraordinary violence. Castor oil, beatings, m and violent occupations of whole towns, ar and killings were the distinctive style of th At first, no journalist failed to notice and features; later they became as routine as tral Park. The violence had a purpose— tion, the smashing of Socialist and trade sometimes the temporary or complete e parliamentary and political leaders. B with a concrete purpose; there was a involved, a display of style and of a imitated among other fascist move bled the violence of the SA and S it. What better way was there to s for parliamentary democracy th hostile deputy by beating him castor oil? When the Nazis we bers to the Prussian diet, they an enormous free-for-all in th they moved into the *Reic*

land, and Poland. The Styrian *Heimwehr* had its March on Vienna, although it was a far cry from Mussolini's successful March on Rome. The German Nazis dreamt of a March on Berlin in 1923, and Gömbös' National Socialists hoped for a *Marcia su Budapest*. The assassinations committed by Ustasha, Lapua, and by the Iron Guard were not far behind the right-wing murders of the early years of the Weimar Republic and of the Austrian Nazis' assaults on Dollfuss. Nevertheless, there were considerable and obvious differences in the degree of political violence unleashed by the different fascist movements prior to their takeover. The Scandinavian, Dutch, Portuguese, and Czechoslovak movements were rather nonviolent during their movement phase, and the Belgian, French, and Swiss fascists showed only moderate levels of political violence. The full display of lawless violence as a style of politics, apart from the *squadristi* and the German stormtroopers, seems to have been limited to the Blue Shirts of Ireland and Spain, the Austrians, especially during their illegal phase, the Arrow Cross and Iron Guard, Ustasha, and Lapua.[15] Violence was common enough to be considered typical of the fascist movements before the takeover.

We are left to contemplate the meaning of the fascist cult of violence in general, and of stormtrooper violence in particular. A piece of the war to the veterans, and a two-fisted response to the challenges of Socialism and democracy to the old middle and upper classes—this lust for violence of the new white-collar classes, and of workers and peasants,

[15] The orgies of violence and exhibitionistic acts of cruelty attributed to the Iron Guard, the Arrow Cross, and the Spanish Falange have also been linked by various native writers to the many "neurotics" in the Iron Guard (Pătrascanu) or the 46 percent convicted criminals in the Arrow Cross (Lacko), which parallels our finding that the SA attracted many unstable, violent, and criminally active persons whose offenses of record were certainly not always political in nature. Their antagonists of the revolutionary left, however, have generally preferred not to probe violent fascist behavior and its psychological motivation, either for reasons of temperament or because their own records were not much better.

still seems obscure at first glance. If we consider, however, that nonpolitical violence such as Saturday night brawls or neighborhood physical clashes were and are quite common to young European peasants and workers, the mystery is lessened. The new white-collar stratum generally came from peasant or worker antecedents, or was in social decline from the better-situated classes. Organized violence of the quasimilitary sort had been the lesson of the war to millions of young people of all social classes. In Weimar Germany and Austria, and among the veterans of other states participating in the war, paramilitary organizations cropped up on a massive scale wherever the authorities were too weak to curb them. The specifically partisan, political violence of the stormtroopers, on the other hand, more likely followed the example of the revolutionary left, which had also experimented with organized violence and attempts at actual conquest and control in Germany and elsewhere. Even the peculiarly symbolic kind of violent posturing of the SA, though without the militaristic trimmings, was common to the left, which thereby hoped to increase proletarian militancy and self-confidence in standing up to the police and to "reaction." Thus fascist violent behavior was neither novel nor without frequent contemporary parallels on the left, which may well have been a major reason why it has not commanded much attention among scholars.

The fascist adulation of violence as manly and heroic, on the other hand, had hardly any contemporary and few historic parallels. Glorying in violence for its own sake, and sneering at the "weak-kneed old aunties" who were shocked by it were typically fascist attitudes. Even the most militant socialist revolutionaries never meant to glorify violence without reference to concrete goals or conquests. Borderline cases such as George Sorel, who in his *Reflections on Violence* eulogized the use of violence as a sign of the *élan vital* of proletarian revolution, constituted a link to fascism. To the average stormtrooper, of course, the cult of violence was not so much an attitude acquired from reading abstruse literature as a fighting posture that naturally grew from

302

unruly emotions or promised to pull together a personality that was on the verge of severe psychological disturbances. The hostile militant youths among our respondents who later became either violently prejudiced or very violent, or both, are clearly a type of person to whom political violence gave an important outlet for their inner tensions. The "politically militarized" youths who made up the bulk of the most active stormtroopers may at first glance appear to have been normal, happy-go-lucky adventurers and brawlers. But this impression is deceptive because their actions were set among an ideological movement; marching, fighting, and proselytizing round the clock for a political movement is hardly a common preoccupation of young people in Germany or anywhere else in industrial society, and no one has as yet demonstrated that it was during the Weimar years in question. Was the Nazi movement of the fighting years imbued with a quasi-religious, utopian consciousness? Or was it a collection of personally maladjusted misfits who sought integration of their personalities through the experience of the struggle? We attempted to gauge the nature of the satisfactions each of the Abel respondents appeared to get out of the movement and arrived at the breakdown in Table VI-2.

The comparison of stormtroopers and party members shows the extent of the utopian expectation, especially

TABLE VI-2   Attitudes toward Nazi Movement of Abel SA/SS and NSDAP (percent)

Attitude toward Nazi Movement	SA/SS	SA/SS Leaders	NSDAP Party
Integration per struggle	16.1	18.9	3.0
Stress on comradeship	23.6	24.5	19.5
Hitler or other leadership cult	20.4	16.8	17.3
Integration per utopia	34.0	34.2	53.1
Expectation of job, rewards (multiple responses)	5.9	5.6	7.1
Totals	100.0	100.0	100.0

among the latter. On the other hand, it also shows the relatively greater share of those oriented toward the struggle as a purpose in itself among the stormtroopers and their lower leaders. Cross tabulation with age, furthermore, divides these groups into an older generation (prewar and war generation) of utopians and people expecting a payoff, and a younger, mostly postwar generation motivated by the struggle and the classless comradeship of the movement. The leadership cultists were the group linking the generations. By occupation, those oriented toward struggle and those oriented toward comradeship tended to be blue and white-collar workers or farmers, and in social decline or static, while the utopians were typically military-civil servants who were upwardly mobile. The struggle-oriented, in particular, had often been in quasi-military organizations and organized or partisan street violence. Their early involvement in political violence, moreover, was accompanied by an obvious liking for it. Unlike many others, who felt they had to rationalize their violent behavior or explain it away, the struggle-oriented obviously gloried in the violence they inflicted upon their enemies (sadism) and liked to refer to them as "murderers," "subhumans," or in other *outré* terms. They shared this language, which takes away the human dignity of the political antagonists, with their comradeship-oriented age mates, who had nearly as large a share of violent stormtroopers among them as those oriented toward struggle. We can regard these two orientations as closely related and, perhaps, at the heart of the stormtrooper phenomenon. One of the Abel respondents (no. 5, born 1908) tellingly describes both orientations in his account of the years 1931 and 1932, after he had switched from the DNVP to the Nazis:

The terror in the streets increased. They had found out that they could not silence us by ignoring us. . . . Very rarely did they manage to get one or the other stormtrooper to want to quit. . . . Those were usually people who had joined us for some reason other than fanatical enthusiasm for our idea. I liked it better every day. *Now I really got to know the spirit of comradeship.* Many people I once had rejected as inferior I now found serving in the ranks, and I learned to appreciate them. I learned in practice the truth that birth and estate mean nothing and merit everything.

I soon became accustomed to the many propaganda rallies where we had to serve as protective squads, the marches and demonstrations which led us through the streets of our hometown or neighboring towns, and the howling of the enemies and *the quiet enthusiasm of our adherents.* I could not imagine a life without them. I became so used to it in fact that *I more and more lost contact with my old friends.* They had become strangers to me and no longer understood me either. They thought that I would in time come back to spending convivial evenings with them as I once used to do every night and considered it odd that I had no time for these pleasures any more. . . .

Thus I had soon lost all contacts of my earlier years and *knew only one thing, the NSDAP and its goals.* My wife —it was 1931 and I had gotten married meanwhile— often anxiously tried to persuade me to quit at least the SA. It was in vain. I had gotten so deeply into it that I simply could not break away. I took part in the great SA rally of October 1931 in Braunschweig and came back more fanatical than ever. *I had seen the size of the movement, its coiled power, and nothing could wean me away.* I never missed an SA service and could not have forgiven myself if I had ever neglected my duty once I knew it. (Italics supplied.)

Concluding Remarks

The current debate about "theories of fascism" and, for that matter, earlier such debates have tended to be couched in misleading terms.[16] To begin with, the word "theory" as it has been used by historians in this connection has been highly ambiguous, often denoting several disparate things. Few have seriously suggested a "theory" of fascism in the sense in which, for example, economists speak of a "theory" of price, supply, and demand.[17] Most writers mean by "theories" of fascism a species of broad interpretations divorced from, or only selectively supported by, historical research on particular movements in particular settings. The philosophical-political character of these "theoretical" interpretations does not easily admit a procedure for empirical proof or disproof such as all scientific theory should have. These interpretations, in fact, are only intended as heuristic models for the imagination of students and the reading public, often connected with a moral or political message. There is something very engaging, though not exactly scientific, about scholars who wish to uphold the whole Nazi experience as a horrifying "counterpoint to the liberal world"

[16] Regarding current and other debates, see Karl D. Bracher, *Zeitgeschichtliche Kontroversen, um Faschismus, Totalitarismus, Demokratie* (Munich: Piper, 1976); Gerhard Schutz, *Faschismus-Nationalsozialismus. Versionen und theoretische Kontroversen 1922-1972* (Frankfurt: Propylaen, 1974); Ernst Nolte. ed., *Theorien über den Faschismus* (Cologne: Kiepenheuer & Witsch, 1967); Paul M. Hayes, *Fascism* (London: Allen & Unwin, 1973); Johannes Agnoli, *Zur Faschismus-Diskussion* (Hamburg, 1973); Helga Grebing, *Aktuelle Theorien über Faschismus und Konservatismus. Eine Kritik* (Stuttgart: Kohlhammer, 1974); and Wolfgang Wippermann, *Faschismustheorien* (Darmstadt: Wissenschaftliches Buch, 1975). On Italian fascism, see especially the sources reviewed by Adrian Lyttelton in Laqueur, *Fascism, A Reader's Guide*, pp. 129-134, and the writings of Renzo de Felice on this subject. On the general debate see also Wolfgang Schieder's introduction in Schieder, *Faschismus als soziale Bewegung*, pp. 11-23, and the October 1976 issue of the *Journal of Contemporary History.*

[17] The closest examples to real theory are "empirical theories" based on comparative sets of data as, for example, in Juan Linz's comparative historical sociology of fascism in Laqueur, *Fascism, A Reader's Guide*, or the theorizing often attached to particular empirical studies such as Bracher, Sauer, and Schulz, *Die national-sozialistische Machtergreifung.*

(Peter Gay), or who are wary of explaining away this embodiment of absolute evil with sociological understanding. Nevertheless, and this is our second point, we should not give in to the temptation of mixing scientific understanding with moral or political purposes. This is not to deny that real scientific insights might sharpen our perception of when and how such sinister developments can be headed off. The ancient exhortation, *principiis obsta*, is predicated on a sound understanding of the processes involved. But scientific understanding should remain divorced from the uses to which society may put it.

Our third point relates to the confusion of different kinds of social causation implicit in most "theories" of fascism. There is not only an extraordinary amount of controversy and well-reasoned doubts about any attempt to apply causal thinking to social processes, but there are even greater objections to monocausal reductionism of any kind. As for causality, this mode of thinking of the human mind is a dubious way of approaching political actions, questions of intent, or meanings in human hearts. No human individual or group is set in motion in the manner in which a billiard cue may push the ivory ball across the green table. Deterministic explanations of the German Nazi movement, or any other fascist party, are bound to ignore not only a large part or what we already know about them, but the nature of politics itself. They are profoundly unpolitical in attempting to explain one of the most politicized groups of people of the twentieth century. At the same time, monocausal determinism of any sort is implausible as an explanation, even aside from the question of causality. Human motivation is far too complex to be reduced to one factor alone,[18] such

[18] The best acknowledgment of this principle can be found wherever well-known experts deny that their own specialty can explain the whole phenomenon. As the economic historian Alan Milward concluded in his survey of literature on the "social basis of fascism," with emphasis on developmental and Marxist theories, "the propensity to join a fascist party was determined more by psychological considerations than by social class"; Milward, "The Fascist Economy," in

as the impact of mass unemployment, the absence of fathers, the violent legacy of war and revolution, or the mobilization of organized youth cultures. Taken together, on the other hand, all these factors and some others can add up to a plausible combination that explains the setting in which the political act of will was conceived that we seek to explain. Reconstructing the world of meaning as the stormtroopers and party men saw it goes a long way toward explaining their decision to march and fight and proselytize, as long as we remember that it was still their free decision to join and work for the movement. In this limited sense, then, as factors influencing political decisions, we can even speak of the "causes of national socialism," although the word "cause" is misleading.

What is true of the individual decisions of stormtroopers to join and fight applies to the macropolitical question of Hitler's triumph with redoubled force. Although the combination of forces and factors at work was infinitely more complex, we can safely say that there was no necessity, causal or other, behind it. A careful examination of all the factors, economic, political, and social-psychological, shows the complexity of the setting, but in the end there remain the free decisions and acts of folly that enabled Hitler to take over Germany and to make war on the world—the folly of von Hindenburg, von Papen, Hugenberg, von Schleicher, and many others, and most of all the folly of hundreds of thousands of violent young stormtroopers whose motives we have sought to explain.

Laqueur, *Fascism, A Reader's Guide*, pp. 385-386. One would hope that psychological interpretations will similarly show their readiness to acknowledge economic and social factors.

Selected Bibliography

Abel, Theodore. *The Nazi Movement*. New York: Atherton, 1965.

Adorno, Theodor W. *The Authoritarian Personality*. New York: Harper, 1950; reissued New York: Science Edition, 1964.

Allen, William S. *The Nazi Seizure of Power*. Chicago: University of Chicago Press, 1965.

Allport, Gordon W. *The Nature of Prejudice*. Garden City, N.Y.: Doubleday/Anchor, 1958.

Angress, Werner T. *Stillborn Revolution*. Princeton: Princeton University Press, 1963.

Arendt, Hannah. *Eichmann in Jerusalem*. New York: Viking Press, 1963.

————. *The Origins of Totalitarianism*. New ed. New York: Harcourt, Brace, 1966.

Arlt, Wolfgang, ed. *Deutschlands Junge Garde*. Berlin: Neues Leben, 1959.

Bade, Wilfrid. *SA erobert Berlin*. Munich: Knorr & Hirth, 1941.

Baeyer-Katte, Wanda von. *Vom Zerstörerischen in der Politik*. Heidelberg: Quelle & Meyer, 1956.

Balle, Hermann. "Die propagandistische Auseinandersetzung der Nationalsozialisten mit der Weimarer Republik und ihre Bedentung fuer den Aufstieg des Nationalsozialismus." Ph.D. dissertation, University of Erlangen, 1963.

Beck, Friedrich A. *Kampf und Sieg, Geschichte der NSDAP in Gau Westfalen-Süd*. Dortmund: Westfalenverlag, 1938.

Bennecke, Heinrich. *Hitler und die SA*. Munich: Olzog, 1962.

Berghahn, Volker R., ed. *Militarismus*. Cologne: Kiepenheuer & Witsch, 1975.

———. *Der Stahlhelm, Bund der Frontsoldaten*. Duesseldorf: Droste, 1966.

Berthold, Lothar. *Das Programm der KPD zur nationalen und sozialen Befreiung des deutschen Volkes vom August 1930*. Berlin: Dietz, 1956.

Bessel, Richard. "The Potempa Murder." *Central European History*, 10 (September 1977), 241-254.

Bettelheim, Bruno, and Janowitz, Morris, *Dynamics of Prejudice*. New York: Harper, 1950.

Binion, Rudolph. *Hitler among the Germans*. Amsterdam: Elsevier, 1976.

Bittner, Egon. "Radicalism and the Organization of Radical Movements," *American Sociological Review*, 28 (December 1963), 928-940.

Bley, Wulf. *SA marschiert*. 10th ed. Stuttgart: Union DVG, 1933.

Bloch, Charles. *Die SA und die Krise des NS-Regimes 1934*. Frankfurt: Suhrkamp, 1970.

Boehnke, Wilfried. *Die NSDAP im Ruhrgebiet 1920-1933*. Bonn: Friedrich-Ebert-Stiftung, 1974.

Botz, Gerhard. *Gewalt in der Politik*. Munich: Fink, 1976.

Bracher, Karl Dietrich. *Die Auflösung der Weimarer Republik*. 4th ed. Villingen: Ring, 1959.

———. *The German Dictatorship*. New York: Praeger, 1970.

———. *Zeitgeschichtliche Kontroversen, Um Faschismus, Totalitarismus, Demokratie*. Munich: Piper, 1976.

———; Sauer, Wolfgang; and Schulz, Gerhard. *Die nationalsozialistische Machtergreifung*. Cologne: Westdeutscher Verlag, 1960.

Brandenburg, Hans-Christian. *Die Geschichte der HJ, Wege und Irrwege einer Generation*. Cologne: Wissenschaft und Politik, 1968.

Braun, Otto. *Von Weimar zu Hitler*. Hamburg: Reinbek, 1949.

Das Braune Heer. Leben, Kampf und Sieg der SA und SS. Berlin: Zeitgeschichte, 1932.

Broszat, Martin. *National Socialism, 1918-1933*. Santa Barbara: Clio Press, 1966.

Buchheim, Hans et al. *Anatomy of the SS-State*. New York: Walker, 1968.

Carsten, Francis L. *The Rise of Fascism.* Berkeley and Los Angeles: University of California Press, 1967.

Cassels, Alan. *Fascism.* New York: Crowell, 1975.

Chakotin, Serge. *The Rape of the Masses: The Psychology of Totalitarian Political Propaganda.* New York: Haskell House, 1976. (First published 1939.)

Childers, Thomas. "The Social Bases of the National Socialist Vote," *Journal of Contemporary History,* 11 (1976), 17-42.

Ciolek-Kuemper, Jutta. *Wahlkampf in Lippe.* Munich: Kommunikation und Politik, 1976.

Comfort, Richard A. *Revolutionary Hamburg, Labor Politics in the Early Weimar Republic.* Stanford: Stanford University Press, 1966.

Conze, Werner. *Die Zeit Wilhelms II und die Weimarer Republik.* Tuebingen: Wunderlich, 1964.

Darré, Walter. *Das Bauerntum als Lebensquell der nordischen Rasse* and *Neuadel aus Blut und Boden.* Muenchen: J. F. Lehmann, 1929 and 1930.

Decker, Will. *Kreuze am Wege zur Freiheit.* Leipzig: Koehler & Amelang, 1935.

De Felice, Renzo. *Fascism: An Informal Introduction to Its Theory and Practice. An Interview with Michael M. Ledeen.* New Brunswick, N.J.: Transaction Books, 1976.

———. *Le interpretazioni del fascismo.* 2nd ed. Bari: Laterza, 1970.

———. *Benito Mussolini.* 3 vols. Turin: Einaudi, 1966, 1968; and Florence: La nuova Italia, 1976.

Delzell, Charles R., ed. *Mediterranean Fascism 1919-1945.* New York: Macmillan, 1970.

Diehl, James H. *Paramilitary Politics in Weimar Germany.* Bloomington: University of Indiana Press, 1977.

Deutsch, Karl W. "Social Mobilization and Political Development," *American Political Science Review,* 55 (June 1961), 493-514.

Deutschland Erwacht, Werden, Kampf und Sieg der NSDAP. Hamburg: Cigaretten-Bilderdienst, 1933.

Dix, Arthur. *Die deutschen Reichstagswahlen 1871-1930 und die Wandlungen der Volksgliederung.* Tuebingen: Mohr, 1930.

Douglas, Donald Morse. "The Early Ortsgruppen. The Development of National Socialist Local Groups 1919-1923." Ph.D. dissertation, University of Kansas, 1963.

Duenow, Hermann. *Der Rote Frontkaempferbund.* East Berlin: MNV, 1958.

Duesterberg, Theodor. *Der Stahlhelm und Hitler.* Wolfenbuettel: Verlagsanstalt, 1949.

Ebenstein, William. *Today's Isms.* 7th ed. Englewood Cliffs, N.J.: Prentice-Hall, 1973.

Eliasberg, Georg. *Der Ruhrkrieg von 1920.* Bonn: Neue Gesellschaft, 1974.

Engelbrechten, J. K. von. *Eine braune Armee entsteht.* Munich: Eher, 1937.

————, and Volz, Hans. *Wir wandern durch das nationalsozialistische Berlin.* Munich: Eher, 1937.

Erdmann, Juergen. *Coburg, Bayern und das Reich 1918-1923.* Coburg: Heimatkunde und Landesgeschichte, 1969.

Erger, Johannes. *Der Kapp-Luettwitz Putsch.* Duesseldorf: Droste, 1967.

Fallada, Hans. *Bauern, Bonzen und Bomben.* Reissued Hamburg: Rowohlt, 1964.

Fasismus a Europa—Fascism and Europe, an International Symposium, Prague, 18th-29th August, 1969. Prague: Institute of History, 1969.

Farquharson, John. "The NSDAP in Hannover and Lower Saxony, 1921-1926," *Journal of Contemporary History,* 8 (1973), 103-120.

Favez, Jean-Claude. *Le Reich devant l'occupation francobelge de la Ruhr en 1923.* Geneva: Droz, 1969.

Fest, Joachim C. *The Face of the Third Reich.* New York: Pantheon, 1970.

————. *Hitler.* Frankfurt: EVA, 1973.

Flechtheim, Ossip K. *Die KPD in der Weimarer Republik.* 2nd ed. Frankfurt: EVA, 1969.

Franke, Otto and Merbach, Paul A., eds. *Deutscher Wille im Entscheidungsjahr 1933.* Berlin: Verlag Deutscher Wille, 1934.

Franz-Willing, Georg. *Die Hitlerbewegung: Der Ursprung 1919-1922.* Hamburg: Schenck, 1962.

————. *Krisenjahr der Hitlerbewegung 1923.* Preussisch-Oldendorf: Schuetz, 1975.

Fussell, Paul. *The Great War and Modern Memory.* New York: Oxford University Press, 1976.

Geiger, Theodor. *Die soziale Schichtung des deutschen Volkes.* Stuttgart: Enke, 1932.

Geissler, Rolf. *Dekadenz und Heroismus.* Stuttgart: Deutsche Verlagsanstalt, 1964.

Gervinus, Fritz, and Wolf, Werner. *Der Weg zum National-sozialismus, Von Weimar bis Potsdam.* Berlin: Militäer verlag, no date.

Gilbert, G. M. *Nuremberg Diary.* New York: Farrar Straus, 1947.

———. *The Psychology of Dictatorship.* New York: Ronald Press, 1950.

Gimbel, A. *So Kaempften wir.* Frankfurt: Verlagsgesellschaft, 1941.

Glaeser, Ernst. *Jahrgang 1902.* Berlin: Kiepenheuer, 1929.

Goergen, Hans-Peter. *Duesseldorf und der Nationalsozialismus.* Duesseldorf: Droste, 1969.

Goote, Thor. *Die Fahne noch.* Berlin: Zeitgeschichte, 1933.

———. *Kameraden die Rotfront und Reaktion erschossen. . . .* Berlin: Mittler, 1934.

Gordon, Harold J. *Hitler and the Beer Hall Putsch.* Princeton: Princeton University Press, 1972.

Grebing, Helga. *Aktuelle Theorien ueber Faschismus und Konservatismus. Eine Kritik.* Stuttgart: Kohlhammer, 1974.

Gregor, A. James. *Interpretations of Fascism.* Morristown, N.J.: General Learning Press, 1974.

Grill, Johnpeter Horst. "The Nazi Party in Baden, 1920-1945." Ph.D. dissertation, University of Michigan, 1975.

Grohe, Josef. *Der politische Kampf im Rheinland nach dem ersten Weltkrieg.* Bonn: Universitaetsdruckerei, 1941.

Grote, Hans Henning Freiherr, ed. *Deutschlands Erwachen.* Essen: Nationale Vertriebsstelle Ruhrland, 1933.

Grzesinski, Albert C. *Inside Germany.* New York: Dutton, 1939.

Gumbel, Emil J. *Verraeter verfallen der Feme. Opfer, Moerder, Richter 1919-1929.* Berlin: Malik, 1929.

———. *Vom Fememord zur Reichskanzlei.* Heidelberg: Lambert Schneider, 1962.

Gurr, Ted. *Why Men Rebel.* Princeton: Princeton University Press, 1970.

Hambrecht, Rainer. *Der Aufstieg der NSDAP in Mittel-und Oberfranken (1925-1933).* Nuernberg: Stadtarchiv, 1976.

Hamel, Iris. *Voelkischer Verband und nationale Gewerkschaft.* Frankfurt: Europaeische Verlagsanstalt, 1967.

Hayes, Paul M. *Fascism.* London: Allen & Unwin, 1973.

Heberle, Rudolph. *From Democracy to Nazism.* Baton Rouge: Louisiana State University Press, 1945.

313

Heberle, Rudolph. *Landbevoelkerung und Nationalsozialismus. Eine soziologische Untersuchung der politischen Willensbildung in Schleswig-Holstein 1918-1932.* Stuttgart: DVA, 1965.

Heer, Hannes. *Thaelmann.* Hamburg: Rowohlt, 1975.

Heiden, Konrad. *Der Fuehrer.* Boston: Houghton Mifflin, 1944.

Heiss, Friedrich. *Das Schlesienbuch.* Berlin: Volk and Reich, 1938.

Heller, Karl. *"Der Bund der Landwirte (Landbund) und seine Politik."* Doctoral dissertation, Wuerzburg University, 1936.

Hermanns, Will. *Stadt in Ketten, Geschichte der Besatzungs- und Separatistenzeit.* Aachen: J. A. Mayer, 1933.

Heyen, Franz J. *Nationalsozialismus im Alltag.* Boppard: Boldt Verlag, 1967.

Historical Institute of the University of Jena. *Die bürgerlichen Parteien in Deutschland, Handbuch.* 2 vols. Leipzig: VEB Bibliographisches Institut, 1970.

Hitler, Adolf. *Mein Kampf.* New York: Reynal & Hitchcock, 1939.

Hochmuth, R., ed. *Nationalsozialismus in der Praxis.* Berlin: Press, 1932.

Hoefler, Karl. *Oberschlesien in der Aufstandszeit 1918-1921.* Berlin: Mittler and Sons, 1938.

Hoehne, Heinz. *Der Orden under dem Totenkopf. Die Geschichte des SS.* Hamburg: Spiegel; and Guetersloh: Mohn, 1967.

Hoegner, Wilhelm. *Der schwierige Aussenseiter.* Munich: Isar, 1959.

Hoepner, Richard. *Braune Kolonne, Ein Buch der SA.* Berlin: Buchmeister, 1934.

Hoersing, Friedrich Otto. *"Das Reichsbanner Schwarz-Rot-Gold"* in Bernard Harms, ed., *Volk und Reich der Deutschen.* 3 vols. Berlin: Hobbing, 1929, 2:178-194.

Horkheimer, Max. *Autoritaet und Familie.* Paris: n.p., 1936.

Horn, Wolfgang. *Führerideologie und Parteiorganisation in der NSDAP 1919-1933.* Duesseldorf: Droste, 1972.

Hornung, Klaus. *Der Jungdeutsche Orden.* Duesseldorf: Droste, 1958.

Hotzel, Curt, ed. *Deutscher Aufstand: Die Revolution des Nachkriegs.* Stuttgart: Kohlhammer, 1934.

Hundhammer, Alois. *Die landwirtschaftliche Berufsvertretung in Bayern.* Munich: Pfeiffer, 1926.

314

Hunt, Richard N. *German Social Democracy, 1918-1933.* New Haven: Yale University Press, 1964.

Ihlau, Olaf. *Die roten Kämpfer.* Meisenheim: Hahn, 1969.

Im Kampf um das Reich. Munich: Eher, 1938.

Jacoby, Fritz. *Die nationalsozialistische Herrschaftsuebernahme an der Saar.* Saarbruecken: Saarlaendische Landesgeschichte, 1973.

Jasper, Gotthard. "Zur innerpolitischen Lage in Deutschland im Herbst 1929," *Vierteljahreshefte fuer Zeitgeschichte,* 8 (July 1960), 280-289.

Jochmann, Werner. *Nationalsozialismus und Revolution. Ursprung und Geschichte der NSDAP in Hamburg 1922-1933.* Hamburg: Forschungsstelle fuer die Geschichte des Nationalsozialismus in Hamburg, 1963.

Jonas, Erasmus. *Die Volkskonservativen 1928-1933.* Duesseldorf: Droste, 1965.

Jones, Larry Eugene. " 'The Dying Middle': Weimar Germany and the Fragmentation of Bourgeois Politics." *Central European History,* 5 (1972), 23-54.

————. "Inflation, Revaluation, and the Crisis of Middle Class Politics. A Study in the Dissolution of the German Party System, 1923-1928," *Central European History,* 12 (1979), forthcoming.

————. "Sammlung oder Zersplitterung? Die Bestrebungen zur Bildung einer neuen Mittelpartei in der Endphase der Weimarer Republik 1930-1933," *Vierteljahreshefte fuer Zeitgeschichte,* 25 (1977), 265-304.

Kaasch, Wienand. "Die soziale Struktur der KPD," *Kommunistische Internationale,* 19 (1928), 1052-1066.

Karl, Willibald. *Jugend, Gesellschaft und Politik im Zeitraum des I. Weltkrieges.* Munich: Stadtarchiv, 1973.

Kater, Michael H. "Ansätze zu einer Soziologie der SA bis zur Roehmkrise," in Ulrich Engelhardt et al., eds. *Soziale Bewegung und politische Verfassung.* Stuttgart: Industrielle Welt, 1976, pp. 798-831.

————. "Quantifizierung und NS-Geschichte. Methodologische Überlegungen über Grenzen und Möglichkeiten einer EDV-Analyse der NSDAP-Sozialstruktur," *Geschichte und Gesellschaft,* 3 (1977), 453-484.

————. "Sozialer Wandel in der NSDAP im Zugen der nationsozialistisch en Machtergieifung," in Wolfgang Schieder, ed.,

Faschismus als soziale Bewegung. Hamburg: Hoffmann & Campe, 1976, pp. 25-67.

――――. *Studentenschaft und Rechtsradikalismus in Deutschland 1918-1933.* Hamburg: Hoffmann & Campe, 1975.

――――. "Zum gegenseitigen Verhaeltnis von SA und SS in der Sozialgeschichte des Nationalsozialismus," *Vierteljahresschrift fuer Sozial- und Wirtschaftsgeschichte,* 62 (1975), 339-379.

――――. "Zur Soziographie der fruehen NSDAP," *Vierteljahreshefte fuer Zeitgeschichte,* 19 (April 1971), 125-137.

Keese, Dietmar. "Die volkswirtschaftlichen Gesamtgroessen fuer das Deutsche Reich in den Jahren 1925-1936," in Werner Conze and Hans Raupach, eds., *Die Staats- und Wirtschaftskrise des Deutschen Reiches.* Stuttgart: Klett, 1967, pp. 35-81.

Keniston, Kenneth. *Young Radicals, Notes on Committed Youth.* New York: Harcourt, Brace and World, 1968.

Kessler, Alexander. *Der Jungdeutsche Orden in den Jahren der Entscheidung 1928-1930.* Munich: Lohmueller, 1975.

Kessler, Harry Graf. *Walter Rathenau, sein Leben und sein Werk.* Wiesbaden: Rheinische Verlagsanstalt, 1962.

Killinger, Manfred von. *Die SA in Wort und Bild.* Leipzig: Kittler, 1933.

Kindt, Werner, ed. *Die Deutsche Jugendbewegung 1920 bis 1933: Die buendische Zeit. Dokumentation der Jugendbewegung, Vol. 3.* Duesseldorf: Diederichs, 1974.

Klemperer, Klemens von. *Germany's New Conservatism.* Princeton: Princeton University Press, 1957.

Klose, Werner. *Lebensformen deutscher Jugend, vom Wandervogel zur Popgeneration.* Munich and Vienna: Olzog, 1970.

Koch, Karl W. H. *Maenner im Braunhemd.* 2nd ed. Berlin: Stubenrauch, 1936. The 1934 edition is *Das Ehrenbuch der SA.* Duesseldorf: Floeder.

Koeller, Heinz. *Kampfbuendnis an der Seine, Ruhr und Spree.* Berlin: Ruetten and Loening, 1963.

Koenigsberg, Richard A. *Hitler's Ideology. A Study in Psychoanalytic Sociology.* New York: Library of Social Science, 1975.

Koennemann, Erwin. *Einwohnerwehren und Zeitfreiwilligenverbaende.* Berlin: Militaerverlag, 1969.

Kornhauser, William. *The Politics of Mass Society.* London: Routledge and Kegan Paul, 1960.

Kracauer, Siegfried. *Die Angestellten aus dem neuesten Deutschland.* Frankfurt: 1930.

316

Krausnick, Helmut et al. *Anatomy of the SS-State.* New York: Walker, 1968.

Krebs, Albert. *Tendenzen und Gestalten der NSDAP, Erinnerungen an die Frühzeit der Partei.* Stuttgart: DVA, 1959.

Krummacher, F. A., and Wucher, A. *Die Weimarer Republik.* Munich: Desch, 1965.

Kuehnl, Reinhard. *Der deutsche Faschismus in Quellen und Dokumenten.* Cologne: Pahl-Rugenstein, 1975.

————. *Die nationalsozialistische Linke.* Meisenheim: Hain, 1966.

Laqueur, Walter Z., ed. *Fascism: A Reader's Guide.* Berkeley and Los Angeles: University of California Press, 1976.

————. *Young Germany.* New York: Basic Books, 1962.

————, and Mosse, George L., eds., *International Fascism, 1920-1945.* New York: Harper Torchbooks, 1964.

Larsen, Stein U., and Hagtvet, Bernt, et al., eds., *Who Were the Fascists?* Olso: Norwegian University Presses, 1979.

Lasswell, Harold D., and Lerner, Daniel, eds. *World Revolutionary Elites.* Cambridge: MIT Press, 1966.

Lebovics, Herman. *Social Conservatism and the Middle Classes, 1914-1933.* Princeton: Princeton University Press, 1969.

Lerner, Warren. *Karl Radek: The Last Internationalist.* Stanford: Stanford University Press, 1970.

Linz, Juan J. "Some Notes toward a Comparative Study of Fascism in Sociological Historical Perspective" in Walter Z. Laqueur, ed., *Fascism, A Reader's Guide.* Berkeley and Los Angeles: University of California Press, 1976, pp. 3-121.

————. "Totalitarian and Authoritarian Regimes," in Fred I. Greenstein and Nelson W. Polsby, eds. *Handbook of Political Science.* 9 vols. Reading, Mass.: Addison-Wesley, 1975. III, 175-411.

Lipset, Seymour M. *Political Man.* Garden City, N.Y.: Doubleday/Anchor, 1960.

Loewenberg, Peter. "The Psycho-Historical Origins of the Nazi Youth Cohort," *American Historical Review,* 76 (December 1971), 1457-1502.

Lohalm, Uwe. *Voelkischer Radikalismus.* Hamburg: Leibniz, 1970.

Lowenthal, Leo, and Guterman, Norbert. *Prophets of Deceit.* New York: Harper, 1949.

Ludin, Hanns. *SA Marschierendes Volk.* Munich: Eher, 1939.

Lyttleton, Adrian. *Italian Fascisms: From Pareto to Gentile.* New York: Harper Torchbooks, 1973.

———. *The Seizure of Power.* New York: Scribner, 1973.

Marx-Engels-Lenin-Stalin—Institut beim Zentralkommittee der SED. *Die Maerzkaempfe 1921.* Berlin: Dietz, 1956.

Maser, Werner. *Hitler: Legend, Myth and Reality,* New York: Harper Torchbooks, 1971.

———. *Der Sturm auf die Republik. Frühgeschichte der NSDAP.* Stuttgart: DVA, 1973.

Masur, Gerhard. *Imperial Berlin.* New York: Basic Books, 1970.

Mattes, Wilhelm. *Die bayerischen Bauernräte.* Stuttgart: Cotta, 1921.

Matthias, Erich, and Morsey, Rudolf, eds. *Das Ende der Parteien, 1933.* Duesseldorf: Droste, 1960.

Matzerath, Horst, and Turner, Henry A. "Die Selbstfinanzierung der NSDAP 1930-1932," *Geschichte und Gesellschaft,* 3 (1977), 59-92.

Mau, Hermann. "The Second Revolution—June 30, 1934," in Hajo Holborn, ed. *Republic to Reich, The Making of the Nazi Revolution.* New York: Random House/Pantheon, 1972, pp. 224-246.

Merkl, Peter H. *Political Violence under the Swastika: 581 Early Nazis.* Princeton: Princeton University Press, 1975.

Merton, Robert et al., eds. *Reader in Bureaucracy.* Glencoe, Ill.: Free Press, 1952.

Michels, Robert. *Umschichtungen in den herrschenden Klassen nach dem Kriege.* Stuttgart: Kohlhammer, 1934.

Milatz, Alfred. *Wähler und Wahlen in der Weimarer Republik.* Bonn: Bundeszentrale fuer politische Bildung, 1965.

Mohler, Armin. *Die konservative Revolution in Deutschland, 1918-1932.* Stuttgart: EVA, 1950.

Moller, Herbert. "Youth as a Force in the Modern World," *Comparative Studies in Society and History,* 10 (October 1967-July 1968), 237-260.

Mommsen, Hans. "National Socialism—Continuity and Change," in Walter Laqueur, ed. *Fascism, A Reader's Guide.* Berkeley and Los Angeles: University of California Press, 1976, pp. 179-211.

Mosse, George L. *The Crisis of German Ideology.* New York: Grosset and Dunlap, 1964.

———. *The Nationalization of the Masses.* New York: Howard Fertig, 1975.

Mosse, Werner, ed. *Entscheidungsjahr 1932, Zur Judenfrage in der Endphase der Weimarer Republik.* Tuebingen: Mohr, 1966.

Neumann, Sigmund. *Die Parteien der Weimarer Republik.* Stuttgart: Kohlhammer, 1965. The original appeared in 1932.

Noakes, Jeremy. *The Nazi Party in Lower Saxony.* Oxford: Oxford University Press, 1971.

Nolte, Ernst, ed. *Theorien über den Faschismus.* Cologne: Kiepenheuer & Witsch, 1967.

————. *Three Faces of Fascism.* New York: Holt, Rinehart, 1966.

NSDAP. *Parteistatistik 1935.* 2 vols. Berlin: Reichsorganisationsleiter, 1935.

NSDAP. *Der Weg zum Nationalsozialismus, Ruhmeshalle der SA, SS und HJ, des früheren Stahlhelm und der für das Dritte Reich gefallenen Parteigenossen.* Fuerstenwalde: Militaerverlag, n.d.

Nyomarkay, Joseph. *Charisma and Factionalism in the Nazi Party.* Minneapolis: University of Minnesota Press, 1967.

Oeckel, Heinz. *Die revolutionäre Volkswehr 1918/19.* Berlin: Militaerverlag, 1968.

Oertzen, F. W. von. *Die deutschen Freikorps 1918-1923.* 6th ed. Munich: Bruckmann, 1939.

Orlow, Dietrich. *The History of the Nazi Party: 1919-1933.* Pittsburgh: University of Pittsburgh Press, 1969.

————. *The History of the Nazi Party: 1933-1945.* Pittsburgh: University of Pittsburgh Press, 1972.

Paulus, Guenter. "Die soziale Struktur der Freikorps in den ersten Monaten nach der Novemberrevolution," *Zeitschrift für Geschichtswissenschaft,* 3 (1955), 685-704.

Pinson, Koppel S. *Modern Germany, Its History and Civilization.* 2nd ed. New York: Macmillan, 1966.

Plum, Guenter. *Gesellschaftsstruktur und politisches Bewusstsein in einer katholischen Region 1928-1933.* Stuttgart: DVA, 1972.

Pool, James, and Pool, Suzanne. *Who Financed Hitler's Rise to Power 1919-1933?* New York: Dial Press, 1978.

Posse, Ernst. *Die politischen Kampfbuende Deutschlands.* 2nd ed. Berlin: Junker & Duennhaupt, 1931.

Pridham, Geoffrey. *Hitler's Rise to Power: The Nazi Movement in Bavaria 1923-1933.* New York: Harper Torchbooks, 1973.

Pulzer, Peter G. J. *The Rise of Political Anti-Semitism in Germany and Austria.* New York: Wiley, 1964.

319

Reiche, Eric G. "The Development of the SA in Nuremberg, 1922 to 1934." Ph.D. dissertation, University of Delaware, 1972.

Roehm, Ernst. *Geschichte eines Hochverräters*. 2nd ed. Munich: Eher, 1930.

———. "SA und deutsche Revolution," *Nationalsozialistische Monatschefte*, no. 31 (1933), pp. 251ff.

Rogger, Hans, and Weber, Eugen, eds. *The European Right*. Berkeley and Los Angeles: University of California Press, 1965.

Rohe, Karl. *Das Reichsbanner Schwarz-Rot-Gold*. Duesseldorf: Droste, 1966.

Roloff, Ernst-August. *Braunschweig und der Staat von Weimar Politik, Wirtschaft und Gesellschaft 1918-1933*. Braunschweig: Waisenhaus Verlag, 1964.

———. *Buergertum und Nationalsozialismus, 1930-1933. Braunschweigs Weg ins Dritte Reich*. Hannover: Verlag fuer Literatur und Zeitgeschehen, 1961.

Rosenberg, Hans. *Grosse Depression und Bismarckzeit*. Berlin: DeGruyter, 1967.

Rosinski, Herbert. *The German Army*. New York: Praeger, 1966.

Salomon, Ernst von. *Die Geaechteten*. Berlin: Guetersloh, 1930.

Sauer, Wolfgang. "National Socialism: Totalitarianism or Fascism?" *American Historical Review*, 73 (December 1967), 404-424.

Schaefer, Wolfgang. *NSDAP: Entwicklung und Struktur der Staatspartei des Dritten Reiches*. Hannover: NVA Goedel, 1957.

Schelsky, Helmut. *Die skeptische Generation*. Duesseldorf: Diederich, 1960.

Schieder, Wolfgang, ed. *Faschismus als soziale Bewegung, Deutschland und Italien im Vergleich*. Hamburg: Hoffmann & Campe, 1976.

Schleunes, Karl. *The Twisted Road to Auschwitz*. Urbana: University of Illinois Press, 1969.

Schoen, Eberhart. *Die Entstehung des Nationalsozialismus in Hessen*. Meisenheim: Hain, 1972.

Schoenbaum, David. *Hitler's Social Revolution: Class and Status in Nazi Germany 1933-1939*. Garden City, N.Y.: Doubleday, 1966.

Schueddekopf, Otto-Ernst. *Linke Leute von rechts*. Stuttgart: Kohlhammer, 1960.

Schulz, Gerhard. *Faschismus-Nationalsozialismus. Versionen und theoretische Kontroversen 1922-1972.* Frankfurt: Propylaen, 1974.

Schuster, Kurt G. P. *Der Rote Frontkämpferbund 1924-1929.* Duesseldorf: Droste, 1975.

Seldte, Franz, ed. *Der Stahlhelm.* 2nd ed. Berlin: Stahlhelm-verlag, 1933.

Smith, Bradley F. *Adolf Hitler, His Family, Childhood and Youth.* Stanford: Hoover Institute Press, 1969.

———. *Heinrich Himmler, A Nazi in the Making 1900-1926.* Stanford: Hoover Institute Press, 1971.

Spethmann, Hans. *Der Ruhrkampf 1923-1925.* Berlin: Hobbing, 1933.

Stachura, Peter D. *Nazi Youth in the Weimar Republic.* Santa Barbara: ABC-Clio, 1975.

———. *The Shaping of the Nazi State.* London: Croom Helm, 1978.

Stelzner. Fritz. *Schicksal SA.* Munich: Eher, 1936.

Stern, Fritz. *The Politics of Cultural Despair.* New York: Double-day/Anchor Books, 1961.

Stierlin, Helm. *Adolf Hitler. A Family Perspective.* New York: Psychohistory Press, 1976.

Striefler, Heinrich. *Deutsche Wahlen in Bildern und Zahlen.* Duesseldorf: Wende, 1946.

Sturm 33 Hans Maikowski. 9th ed. Berlin: Deutsche Kultur-wacht, 1940.

Sugar, Peter F., ed. *Native Fascism in the Successor States, 1918-1945.* Santa Barbara: ABC-Clio Press, 1971.

Thimme, Annelise. *Die Flucht in den Mythos: Die deutschnationale Volkspartei und die Niederlage von 1918.* Goettingen: Vandenhoeck and Ruprecht, 1969.

Tilly, Charles; Tilly, Louise; and Tilly, Richard. *The Rebellious Century, 1830-1930.* Cambridge: Harvard University Press, 1975.

Tilton, Timothy A. *Nazism, Neo-Nazism, and the Peasantry.* Bloomington: Indiana University Press, 1975.

Toland, John. *Adolf Hitler.* Garden City, N.Y.: Doubleday, 1976.

Tracey, Donald R. "The Development of the National Socialist Party in Thuringia," *Central European History,* 8 (1975), 23-50.

Turner, Henry A., Jr., ed. *Nazism and the Third Reich.* New York: Quadrangle, 1972.

Turner, Henry A., Jr., ed. *Reappraisals of Fascism*. New York: New Viewpoints (Franklin Watts), 1975.

Tyrell, Albrecht, ed., *Führer Befiehl . . . , Selbstzeugnisse aus der Kampfzeit der NSDAP*. Duesseldorf: Droste, 1960.

Uhlemann, Manfred. *Arbeiterjugend gegen Cuno und Poincaré, das Jahr 1923*. Berlin: Neues Leben, 1960.

Vagts, Alfred. *Hitler's Second Army*. Washington, D.C.: Infantry Journal, 1943.

Vogelsang, Thilo. *Reichswehr, Staat und NSDAP*. Stuttgart: DVA, 1962.

———. "SA," in *Staatslexikon*. 6th ed. Freiburg: Herder, 1965, pp. 1034-1035.

Volz, Hans. *Daten der Geschichte der NSDAP*. 10th ed. Berlin: Junker & Duennhaupt, 1939.

Waite, Robert G. L. *Vanguard of Nazism: The Free Corps Movement in Postwar Germany, 1918-1923*. Cambridge: Harvard University Press, 1952.

Waldman, Eric. *The Spartacist Uprising of 1919 and the Crisis of the German Socialist Movement*. Milwaukee: Marquette University Press, 1958.

Walker, Lawrence D. *Hitler Youth and Catholic Youth, 1933-1936*. Washington, D.C.: Catholic University of America Press, 1970.

Weber, Eugen. *The Varieties of Fascism*. Princeton: Van Nostrand, 1964.

Weber, Hermann. *Die Wandlung des deutschen Kommunismus*. 2 vols. Frankfurt: EVA, 1969.

Weberstedt, Hans, and Langner, Kurt. *Gedenkhalle für die Gefallenen des Dritten Reiches*. Munich: Eherverlag, 1935.

Weiss, John. *The Fascist Tradition: Radical Rightwing Extremism in Modern Europe*. New York: Harper & Row, 1967.

Wehler, Hans Ulrich, ed. *Geschichte und Soziologie*. Cologne: Kiepenheuer & Witsch, 1972.

———. *Krisenherde des Kaiserreichs 1871-1918. Studien zur deutschen Sozial- und Verfassungsgeschichte*. Goettingen: Vandenhoeck & Ruprecht, 1970.

Werner, Andreas. "SA und NSDAP. SA: 'Wehrverband,' 'Parteitruppe,' oder 'Revolutionsarmee'?" Ph.D. dissertation, University of Erlangen, 1964.

Winkler, Heinrich August. "From Social Protectionism to National Socialism: The German Small Business Movement in

Comparative Perspective," *Journal of Modern History*, 48 (1976), 1-18.

————. *Mittelstand, Demokratie und Nationalsozialismus. Die politische Entwicklung von Handwerk und Kleinhandel in der Weimarer Republik.* Cologne: Kiepenheuer & Witsch, 1972.

Wippermann, Wolfgang. *Faschismustheorien.* Darmstadt: Wissenschaftliches Buch, 1975.

Wolf, Dieter. *Die Doriotbewegung. Ein Beitrag zur Geschichte des franzoesischen Faschismus.* Stuttgart: DVA, 1967.

Woolf, S. J., ed. *European Fascism* and *The Nature of Fascism.* Both New York: Vintage Books, 1969.

Wunderlich, Frieda. *Farm Labor in Germany, 1810-1945.* Princeton: Princeton University Press, 1961.

323

Index

Abel Collection, xvii-xviii, 8n
anti-republicanism, 19, 49-51
antisemitism (*Judenkoller*), 119-21, 123, 222-28; influences of, 228-31; and paranoia, 229-30; and political mobilization, 226-28; taxicab theory of, 8-9
anti-Western sentiment, 13-14
authoritarian political thought, 15

beer-hall putsch, 127-28
Bruening, Heinrich, 10, 14, 15, 21

colonists (German), 130-31
communist organizations, 34-38
Communist Party (KPD), 20, 34n, 34-37, 52-57; against fascism, 64-65; age distribution, 60-61; bid for power, 35-38; confrontation with SA, 169-70; educational level, 156; electoral support, 63; factions, 62-63; final phase, 63-66; "German October revolution," 37-38; labor support, 59-60, 64; membership, 62; occupations, 61-62, 155; rivalry with SPD, 59-60; "Schlageter policy," 36-37n; unemployment, 11, 62-63

counterrevolutionaries, 121-28

demographic trends, 284-85; German males, 185-87; Weimar youth, 71. *See also* generational groups

educational level, 156t
elections (1919), 19; (1920), 33-34; (1932), 24-29, 33-34, 63
enforcement careers, 259-82; and political participation, 277-79; and socialization, 275-77, 279-82
extremist attitudes, 219-21

family loyalties, 94-95
fascism, theories of, 305-308
fascist movements: compared, 292-99; age factor, 298; ideology, 298-99; violence in, 296-97, 299-305
freecorps, 18, 19, 31-32, 86n
french occupation, 133-37
fronterlebnis, 102, 112-13, 118

generational groups, 108-109; front generation, 109; prewar generation, 144; postwar generation, 111-113. *See also* vet-

325

generational groups (*cont.*)
erans; paramilitary organization
German ethnics, 131-32
German Nationalists (DNVP),
71-72

Hitler, Adolph, 160-62
Hitler Youth (HJ), 212-17

ideology of front-line soldiers, 15
interest groups, Nazi, 11-12
Iron Front (IF), 27, 28

Knapp putsch, 32-33

labor organizations, Nazi, 11-12
leadership cult, 117-19

military or civil servants, 102-15

nationalism, 13-14, 101-102,
129-30; and ethnic friction,
128-38; *voelkisch*, 14n
Nazi movement: as class conflict, 139-40; attitudes toward,
303-305; converts from left,
88-92; converts from right,
92-94; revolutionary character,
148. *See also* paramilitary organizations
Nazi party (NSDAP); age distribution, 185; antisemitism,
222-28; alliance with *Stahlhelm*, 72-75, 83-84; casualties,
98, 99; development of, 283-
84; emergence of, 20; friction
with *Stahlhelm*, 74n, 84; generational groups, 107-109; intensity of participation, 232-
44; military elements pre-1933,
109t; motive force, 102-103,
138; motives for joining, 245-
49; occupational analysis, 70n,

156-59; "party of youth," 12;
recruitment, 250-57; reestablishment of, 162; social mobility, 145-53; social motivation,
142-44; voter support, 23,
24n, 244; working class, 152-
53
neoauthoritarianism, 140-41

occupational analysis, 98-99,
149-53, 154-56

paramilitary organizations, 26-30,
124; common characteristics,
86-88; Communist Red Front
Fighters League (RFB), 20-
21, 52-57; formation of, 31-34;
German Nationalists (DNVP),
20; Iron Front (IF), 27-28;
of the left, 32-33; Proletarian
Hundreds, 36-38; *Reichsbanner*, 21, 28, 49-52; *Stahlhelm*,
20-21, 28, 38-49; unemployed
youth, 189; violence among,
95-96
party membership: age distribution, 60-61; occupational composition, 61-62
physical aggressiveness, 120-21
political development, 13-15
political mobilization: and unemployment, 7-10; rural, 9.
See also youth movements
political motivations and history,
287-91
political participation: intensity
of, 232-44; recruitment, 255-
57
political socialization, 203-10.
See also youth
political violence, 95-100; and
adolescence, 184; casualties of,
96-99. *See also* paramilitary
organizations

politicization, 192-94, 246-49
postwar generation, 110-13
prewar generation, 144
private armies, *see* paramilitary organizations
Proletarian Hundreds, 36. *See also* Communist Party (KDP)
propaganda (marching, fighting, proselytizing), 231-32
Prussia, 21-22, 80-81, 95

Rathenau, Walter, 138-39
recruitment, 249-57
Red Front Fighters League (RFB), 52-57; agitation and propaganda, 53-55; formation of, 53; outlawed, 57-58; political position, 58-59; street warfare, 57-58; women of, 55-56; youth organization, 56-57. *See also* paramilitary organizations
Reichsbanner: challenge to Nazis, 76, 78-82; internal crisis, 51-52; protective formation (*Schufo*), 76-78, 80; rise of, 49-52
Reichstag, 22-24, 61, 175
republican loyalties, 16
republican parties, 19, 33-34. *See also Reichsbanner*
Roehm, Ernst, 84-85, 103, 161, 178-79, 181, 183
Ruhr uprising, 32-33
rural-urban migration, 144-45. *See also* politicization; youth

Saalschutz (SS): antisemitism, 222-28; generational groups, 109-10; intensity of participation, 232-44; leaders, 156; motives for joining, 245-48
Social Democratic Party (SDP), 59-62. *See also* party membership

social deviance, 196-203
social mobility, 145-48, 153; and extremism, 147-48. *See also* enforcement careers
social tension, 138
Spartacists (Spartakus), 32, 34-35. *See also* Communist Party
Stahlhelm, 38-49; composition of, 40-41; end of, 82-85; leaders, 41, 82-86; and Nazi Party (NSDAP), 72-74, 83-86, 92-94; retreat from politics, 75-76; spirit of, 39-40; occupational composition, 70n; outlawed, 42; women and youth, 42; youth organization, 70n, 73. *See also* paramilitary organizations
Stormtroopers (SA); ban on, 26-27; converts from left, 88-92; converts from right, 92-94; discipline, 170-75; extremist identities, 194-203; growth of, 163, 173-75, 179-80, 244; Hitler's conception of, 105-107; homes for, 201; ideology, 170-71, 221-22; outlawed, 172; and party leadership, 107, 175-80; political socialization, 191, 203-10, 220-23; propaganda and agitation, 164-69; purpose of, 163-64; recruitment, 249, 250-57; reduction of, 181-83; rise of, 185; spirit of, 170-75; street warfare, 26-30. *See also* paramilitary organizations

Third Reich: careers in, 257-63; support of big business, 7-8n
Treaty of Versailles, 18-19

unemployment: exploitation of, 7-10; German males, 187-89;

unemployment (*cont.*)
and political unrest, 9-10; and
politicization, 190-94; the
Great Depression, 4-7; of the
young, 10-12, 191

veterans, 112-13, 114-18; associations, 38-39; culture shock,
113-18; militant groups, 20-21;
sex role socialization, 116-17.
See also paramilitary organizations
Von Hindenburg, Paul, 14, 15,
22, 72, 81, 85
Von Papen, 21, 22, 80, 81, 83

Weimar democracy: effects of
WW I, 13-15; leaders of, 14-
15; support of, 12-15
Weimar Republic, fate of, 18-25

Young Plan of Reparations, 71-72
youth: demographic trends, 71;
groups, 211, 262-63; in
NSDAP (Nazi Party), 12;
mobilization of, 66-71; politicization, 15; *Reichsbanner*,
49-50; unemployed, 10-12
youth movement (Jungdo), 17,
66-71, 69n-70n; socio-economic differences, 212

Library of Congress Cataloging in Publication Data

Merkl, Peter H
The making of a stormtrooper.

Bibliography: p.
Includes index.
1. Nationalsozialistische Deutsche Arbeiter-Partei.
Sturmabteilung—History.
2. Nationalsozialistische Deutsche Arbeiter-Partei.
Hitlerjugend—History.
3. Nationalsozialistischer Deutscher Frontkämpferbund
(Stahlhelm)—History.
4. Paramilitary forces—Germany—History.
5. Violence—Germany—History.
6. Germany—Politics and government—1918-1933.
I. Title.
DD253.7.M47   943.085   79-3223
ISBN 0-691-07620-0